BEST SERMONS

BEST SERMONS

Volume VII

1959–1960 PROTESTANT EDITION

EDITED BY

G. Paul Butler

Introduction by

SAMUEL MC CREA CAVERT

THOMAS Y. CROWELL COMPANY
New York · Established 1834

To the Memory of
MY MOTHER
who gave me a
faith to live by

Acknowledgments

FOR SIXTEEN YEARS I have searched for the finest sermons preached anywhere. Clergymen of 165 denominations in 65 different countries and 21 languages have sent their sermons for reading and selection. For this volume 7,785 sermons were received, read and considered, making a total of 47,208 sermons received and read for the seven volumes of *Best Sermons* published between 1943–1944 and 1959–1960. I am most grateful and hereby express my deep appreciation to each individual who has given me the privilege of reading his sermon.

To laymen who have written me that they read each volume, I trust that this volume will be the most inspiring of my series. It has been a joy to hear from judges, lawyers, teachers, librarians, businessmen, housewives, and students that the books fill a need in their lives for devotional reading and study.

An increasing number of theological seminaries have adopted *Best Sermons* for use in homiletics classes and for analysis of current religious thinking in other courses. Equally gratifying are the letters and reports from college professors and presidents that *Best Sermons* is used for collateral reading and study in classes in religion, philosophy, and religious education. I am happy to hear of such an increasing use of my collection.

This seventh volume contains forty-two Protestant sermons. A separate Catholic volume is in preparation.

To my advisory committee I am deeply obligated; their reading of sermons for inclusion was an invaluable help. To Dr. Joseph R. Sizoo, Dr. Paul E. Scherer and Dr. Thomas S. Kepler my heartfelt thanks for their wisdom, kindness, and careful judgment in advising me. Though they are not ultimately responsible, the book is indubitably better because of their guidance and advice, and I am grateful to them.

Publishers have been most cooperative in granting permission to quote poetry or prose from other published works. I thank them for the use of copyright materials which are acknowledged in footnotes on the pages where they appear.

To my friend, Fred Packer, the Pulitzer Prize-winning cartoonist of the *New York Mirror*, I wish to express my special appreciation for a drawing he made for me for the cover of my book before his death. I believe everyone will enjoy the pulpit on the dust jacket. It shows Fred's art excellently.

To David H. Scott, my editor, and the staff of Thomas Y. Crowell Company; to my wife, Erica, who helped with reading, typing, correcting, checking night after night; and to Renate and Eric, for their help with the index, my thanks.

G. PAUL BUTLER

Contents

viii

Foreword

TO LABEL an utterance as "preaching" or to describe it as "preachy" is, in popular parlance, to give it a depreciatory meaning. To say, "Don't preach at us," is a way of shrugging off counsel to which we do not care to listen. Even among those who share faithfully in the services of the Church, voices are often heard protesting against the preponderant amount of talk from the pulpit. An old teacher of mine, himself a magnificent Scottish preacher, G. A. Johnston Ross, used to complain about "the uninterrupted garrulity of Protestant worship."

Perhaps, however, as a ruminative minister has remarked, "people are not tired of preaching but tired of *our* preaching." They may not be interested in my moral exhortations, my comments on the state of the world, or my ideas about managing one's feelings. But they are open and receptive toward anything which seems to bring them "a word from Beyond." Probably there never was a time when men were more religious in the sense of having (to use Paul Tillich's phrase) "an ultimate concern" about the meaning of our existence and the destiny of mankind.

I am convinced that it is this hunger for some fundamental understanding of human life that chiefly accounts for the current revival of religious interest and upsurge in church attendance. Part of it may be explained merely as a superficial response of "other-directed" men to a trend of social conformism. But no reflective observer can fail to detect a widespread mood of anxious concern in the man of today as to whether he can really believe in any divine purpose that gives significance to our chaotic human scene.

In this situation it is well to be reminded that Christian preaching, as a distinctive form of public utterance, is always *proclamation*. It is not good advice. It is not theological opinion. It is not psychological observation. It is not ethical idealism applied to contemporary events. All these may have a place in the pulpit, but only in relation to the preacher's pivotal role as an announcer of a gospel. He is a herald of good news—the good news of what God has done for man. It is in this sense that "Jesus came preaching," and it is in this same sense that His representative today is to be a preacher.

Too much of our preaching is directed to urging people to have high ideals and to make great effort to achieve them. "We must" and "you ought" are too characteristic of it. "Must" and "ought" do not convey good news to men who are already inadequate to meet the anxieties and strains of living. Their need is not to be told what ought to be, but to be helped to a deeper sense of what *is*—as seen in the light of the Gospel. As Baron von Hügel has put it, "No amount of *Oughtness* can be made to take the place of *Isness*." If a man is genuinely convinced about the nature of reality, his conduct will follow accordingly. This is why the proclamation of the Kingdom of God, as what really is, is of crucial moment.

Christian preaching is therefore always Biblical in its basic thought. It is grounded in that understanding of God which is given to us in the Scriptures that interpret His dealings with His people and His saving work in Jesus Christ. Whatever excellent qualities a sermon may have, it is not truly Christian preaching unless it conveys some insight into that Word of God which is historically mediated to us in the Bible and is the creative source of the Christian community.

Preaching does not become Biblical just by using the Bible as a source of texts. It is Biblical only as it is rooted in God's self-revelation as recorded in the Scriptures. This is something wholly different from the clever use of a casual verse. A Y.M.C.A. secretary who was eager to emphasize the spiritual values of physical fitness is said to have begun his talk to a tennis club by taking as a text, "And Joseph served in Pharaoh's court!"

Nor does the insistence that preaching be Biblical mean that it is to be preoccupied with the exposition of an ancient passage without discovering its relevance for life today. When Harry Emerson Fosdick and Johnston Ross, colleagues at Union Theological Seminary, were once having a friendly argument over the best kind of introduction to a sermon, the American said to the Scot, "You take your texts from the Bible but I take mine from Broadway." It would be unfair, however, to infer that Dr. Fosdick was less a "Biblical preacher" than Dr. Ross. The difference between them was only in the method of being Biblical. Dr. Ross began with a careful exposition of Scripture and ended by suggesting what it meant for present living. Dr. Fosdick began with the present conscious needs of his audience and ended by showing that any final solution carried them back to the Bible. Both methods are equally Biblical; the question is which method, in a given situation, will be most effective in bearing witness to Biblical truth. This is a problem of communication, not of the nature of the Message which is to be communicated.

Whatever the method, the preacher needs the fullest possible grasp of the Message that he seeks to communicate. The minister who says, "I preach the fatherhood of God and the brotherhood of man without any supernatural accretions or assumptions," is simply not preaching in any adequate New Testament sense. He is defining the message in a way which leaves out the heart of the apostolic testimony as to what God has done in Christ. Moreover, as James S. Stewart has remarked, such a viewpoint betrays confused and muddled thinking since "the existence of a living personal Father God is the most supernatural view of all."

There is a decisive difference between good preaching and effective preaching. A sermon may be good in structure, in style and in delivery and yet lamentably fail to achieve its essential goal. That goal is to bring about a direct encounter between God and the man in the pew. It is to give reality to the "I-Thou" relationship, in which God confronts man with what He has done for man and seeks man's response. It is this which Henry Sloane Coffin had in mind when he called his last book *Communion Through Preaching*. By this title he was intimating that effective preaching has a sacramental quality, being the means through which God approaches the souls of men.

I am sure that all of my fellow-ministers who contribute to this volume would like to have their efforts judged by the extent to which they meet this test.

SAMUEL MC CREA CAVERT

Introduction

THIS VOLUME OF *Best Sermons* represents two new features which we trust readers and users of previous volumes will find helpful. Both are based upon requests in person and by letter from clergy all over the country. First, we have included several lay sermons, chosen from hundreds submitted for consideration. We believe readers will welcome the messages by the Honorable John Foster Dulles, whose recent death was mourned in most of the Western world, by Dr. Nathan M. Pusey and by Dr. Irwin Jacob Lubbers. Second, in order to meet requests for more sermons, we will now publish two volumes instead of one: this volume devoted to forty-two Protestant sermons, and a separate volume for Catholic sermons to be issued by another publisher.

It is, therefore, a privilege to present this seventh volume of *Best Sermons* with more Protestant sermons than I have been able to include in any previous volume. It is my belief that the sermons included meet Dr. Cavert's principles of Christian preaching as outlined in his foreword. There is a strong trend today toward preaching which emphasizes the nature, need, and value of religious faith. In thousands of sermons this has stood out like a beacon on a high hill. Bishop Bo Giertz's sermon from Sweden, "Faith Which Can Never Die," Dr. McCracken's "The Unseen Presence," and Mr. Dulles' "Faith of Our Fathers" well illustrate the emphasis upon faith in current preaching.

Dr. Sockman's distinguished sermon on immortality, James Stewart's solid discussion of "Life's Most Indispensable Possession," and Leslie Weatherhead's inspiring message on "The Religion of the Dawn" all proclaim a Gospel needed for life today and set a high standard for contemporary sermonizing. The literary touch in James T. Cleland's sermon, the blank verse used by Herman J. Smith, and the autobiographical type of sermon preached by David O. Woodyard are good examples of different homiletical approaches.

The sermons on education can be used as models for baccalaureate addresses for high school or college groups; these were chosen from several hundred preached to graduating classes at colleges or universities.

In the search for the finest preaching being done anywhere, thousands of invitations were sent to ministers, and thousands of sermons were received and read to select the forty-two included. *Our first search was among pastors,* "preaching ministers," and we are happy to include the sermon manuscripts of the men who are excellent in their own pulpits. The first test has always been, "Is this truly one of the best sermons preached this year?" To meet this requirement we have also read sermons by professors of homiletics, church executives, bishops, evangelists, seminary presidents. The great majority of the sermons included were preached during 1958 or 1959, only a few in 1955, 1956, or 1957.

After reading nearly fifty thousand sermons in the preparation of the seven volumes issued to date, I am convinced that every man in the pulpit is anxious to preach his best. But there are so many things to interrupt a minister's sermon preparation: calls, funerals, counseling, his family, speeches, board meetings. The congregation owes it to its minister to keep inviolate his stated sermon-preparation time, probably Monday, Tuesday, Wednesday, Thursday mornings. Whatever the time, he should let it be known in the church bulletin or otherwise, so that he is not disturbed except in emergency. In this the preacher must be firm with others and even more firm with himself, for he bears the responsibility of preparing and delivering the finest possible sermon to his congregation every Sunday. Millions of people go to churches, and it is the preacher's challenge to give them stimulation and inspiration every time they come. Wherever there is excellent preaching there is always a full church, a happy preacher, an inspired congregation. Preaching, in my deepest conviction, is the most important function of the Christian church. Worship, ritual, prayer, fellowship—all are important, but preaching for our Protestant church is the key to bringing all men to faith in Christ.

* * * * *

In closing I would like to have all ministers and laymen know that ministers of all denominations are invited to send sermons for consideration for later volumes of *Best Sermons.* We want to include new men in every volume. "And as ye go, preach."

G. PAUL BUTLER

Bookmere
Little Silver, N.J.
June 30, 1959

Life Can Be Eternal

Reverend Ralph W. Sockman, Ph.D., D.D., Litt.D., LL.D.
MINISTER, CHRIST CHURCH, METHODIST, NEW YORK CITY
AND PREACHER ON THE NATIONAL RADIO PULPIT

Dr. Ralph Sockman is one of the great preachers in the con-
temporary world. His forthright questions in "Life Can Be Eternal,"
and his equally honest—and scriptural—answers bring new aspects
of his thought to readers of BEST SERMONS. *His searching questions*
probe deeply into both philosophy and religion, and look back into
history; his clear-cut statements will satisfy the hearts and minds
of many who wonder what they can believe about immortality.

Dr. Sockman was born in Ohio and is a graduate of Ohio Wes-
leyan University. He did his theological study at Union Theological
Seminary, New York, and took his Ph.D. at Columbia University. His
doctoral dissertation was in the field of history, which he has since
used to light up his sermons and to give perspective to his preaching.
He preaches all over America every year, has appointments with
thousands of people, and corresponds with hundreds. His National
Radio Pulpit congregation is numbered in millions, probably the
largest in the world.

In 1916, while still studying at Union and Columbia, he became
associate minister of Madison Avenue Methodist Episcopal Church;
in 1917 he was invited to become the full-time minister, where he
has remained for forty years. He is a member of innumerable com-
mittees which he serves actively, with clarity and vision. He is the
Director of the Hall of Fame for Great Americans. Every Sunday he
preaches two sermons at eleven and at five, and is Associate Pro-
fessor of Practical Theology at Union Seminary.

He is the author of many books, including THE HIGHER HAPPI-
NESS, THE UNEMPLOYED CARPENTER, THE PARADOXES OF JESUS, DATE
WITH DESTINY, THE HIGHWAY OF GOD, *and* HOW TO BELIEVE. *He has
been honored with the honorary doctorate by some twenty universities and colleges, including Ohio Wesleyan, Wesleyan University,
Rollins, Florida Southern, Washington and Jefferson, Northwestern
University, Miami University, Columbia University, and Duke University. In 1941 he gave the Lyman Beecher lectures at Yale, and
during 1947–48, he was Visiting Professor of Homiletics at Yale
Divinity School. He is President of the Church Peace Union and,
since 1928, has been chairman of the World Peace Commission of
the Methodist church. He is a member of the Harvard University
Board of Preachers and is chaplain of New York University.*

*Dr. Sockman has received thousands of people into membership
at Christ Church and now has members of his church in countries
around the world, retaining an associate membership in Christ
Church. His preaching is the kind that attracts people from all over
the United States and visitors from all over the world, for it is an
event to hear Ralph Sockman preach.*

SERMON ONE

WHY DO WE SEEK ETERNAL LIFE?

WHY HAS MANKIND through all ages and all cultures yearned for
immortal life? Why have the noblest spirits been convinced in their
highest moments that death is not the end but only a passing through
the door? Why do you and I, faced by the piercing reality of a
loved one's death, feel sure that the beloved spirit must go on, and
that, by the same token, we too can be worthy of the after life? The
answer to all these questions is the same: it is *love* that creates the
longing and carries the conviction that life is too great for the grave.

Faith, yes; hope, yes; but the greatest of the abiding sources
of assurance is love. It is love which knocks at the door of death
and asks for an answer. We want to know whether those we love live
on. We may be brave enough not to be deeply concerned about
prolonging our own lives, but can we stand beside the grave of a
beloved wife or beside a brave little boy fighting for life, and say
immortality does not matter? No, it is love that cries out for life
eternal.

What makes us dread the thought of death? It is not the pain involved in the act of dying, is it? Those who have witnessed death know that the pain at the moment of passing is usually trifling. Most of us endure far more physical suffering during life than we shall experience in the hour of death. In my opinion, it is the fear of loss rather than the fear of pain which we dread. We hate to give up these beloved associations. We cannot imagine life's being worth while without them.

CAN WE BELIEVE IN IMMORTALITY?

The foundation of my belief in life immortal reaches further back than the resurrection of Christ. The belief in life beyond has persisted through all ages and is practically universal in all races. The Egyptians storing the tombs of their beloved with rich treasures for future enjoyment; the American Indians placing in their burial mounds their bows and arrows for use in the happy hunting grounds hereafter—are examples of the pervasive conviction that death is not the end.

This belief involves the very integrity of the universe itself. The Creator has endowed us with the power to love, to evaluate, to hope. These powers are as integral to human nature as the hunger of the body or the air we breathe. Certainly the Creator Who keeps faith with the cravings of our bodily instincts will not play false to the other half of our natures. Certainly the Creator Who guides through the boundless sky the path of the migrating bird on its unerring flight has not planted in man a migrating instinct only to mislead him when he sets out for the larger home of his soul.

If life ended at the grave, this would indeed seem an irrational world. We should then have to believe that the universe, having struggled through aeons of time to evolve its highest creation, that of human personality, having nurtured this human being with parental care, having rounded him into maturity and enriched him with grace, then after all that infinite labor throws him on the dust heap, a piece of rotting flesh less valuable than rusting iron which can be salvaged for further use. We should have to believe that the genius of a Beethoven composing a Ninth Symphony, or the spirit of St. Francis leavening with love the sodden life of the Middle Ages, is of no more value than the leaves which go flying down the street before the autumn wind, "cast as rubbish to the void."

Some years ago during Holy Week, Dean Inge of St. Paul's Cathedral, London, lost his eleven-year-old daughter. Out of his grief Dean Inge, whose mind was rated the most brilliant in England at

3

the time, wrote: "If we are right in claiming for our judgments of value an authority no less than we allow to our judgments of fact, which come to us through the senses, we may assert with confidence that the souls of the righteous are in the hand of God, and that what is dear to Him will never be plucked out of the land of the living."

I should hold the hope of immortality had Christ never risen. But Christ enhances my belief in the fidelity of this world's government. In His view, this is our Father's world, a world that clothes the grass of the field, and feeds the fowls of the air, a world wherein earthly fathers give good things to their children, a world wherein our Heavenly Father gives even so much better things to those who love Him. As I catch the spirit of Christ's integrity, I feel convinced that I can trust Him when He says about the hope of a life beyond: "If it were not so, would I have told you that I go to prepare a place for you?" When I add the conviction of Christ's integrity to my belief in the world's integrity, I should believe in immortality, if the career of Jesus had ended at the cross.

But the record of Christ did not end on Calvary. When I let my mind lie open to the record and allow each Gospel to send its wave of testimony in on my thought, I feel a rising tide of conviction in the truth of Christ's triumph over the grave.

The sad-hearted women going out in the misty morning to anoint the body of their departed leader; the experience in the garden which sent them rushing back to bring the disciples; the evening walk to Emmaus when a mysterious presence seemed to accompany them and to make their hearts burn within them on the way; the upper room a week later with the disciples gathered about the still doubting Thomas, and then his cry of conviction, "My Lord and my God" —these Easter reports are told with such reserve and artlessness that I cannot believe they were inventions. If not invented, may these resurrection reports constitute just another ghost story to be added to the world's collection? But what ghost ever had the effect of producing moral grandeur in the people who thought they saw him? When did a ghost drive men from abject terror to flaming, ringing courage? Yet that is what the Resurrection did for the disciples. It transformed them from defeated refugees trying to slip out of Jerusalem's back streets into triumphant radiant apostles proclaiming the Risen Lord.

Something happened which made Jesus more alive in the streets of Jerusalem at Pentecost than He was on Palm Sunday. Was it all a delusion or was it a divine revelation? The conviction that Christ triumphed over death has carried the Christian movement

4

for nineteen centuries. It sustained the hunted Christians hiding in the catacombs. It comforted the Christians in the blacked-out cities of war-torn regions. It is sending its Easter hopes through the hearts of six hundred million followers of Christ today.

Jesus so lived and taught that He brought glimpses of the kingdom of heaven into the here and now. He said, "The kingdom of God is in your midst."

Have we not all enjoyed some snatches of eternal life? Have we not all had some experiences so engrossing that we became oblivious to time, and "one crowded hour of glorious life is worth an age without a name." And we exclaim, "Ah, this is heavenly," and we have those moments of rare insight and lofty feeling when, as the Scripture says, we taste "the powers of an age to come."

Have we not discovered that hours spent with loved ones flash by with never a look at the clock, while hours spent in a hospital corridor awaiting the outcome of a serious operation drag by on leaden feet? There is a quality of life which is independent of the quantity. And that quality which lifts us above the limitations of time and lessens the fear of death, which makes us feel the nearness of heaven and the nowness of eternity—that is what Christ imparts to those who cultivate His company.

Christ lifts our spirits above the limitations of the body by enlarging our lives and setting our hearts on things invisible and eternal. And I feel that some of this universal, imperishable, on-going life is in me. How it came to me I do not know. To be sure, that spark of life was passed on to me by my parents at birth, but that power of generation is a mystery. It is a mystery, too, where the seat of life is.

Ten years ago on Easter morning a little girl made her first appearance on the stage of this world. On that first day she was flesh of her mother's flesh and blood of her mother's blood. Now she is a little individual self, forming her own ideas, making up her own mind, headed for her own life.

If, as we are told, the human body changes its tissues every seven years, three years ago all of the mother's body which was born in that little girl was gone, but more and more of her mother will be in her mind and heart as the years pass. As I watch that little girl gradually losing the elements of her mother's body but steadily growing into the attitudes of her mother's mind, I realize how, as Jesus said, "life is more than meat," and how love leaps over the limits of the body. Now that mother can feel the presence of her child in the next room, and the time will come when that daughter grown to womanhood will feel her mother's presence in the next room, or even, as we say, in the next world. Who shall separate us from the love of mother? "Shall tribulation, or distress, or persecution, or famine, or nakedness, or peril, or sword?"

John Henry Newman put our Christian faith in his beloved hymn:

> So long thy power hath blessed me, sure it still
> Will lead me on,
> O'er moor and fen, O'er crag and torrent, till
> The night is gone;
> And with the morn those angel faces smile,
> Which I have loved long since and lost awhile.

HOW ARE WE TO PICTURE THE LIFE ETERNAL?

A few years ago one of my best parishioners wrote me a very lovely letter telling of her twenty-one years' membership in my church. In it she modestly said: "I wish I were more spiritually minded, for as life goes farther and farther, the beyond gets closer but not clearer." I suppose most of us share her feeling, for as long as we are in this physical room of our Father's many-mansioned house, we "see through a glass darkly." We see and talk in material terms, and these are not adequate to describe the life beyond the body.

Hence we have projected our most precious material things, such as golden streets and pearly gates, into our pictures of heaven. All this is, of course, not justified by Jesus' own teaching. What He said was, "I go to prepare a place for you." And from this all we can conclude is that heaven is the kind of place our kind of Christ would choose.

How can we make the future life seem alive and real? Let me use a very inadequate analogy. Suppose a Californian became stranded among the Eskimos in some snow-bound region of Alaska. How would he make Southern California understandable to the Eskimos? He would have to describe his home to the Eskimos mostly in negatives, because they could hardly comprehend palm trees and oranges. So he would say to them that there is no ice there, no igloo, no whale meat there, no midnight sun.

Similarly the Scripture describes heaven mostly in negatives. There will be no night there, no weeping, no walls. The Bible can only say that this natural body will be raised a spiritual body, and "this corruptible body will put on incorruption," that "if the earthly tent we live in is destroyed," we shall have a "house not made with

6

hands, eternal in the heavens." All this is rather hard to make real and living, isn't it?

Since Jesus was a teacher here on earth, I believe heaven will be a kind of school, where we go on growing in grace and advancing in knowledge. Since Jesus was just, I believe there will be justice which punishes us for our sins and rewards us for our virtues; but I think heavenly justice will be aimed at redemption rather than at vengeance, and that our Heavenly Father will ever hold the light of hope before His children. Since Jesus was full of love and compassion, I believe there will be infinite mercy in the hereafter.

Since God is love and Christ craved comradeship, we can believe that there will be fellowship in the hereafter. I believe that we shall know our loved ones better in the spirit realm than here where we see through a glass darkly, and where we often are too hurried to look at them. I agree with Frederick William Faber when he sang:

> For the love of God is broader
> Than the measure of man's mind;
> And the heart of the Eternal
> Is most wonderfully kind.

WHAT MUST WE DO TO INHERIT LIFE?

Granted that we shall survive death, will we do so *victoriously?*

There is nothing in the logic of the universe's fidelity nor in the teachings of Christ to warrant the belief that eternal life is given to everyone as a sort of universal insurance policy guaranteeing us against want and hardship. The teaching of the Bible is that eternal life is something that we "lay hold on." We enter the hereafter, as I see it, by way of a schoolroom rather than a courtroom. And if we have not learned much of good in this life, we shall have to start the next life without much of good. If we have not learned to like what Jesus liked, we cannot enter very far into the joy of our Lord. We may survive death and be defeated by it. We may wake up beyond the grave and wish we had not. We may reach the realm of the Spirit and be as little able to appropriate it as a South Sea savage could appreciate the discussions of a convention of scientists. And to be where we do not fit—that is hell. We might go where Christ had prepared a place for us, and be as ill at ease as a night-club roué amid the meditations of a religious retreat. And that would be hell. To be worldly where things are pure and true, to be filled with hate in a realm attuned to love—that would be hell.

7

Let us not torture ourselves with old pictures of hell as a place of unending punishment. God is love, and love chastens only to redeem. Hence, unending punishment can hardly be reconciled with the Father of our Lord Jesus Christ. But on the other hand, let us not fool ourselves into thinking that to get by the gate of death is the guarantee of eternal bliss. Emerson remarked that people clamor for immortality when they have not shown ability to use this life. And Dr. Samuel Johnson once looked back on a day when he had been peevish and fretful, and asked himself, "Is this the kind of life to which eternity is promised?"

Christ could say, "Be of good cheer, I have overcome the world," because He had conquered the fear of losing it. He had learned to live with the values which do not have to be left behind in this world. So can we.

In short, do we in the worldly sense love to live or do we live to love? Love has eternity in its heart. Love is above the ravages of time. Love peoples the shore of the next world with those we "have loved long since and lost awhile," and after a time the company of those who await us yonder is larger than the circle of those we must leave here. Thus, as Paul said, "love never ends" in this world or the next.

Christ came to make men alive to beauty, to enrich the joys of human comradeship, to set men loving the laughter of little children and copying the contentment of birds, to help men feel the thrill of seeking truth and pursuing the perfection of goodness. His enjoyment of life seemed so independent of physical limitations. And He came to impart that quality of eternal living to us so that we might be full of life, full of the kind of life which we can take with us. Thus Christ prepares His followers for the invasion of death.

Christ makes foretastes of the future available to us if we learn to like what He liked, if we look on the things that are invisible and eternal until they become real to us. It is by giving attention to things that we make them real to us. In my boyhood community when a young man was making love to a girl, the neighbors said that he was "paying attention to her." True, that is the way we make love. And if we would make eternal life real and appealing to ourselves, we must give attention to whatever things are true and honest and just and pure and lovely, we must set our values on the inner qualities of life, on character rather than reputation, on being something rather than having something. *The richness of our future life is in our hands today.*

8

Can life be eternal? In my work as a minister, almost every week a window opens to let in clearer light on my conviction of immortality. As I was finishing this Easter message, a friend passed away. He was a scholar, Doctor of Philosophy from Columbia University; he was a distinguished missionary, doctor of souls in China for forty years. The guiding prayer of his life was: "Oh God our Father, I accept Thy gift of love; help me to pass it on for Jesus' sake." On the morning of his death at ninety-two, Dr. Lacey Sites said to those at his bedside: "If we live the eternal life now, we will always."

Such is the confidence Christ's love has kindled in His devoted followers from St. Paul to the present. Surely God will keep faith with those who love Him most. *"Love never ends."*

ASSURANCE

The Religion of the Dawn

Reverend Leslie D. Weatherhead, Ph.D., D.D., Litt.D.
MINISTER, CITY TEMPLE (CONGREGATIONAL), LONDON, ENGLAND, AND HONORARY CHAPLAIN TO HER MAJESTY'S FORCES

Dr. Weatherhead belongs on any list of the great preachers of our day, and his church in London is filled whenever he is in the pulpit. His popularity in the United States is also tremendous. He has the great ability to interpret the Christian story with fresh meaning and power for his hearers, to comfort or convert, to stimulate or to inspire, to lead or to direct.

"The Religion of the Dawn," preached in Marylebone Presbyterian Church, London, on Sunday, June 29, 1958, shows the Christian religion as a religion of faith, comfort, hope, and assurance. The illustrations he uses are especially pertinent.

Although City Temple was destroyed during World War II, Dr. Weatherhead kept his congregation together through his preaching and leadership all through the eleven years in which they were without their own church building. On August 1, 1958, the church offices were finally moved into the new building; on August 10 they held their closing service in Marylebone and the first service in the new church was held on August 17.

Leslie Weatherhead was born in London in 1893. He studied at Richmond Theological College, London University, and Manchester

9

University. During World War I he was a second lieutenant in India, Mesopotamia, Kurdistan, and Persia. He went to Madras, India, in 1919 for the English Methodist Church, and in 1922 returned to Manchester and Leeds. After some years with the Wesleyan Methodist Church in England, he was called to be minister of City Temple in 1936. He has been the minister of this great church ever since.

Among his books are AFTER DEATH, PSYCHOLOGY AND LIFE, JESUS AND OURSELVES, HOW CAN I FIND GOD?, WHY DO MEN SUFFER?, PERSONALITIES OF THE PASSION, DISCIPLESHIP, *and* A PLAIN MAN LOOKS AT THE CROSS. *He has been honored with the doctorate by Edinburgh University, the Pacific School of Religion, and the College of Puget Sound.*

SERMON TWO

"Weeping may tarry for a night, but joy cometh in the morning," Psalms 30:5, E.R.V.

IN THAT EXCELLENT MONTHLY PUBLICATION, *The Reader's Digest*, I read in the April, 1958, number an article called, "You Can't Hold Back the Dawn." The writer, Clarence Hall, tells of a journey he made some years ago to the Holy Places of Palestine. He very much wished to attend the Sunrise Service on Easter Morning held at the Garden Tomb, one of the two traditional places of Christ's burial, and, as I think, the more likely. The night before seemed endless. He was restless and could not sleep. Querulously he turned to the Christian Arab who had promised to be his guide, and asked him if the night would ever pass. He writes, "Abdul's face in the candlelight rebuked me. 'Never fear, my friend. The day will come. You can't hold back the dawn.' Two hours later at the Garden Tomb, the service began. The minister read from the Bible with the aid of an electric torch and the choir sang Easter anthems. Then, with dramatic suddenness, the sun burst over the horizon, banishing the gloom and flooding the sky with light. I remembered Abdul's phrase: 'You can't hold back the dawn.'"

❋ ❋ ❋ ❋ ❋

I call Christianity "The Religion of the Dawn" because, if I may so put it, it has a Dawn-Answer for every situation. It does not pretend that there is no night. Nor, though here we must desert the figure, does it counsel that nothing can be done to hasten the

10

dawn. But it is a religion of unquenchable faith and hope and patience; unquenchable because it believes that the permanent thing is light and the passing thing is darkness; that however long the night, whether it be in world affairs or the poignant private world of the human heart, the night will pass. "You can't hold back the dawn." All affairs, private and world-wide, are in the hands of a God who is in complete and final control and Who has decreed the entire conquest of all evil and the final emergence of indescribable good.

* * * * *

I think my description of Christianity, "The Religion of the Dawn," is not ill-chosen, for Christianity was born in the most wonderful dawn in the world's history.

Cast your mind back, if you will, to early beginnings. Watch those young men whom Jesus called to Him—Andrew, Peter, Matthew, John and the rest. I suppose we shall never be able to enter into the darkness of the night that overwhelmed them when they shivered behind shut doors on the night when their Master was taken and on the next day when He was brutally put to death. They had heard His words of new life. They had watched His marvelous deeds. They had seen Him raise the dead. Who would have thought he would let himself be taken, tortured and murdered by a handful of Jews? Was He not in command of supernatural forces? Had He not spoken of legions of angels ready to do His bidding? And now it was all over! He was dead and they were disillusioned. Where were all His promises about a new kingdom and their privileged places in it? What now of His talk about the whole world responding to His message?

And then, at dawn on Easter morning the Resurrection! After the great darkness, this amazing dawn! Within seven weeks they—the hunted, frightened fugitives—had become flaming missionaries and willing martyrs ready to lay down their lives rather than deny the truth of His risen glory and His transforming power. Christianity was launched on its world mission. From the East the dawn-light spread across the skies of the world. The religion of the dawn!

* * * * *

But there was a second darkness. They thought He would return in their own lifetime and that that return would be the end of the world they had known. Some of His own words lent credence to

11

this. St. Paul preached at one time this very message. Men actually left their work. It seemed silly to go on making pottery that would never be used, or plows that would make furrows for seed that would never come to harvest. It seemed futile to slave for a master when *the* Master would soon return and open a new era on a new plane of heavenly existence.

But He came not. What did come was persecution. The first epistle of Peter was written against a background of the terrible persecution of A.D. 65 when saints were martyred, not delivered, and when to confess Christ's name meant certainly a new life in one sense, but a quick death as well. Says the letter to the Hebrews (11:35 *ff*): women were tortured, mocked, scourged. Men were stoned, sawn asunder and slain with the sword. "They went about in sheepskins and goatskins; being destitute, afflicted, evil entreated of whom the world was not worthy, wandering in deserts and mountains and caves and holes of the earth."

What sort of new day was this? They were happier before it dawned.

One is reminded of a story told by Hilaire Belloc. With a friend he set out one evening to climb in the Pyrenees. They were caught in a terrible storm and the night came on. Thunder roared and lightning flashed. Rain drenched them and tempest all but dragged them from their hold on the rocks among which they sought to shelter through the long and terrifying night. Belloc's friend was new to the experience. "Isn't this terrible?" he shouted to his friend. "It seems like the end of the world." Back came the reassurance of the more experienced traveler. "This is how the dawn comes in the Pyrenees," he said.

And again and again in Christian history, both widespread and personal, the dawn has seemed born of storm and tempest, danger and horror, tears and death, but it has come, and its light has spread across the world.

* * * * *

Is it merely wishful thinking to suppose that Christianity is really like the dawn? Is it as certain? Is it as all-conquering?

I think we may say that it is not merely wishful thinking to believe in its power when we consider three points.

(1) *What Christianity has done.*

Admittedly it has been the cause of much quarreling, strife and bloodshed, of cruelty, persecution and intolerance. But it has always fought evil, when it was recognized to be evil.

12

It tackled slavery and overcame that darkness. It tackled the evils of disease and suffering, and while it did not originate the hospital, it immensely enlarged the scope of tackling disease. The very names of some of our oldest London hospitals—St. Bartholomew's, St. Thomas's, St. Mary's—testify to the support of religion. It tackled ignorance. The first schools were church schools and the Church kept the torch of education alight through the darkness of the dark ages. It tackled injustice. The phrases we still use reveal the part the Church played. Justice was first of all administered in church, and the "bar" to which counsel were "called" was the communion rail. The judge sat below the high altar and the bow of the advocate is a relic of the earlier bow, not to the judge, but to the crucifix above his head.

As Christianity has been like a dawn dispelling slavery, disease, ignorance, and injustice, it will, as it is promoted and extended, banish class distinction, color bars, prostitution, married unhappiness, poverty, industrial strife and war.

(2) *Where the dawn of Christianity cannot yet banish darkness, it shines in judgment upon evil.*

Look for a moment at this imaginative picture. "Here is a great banqueting hall in ancient Rome, on the tables is every possible thing to eat and drink; round the tables are noblemen and women, wearing wonderful robes and glittering dresses, enjoying themselves to the full. Imagine the scene to be full of pagan splendor, with wonderful music stealing through the room. Imagine that feast going on and on through the night, an orgy of eating and drinking and making merry. Then imagine that through the windows facing the East, there rises the slow, majestic, steady, certain light of dawn, until the guttering candles seem an insult to its glory. As the sun rises higher in the sky, what a dejected, vulgar, dismal scene it is, with men drunk and women disheveled, with candles guttering and people stupid with wine! Yes, when the Dawn comes, all other lights fail and *all false ways of living are betrayed.*" [1]

In the blessed dawn-light of Christianity, how mean and sordid, how shabby and meretricious, unworthiness looks! No one, since Christ rose with a glory like the sunrise, will ever be satisfied with things that belong to the darkness. Where Christianity has not banished evil, it has made us ashamed of evil. "This is the judgment that the light has come." [2] And as men cannot pluck the sun from the summer sky and push it back so that the night that is past once

[1] From my book, *Over His Own Signature*, Epworth Press, pages 85–6.
[2] John 3:19.

13

more overcomes the day, so no one will ever live again as though Jesus Christ had never lived.

Christianity is a Dawn Religion, and you can't hold back the dawn.

> Whatever clouds may veil the sky,
> Never is night again.

(3) *The third factor we must remember is that of the character of God.*

It is this that makes the dawn certain. As we *know* that the dawn will come tomorrow because of those unalterable majestic laws by which God governs His universe, so we may *know* that that same omnipotent hand is on man's affairs, yes, on every man's life, and on them for good, to banish all that is evil and to establish all that is good.

If the history of the world ended in a welter of atomic wars and the incredible horrors of which we have been warned; if cancer and polio, pain of body and madness of mind, frustration of personality and unredeemed disappointment, if these things of the night had the last word, then, indeed, there would be at the heart of the universe either nothing at all or a feeble and purposeless obscenity instead of a loving, wise and finally omnipotent Spirit. We might as well sing in such a case a new Nunc Dimittis—"Lord, now lettest Thou Thy servant depart in tears, for mine eyes have seen hell."

Our certainty about the dawn is firmly based on the character of God.

I heard, many years ago, a sad but true story. Try to picture the scene. It was Christmas Eve in a middle-class home. There was no poverty, no real need. Three children had gone to bed. But they were much too excited to sleep. They did not believe any longer in Father Christmas, but they did believe in Daddy. Their mother, too, had given them reason to hope. Daddy had promised that when he was up in town he would get the presents which were to fill their stockings.

Then, very late, there was the sound of unsteady feet and a rough voice which they hardly recognized. Daddy was drunk. He had spent all his money on drink. He had completely forgotten his children. When he got home, it was too late to do anything about it, and he was much too fuddled, even if a shop here and there had still been open. The mother could do nothing. The next morning three little stockings were empty. The children crept together into one bed and wept out their disappointment under the bedclothes. Having dressed, they loyally tried to keep back further tears, tried to behave as though nothing had happened, tried to love the one who had brought such disappointment to their home. They had hoped, they had had reason to hope, but the character of the person concerned, the character which was the basis of their hopes, had broken down. All through the night they had hoped that the dawn would bring happiness, but he on whom all depended let them down.

For us, the character of God is the supreme assurance of the blessedness of a satisfying dawn.

* * * * *

I dare not leave my message there, however. We must remind ourselves of two facts, one challenging, one comforting.

(1) God uses men to bring light to them that sit in darkness. Ah, you say, your imagery breaks down there, for God does not require man to help Him make the dawn. But God often wants men to tell their fellows that the dawn is in the sky. How many times have great men pulled up a blind that men may see what God can do; aye, what God has done! How many times have wise men opened a door and urged their fellows to turn their backs on darkness and turn east toward the dawn light! Moses told Israel that the dawn was in the east, and they found the light of liberty; and so we could go on through the great names of the world—Augustine, Luther, Wilberforce, Lincoln, Wesley.

Congregations misunderstand the preacher's use of famous names. They think, "Yes, but I am not great like that." But the preacher uses these names because he has access to these lives. Everybody knows about them. But you and I can visit a lonely heart, a sick soul, an unhappy spirit and carry the Dawn-Religion in our eyes, our handclasp, our gift of flowers, our simple word of love. We can say, "You are facing the wrong way. The dawn is in the sky."

(2) So I come to this last word of comfort. Because I believe in God and because I believe in the character and might of God, I believe that for everyone, *everyone*, EVERYONE, life is working out toward an indescribable good. Nothing less than this would satisfy the God I believe in. He is such a good Shepherd that He will never be content if a sheep be lost. He will search and search *"until He find it,"* as Jesus said (Luke 15:4).

There will come, after however long a night and dark a road, a sense of being safe, of being secure, of utter well-being. God is good beyond our dreams, and the universe is finally friendly to all

15

that we value most. The values we cherish like love, beauty, truth, humility, unselfishness, will triumph over every force of evil, however blatant and powerful that evil may seem to be. All things work together toward an indescribable good, to all who do not finally close their hearts against God, and surely no one will *finally* do that; see the splendor and beauty and meaning of Love and repudiate it. Oh, yes! I too believe in hell. But there is not a word in the Bible which proclaims that it is endless. We may suffer in the next world. I think we shall as we realize how our sins here have hindered God's Kingdom, hurt other lives, hampered our usefulness and retarded our progress. We shall all suffer the pains of discipline and remorse. But we shall still be free to turn to the light and all men will do so at last, however distant that "last" may be. The alternative is a God Who has failed and is eternally mourning His lost sheep and eternally deprived of the fullness of joy.

Every man and woman, whatever trouble they may be facing, may say with utter conviction—feeling as sure as they are sure of the dawn—this will not only pass, but be woven into a pattern of indescribable beauty. Sorrow, disappointment, physical pain, mental anguish and spiritual desolation, these things are of the night and the night will pass. The joy of all men is finally absolutely certain.

Now having listened so long, you deserve to hear the text! It is in Psalm 30, verse 5: "Weeping may tarry for a night"—the Hebrew word "tarry" means "spend the night as a lodger";—"but *joy cometh in the morning*" and the morning is *certain*.

Ours is the Religion of the dawn.

Life's Most Indispensable Possession

Reverend James S. Stewart, D.D.

PROFESSOR OF NEW TESTAMENT, LANGUAGE, LITERATURE AND THEOLOGY, NEW COLLEGE, UNIVERSITY OF EDINBURGH; (FORMERLY MINISTER, NORTH MORNINGSIDE CHURCH, CHURCH OF SCOTLAND), EDINBURGH, SCOTLAND. ONE OF THE CHAPLAINS TO HER MAJESTY THE QUEEN IN SCOTLAND.

Dr. James Stewart is surely one of the great preachers of our day. His sermons are a combination of profound thought and

*spiritual insight to which is added a simple persuasiveness that brings
the Gospel near men's hearts and men's hearts near the love of God.
In "Life's Most Indispensable Possession" he discusses man's urgent
need of the Spirit of God in his day-by-day living and shows how
men miss the finest things of life if they do not have God and Christ
with them always.*

*Preaching has been important in Scotland for at least four or
five hundred years. The Scots grow up on good preaching, and the
Kirk of Scotland has developed preaching of a high quality. From
John Knox to James Black, John Baillie and James Stewart there has
been a long line of great Scottish preachers who have spoken the
Gospel as they learned it in school and study and prayer.*

*James Stewart adds to the glory of this line of pulpit masters
with his own great preaching.*

*In Edinburgh people go to hear him wherever he preaches. It
it worth a pilgrimage anywhere to hear Stewart of Edinburgh. Now
his work at New College allows him to teach others who may one
day join the long line of great men who have made New College-
trained ministers world-famous.*

*People in America like Dr. Stewart's preaching almost as much as
his own people in England and Scotland, and when he comes here
for his periodic visits, he is always sure of a warm welcome in New
York or Boston or Chicago or Brooklyn or Los Angeles. When he gave
the Lyman Beecher lectures on preaching at Yale, he added stature
to the long line of distinguished ministers who have given these great
lectures.*

*Several of his books have had wide influence on contemporary
religious thinking:* A MAN IN CHRIST (*a discussion of the vital elements
of Saint Paul's religion*), THE GATES OF NEW LIFE, THE STRONG NAME,
HERALDS OF GOD, A FAITH TO PROCLAIM *and* THINE IS THE KINGDOM.

*In 1959 he was invited to Australia to be guest preacher for three
months in the Scots Church, Melbourne.*

SERMON THREE

". . . take not thy holy spirit from me," Psalm 51:11

THAT IS AN ABRUPT CRY from the edge of the abyss. It is the
cry of a man suddenly feeling that the foundations of his world are
in danger of being swept away. "Take anything else I have, but not

17

the one thing that makes life livable! Take not Thy Holy Spirit from me."

You may call this picture in the Psalm overdrawn. You may feel it has very little connection with ourselves, worshiping God here today in tolerable comfort and security. You may think this man's shattering experience is right outside the orbit in which we normally live and move and have our being. We are not crying to God from the edge of any abyss. This is irrelevant.

But wait a moment.

You and I have our faith today—thank God for that! But—do we never find ourselves wondering how we should fare if for one reason or another that faith in God were gone and we were left spiritually unsupported? Do we never have moments when we feel that the mounting pressure of life, its frustrations and vexations, its deadly wear and tear, its hard humdrum necessities, are threatening to dim down or even extinguish many a heavenly vision that once cheered us on our way?

When Robert Browning breaks in boisterously, crying,

> "Grow old along with me!
> The best is yet to be—"

are there not moods in which we want to raise an angry, disbelieving question mark against that confident philosophy, and tell him bluntly it is not true? St. Paul put it another way: "Though our outward man perish, yet the inward man is renewed day by day." Yes, Paul, it is lovely, no doubt, when it happens like that. But suppose it does not? Suppose our inward spiritual man is not renewed to match the dwindling of the physical enthusiasm, suppose the inner man goes on dwindling too and the fire of the spirit burns low, what are the prospects then?

You see, the Psalmist's cry is not really so strange and unfamiliar after all. At some time most of us have stood or will stand just where he stood then. "Take not Thy Holy Spirit from me."

✤　✤　✤　✤　✤

Now what I want to do is to let the light of the Gospel fall upon this text and this experience. Consider, first, *what it means to possess and to lose the Spirit.*

I would put it like this. To be aware of and obedient to the inner voice that speaks in conscience, to be alert and sensitive to the mind of Christ—this is what it is to have the Spirit. To have a faith that takes God at His word, to have a hope that looks beyond the darkness to the dawn, to have a love that sees in every human creature a brother for whom Christ died—this it is to have the Spirit. To be alive to the existence of a world unseen; to realize that the common ways of life are continually being interpenetrated by another dimension, the dimension of the Eternal; to have glimpses, even in the here and now, of a supra-human quality of life—this it is to have the Spirit.

> And every virtue we possess,
> And every victory won,
> And every thought of holiness
> Are His alone.

Well may the Psalmist cry—"Take not Thy Holy Spirit from me!"

But now look at the other side of it. What does it mean to lose the Spirit?

This. To be unresponsive to the still small voice, insensitive to the Living God, and weary of the irksomeness of Christ—this is what it means to lose the Spirit. To grow skeptical about faith, disillusioned about hope, cynical about love—this it is to lose the Spirit. To feel that the struggle between good and evil is not worth the battle; to find your spiritual zest and idealism smothered by the dust and dreariness of life, replaced by moral lassitude and inertia and debility; to stop caring for religion, to find prayer weariness and belief a sham, to record as the final verdict on it all "Vanity and vexation of spirit and a striving after wind"—this it is to lose the Spirit. Well may any of us cry—"Take not Thy Holy Spirit from me!"

* * * * *

Consider, in the second place, that *thus to lose the Spirit is of all deprivations the most far-reaching and calamitous.* I can illustrate this best by some analogies.

Think, for example, of a musician deprived of the music that is his life. The tragedy of Beethoven was that he went stone-deaf; he never heard, except intellectually, his own greatest melodies. I have visited several times the house in Bonn on the Rhine where Beethoven was born and lived. It is now a museum; and one of the most poignant exhibits is a big glass case full of the strangest ear trumpets, of all shapes and sizes, from an inch or two in length to two or three feet. This was the composer desperately trying to hear the music he would never hear again. Well might Beethoven have cried—"Take not my music from me!"

Or think of a devotee of Nature being deprived of Nature's

beauty. Some of you will remember the scorching, tumultuous words that Bernard Shaw puts into the mouth of St. Joan when her judges have sentenced her to perpetual imprisonment. "Send me to the stake rather than that," she cries. "To shut me from the light of the sky and the sight of fields and flowers; to chain my feet so that I can never again climb the hills—this is worse than the furnace seven times heated. Without these things I cannot live; and by your wanting to take them away from me, I know that your counsel is of the devil, and that mine is of God." So might any devotee of beauty cry— "Take not this fair world of Nature from me!"

Or you might think of an exile deprived of country and home. All exiles in every age speak the same language: whether it is Robert Louis Stevenson far away in the South Seas dreaming of the moors of Scotland:

> Blows the wind today, and the sun and the rain are flying,
> Blows the wind on the moors today and now,
> Where about the graves of the martyrs the whaups are crying,
> My heart remembers how.

Or whether it is the Hebrew poet of Israel's captivity—"By the rivers of Babylon, there we sat down; yes, we wept, when we remembered Zion. We hanged our harps upon the willows in the midst thereof. How shall we sing the Lord's song in a strange land?" "Take not my country and my home from me!"

Or just once again you could think of a loving heart deprived by death of the dear object of its love. There are partings that pierce life with pain unspeakable, the aching elemental poignancy of that last farewell, the grief that binds all generations into one, the same yesterday, today, and forever: "O my son Absalom! my son, my son Absalom! Would God I had died for thee, O Absalom, my son, my son!" "Take not my love from me!"

These are analogies. But now this has to be said: desolating as such privations are, the one of which the Psalmist speaks is more desolating still. After all, Beethoven could triumph in affliction, and Joan of Arc go through the fire to victory, and exiled Israel lead captivity captive, and love and heartbreak look beyond parting to a wonderful reunion where there shall be no more parting again forever. As long as you have the Spirit of God, all these other desolations are at least bearable. As long as that Spirit remains, you can see life through with honor. But if once that Spirit should go, then gone is all the reinforcement: no light to guide, no voice to interpret and give meaning, no hand to steady and control. Then indeed is Paradise lost and chaos is come again. This is the last intolerable loneliness. This is life's uttermost of desolation. "Take not Thy Holy Spirit from me."

* * * * *

Consider, in the third place, the question: *But is this risk real? Can* this thing happen? Does God ever remove His Spirit? Would He ever think of taking His Spirit away from anyone?

What of all the texts that say—"I will never leave thee nor forsake thee. Lo, I am with you alway, even unto the end"? Surely the Psalmist is imagining the impossible! Surely in this risky world, here is one risk for which we are guaranteed immunity! For surely you cannot conceive of God looking out from heaven and seeing some poor unhappy creature stumbling through the dark, and God saying, "I am finished with that man! Henceforth I leave him to his own devices"! Can that happen? Does God ever take His Spirit away? This is the question.

There was an old Jewish tradition about the final destruction of Jerusalem and its temple by the Roman legions in the great siege of the year A.D. 70. It was said that just before the final assault loud mysterious voices had been heard echoing through the temple, crying "Let us depart!"—and there had been a sound of great unearthly wings sweeping out across the darkening skies; and this was Jehovah and His attendant cherubim and seraphim abandoning the disobedient city to its fate, God finally withdrawing from the temple that had failed to do Him honor. Legend? No doubt. But what of God's human temples? "Ye are the temple of the Holy Ghost," says the Bible. Is it perhaps not legend there, but fact—the departing Deity, the retreating wings, the irretrievable abandonment?

There is no simple answer to that question. But part at least of the answer would have to be this. There are things in life that certainly break our fellowship with God. They interpose a barrier, and disqualify us for any living awareness of his Spirit.

One is *neglect*—neglect of prayer, neglect of the faculty of spiritual vision. For neglect of this faculty, as of any faculty, inevitably spells its atrophy and decay. There is one significant, pathetic passage in Charles Darwin's *Life and Letters* where the great scientist tells how in his younger days he had loved music and art and literature, having a real faculty for them all and finding intense delight in them; but how latterly he had lost all taste for them, be-

21

cause of his constant one-sided concentration on his scientific calculations. He had in fact reached the point where he could not endure to read a line of poetry, and found even Shakespeare nauseatingly dull. "If I had my life to live over again," wrote Darwin, "I would make it a rule to read some poetry and listen to some music at least once every week"—just to keep the faculty alive. So on a deeper level, to neglect the faculty of spiritual vision is to condemn it to a similar degeneration. "Take the talent from him," said the master in Jesus' parable of the man who would not use his gift, "take it away from him!" If we will not use our capacity for the Spirit nor exercise our faculty of faith, we need not hope to keep them. This is the nemesis of neglect.

But neglect is passive. There is a more active attitude that tells in the same direction, breaking fellowship and destroying a man's openness to the divine Spirit—the attitude of *rebellion*, the secret revolt, the sin that clouds the soul.

Now this is the clue to the Fifty-first Psalm. For according to tradition, this Psalm was written by David after the blackest hour of his life. David, shepherd-king of Israel, had broken the vows which in the day of his anointing he had made to the high God of his salvation. He had stolen Bathsheba and sent the brave soldier Uriah to his death. He—David—had done this. "How are thou fallen from heaven, O daystar, son of the morning!" And all these months since, a restless remorse had been rankling in his heart. He had tried to pray, and no prayer would come. He had bowed in worship before the throne of heaven, and God was silent to him and gave him no sign. And so the dark cloud lowered and the black mood deepened. And then one day at last Nathan the prophet had come with one swift rapier thrust had pierced the king's defenses: "Thou art the man!" And in that instant, as in a sudden lightning flash across the darkness, David saw where these past months of unrepented, unforgiven sin had brought him—to the verge of a terrible abyss, from which now, shuddering, he recoiled.

Martin Luther once on a similar day was heard to cry beseechingly: "Punish us, O God, punish us, but be not silent towards us!" For anything is more bearable than that ominous silence of heaven; any discipline of punishment, any fire of judgment more tolerable than that fading out of the vision, that growing dumb of the voice, which are the nemesis of the soul's rebellion. It was with the realization of how near he had come to being a castaway that David raised beseeching hands to heaven: "Take not Thy Holy Spirit from me!"

Now let us see the point we have reached. We have considered, first, what it means to lose the Spirit; second, the magnitude of this deprivation; and third, its possibility.

But when we have reached this point, suddenly a great burst of Gospel light comes breaking from this text. This is the last thing I ask you to consider; and it is the most important of all. *The very fact that the Psalmist could make this cry proved that the Spirit was still there.* For, you see, it was precisely God's Spirit within him that made him cry like this. This is in fact an instance of what Paul described to the Romans as "the Spirit Himself making intercession for us with groanings that cannot be uttered."

Here on the day when David miserably felt he had reached rock bottom, he suddenly discovered that he had reached the Rock of Ages. In the moment of his despairing cry, "Take not Thy Holy Spirit from me," he was nearer the heart of God than he had been for months. This, I repeat, is the Gospel shining through; and it means that when you have touched the depths, you have touched the everlasting arms.

Take any of us here today. How comes it about that we are here? Surely our broken vows, our frequent failures, would long ago have justified God in removing His Spirit from us once for all. And yet —the very fact that we are here in God's House is evidence of His Spirit still operating in our lives. And therefore to the most discomfited soul here today the word of the Lord would be precisely Jesus' word to His disconsolate disciples long ago: "Look up, and lift up your heads, for your redemption has come nigh!"

May I say a special word in closing to anyone whom the pressure of these days has been victimizing? You have had your share —perhaps more than your share—of the elemental facts of pain and discipline and trial and loneliness. You have felt faith strained to the point where it begins breaking down into unbelief. It may be you have been brought quite near to the breaking point, almost (humanly speaking) to the end of your tether. You have experienced the same forsakenness that the Psalmist knew, and Job and Elijah and Jeremiah. Be of good courage! For that is precisely the kind of experience that gives God His best chance. It is far opener to His Spirit than any amount of glib, facile religious profession.

For once there walked this earth a Man Who had not where to lay His head. In nakedness and pain and desolation He tasted death for every man, and out of the last darkness cried, "My God,

My God, why hast Thou forsaken Me?" And God in everlasting mercy brought Christ through, and set Him on high, and shattered death with resurrection: so that today wherever the name of Jesus is called upon—even if it is only a half-articulate cry, "Jesus, from Your cross have mercy!"—He is veritably present in the midst. This is not pious metaphor. It is sober fact.

You may have been having a difficult time in all conscience, and life may have hurt you sore. But do you not see that it is just there through the tender mercy of your God that the dayspring from on high has visited you? And the secret of weathering the storm in the day when the rain descends and the floods come and the winds blow and beat upon the house—the secret is not your tenacity and endurance; it is God's constancy, Christ's fidelity. Place your confidence there, and you build on the rock that nothing can move.

There was a night sixty years ago when one of Henry Drummond's great student meetings was nearing its end, and Drummond was appealing for decisions. "I cannot guarantee," he said, "that the stars will shine brighter when you leave this hall tonight, or that when you wake tomorrow a new world will open before you. But I do guarantee that Christ will keep that which you have committed to Him." He will keep His promise, right on to the unknown end.

I should be a fool to stand here today and talk to you about religion, if I were not dead sure of that elemental fact. I know Whom I have believed. I know that His promise stands fast forever.

> Jesus, my Lord! I know His Name,
> His Name is all my boast;
> Nor will He put my soul to shame,
> Nor let my hope be lost.
>
> I know that safe with Him remains,
> Protected by His power,
> What I've committed to His trust,
> Till the decisive hour.

A Man with Two Sons

Bishop Gerald Kennedy, Ph.D.
RESIDENT BISHOP OF THE METHODIST CHURCH, LOS ANGELES AREA,
LOS ANGELES, CALIFORNIA

Bishop Kennedy is one of the most dynamic preachers of the American pulpit today and has won respect and confidence everywhere he preaches. "A Man with Two Sons" was first given at the Chicago Sunday Evening Club in Orchestra Hall, Chicago, Sunday, January 19, 1958, and was broadcast over Radio Station WIND. The sermon discusses the story of the Prodigal Son as a drama with four key actors, showing its spiritual application to personal lives. But he has gone beyond the ordinary interpretation of this parable and points out the great need in the world today for understanding among men and nations.

Born in Michigan, Bishop Kennedy studied at the College of the Pacific and the Pacific School of Religion, and took his Ph.D. at Hartford Theological Seminary in 1934. He was ordained a Methodist minister in 1932, and began his ministry at First Congregational Church, Collinsville, Connecticut, where he served from 1932 to 1936. He was appointed to Calvary Methodist Church, San Jose, California, in 1936, and to the First Methodist Church, Palo Alto, California, in 1940. He was Acting Professor of Homiletics at the Pacific School of Religion from 1936 to 1940. He entered into national leadership while he was pastor of St. Paul Methodist Church, Lincoln, Nebraska, from 1942 to 1948. In 1948 he was elected a bishop of the Methodist Church by the Western Jurisdictional Conference, the only time a man has been elected while serving in another jurisdiction. He was first assigned to the Portland Area and then in 1952 to the significant Los Angeles Area, which includes Southern California, Arizona and the Hawaiian Islands.

He has spoken in many parts of the world, lectured on twelve important university foundations, and traveled around the world twice, visiting mission fields and foreign countries in the interests of the church. He is also known as an administrator, leading his church in the establishment of a theological seminary and a university and in the building of new churches, and helping his pastors to become

*better preachers while pointing out the necessity of disciplined study
and pastoral work.*

*Bishop Kennedy is a director of the Rockefeller Brothers The-
ological Fellowship Program and a trustee of the Pacific School of
Religion, Southern California School of Theology, the College of
the Pacific, and California Western University. He is the author of
several significant books, including* HIS WORD THROUGH PREACHING
(a handbook on preaching), THE LION AND THE LAMB *(the Peyton
Lectures at Southern Methodist University),* WITH SINGLENESS OF
HEART, GO INQUIRE OF THE LORD, GOD'S GOOD NEWS *(the Beecher
Lectures at Yale University),* I BELIEVE *and* THE METHODIST WAY OF
LIFE. *His latest book is* THE SECOND READER'S NOTEBOOK. *He is an
omnivorous reader, which is clearly reflected in his preaching.*

SERMON FOUR

> "It was fitting to make merry and be glad, for this your
> brother was dead, and is alive; he was lost, and is found,"
> Luke 15:32, R.S.V.

IF ANY MAN DOUBTS that the Bible has made an impression
on contemporary life, let him note the number of references to the
Parable of the Prodigal Son which appear in secular places. In
books, magazines, newspapers and ordinary conversation, we are
forever assuming a common knowledge of this wonderful story. It
is our common heritage and yet as with all of these marvelous
parables of our Lord, familarity can never dim the luster of its
beauty. This familiar, family situation speaks with old wisdom and
fresh meaning. Here we have illumination to live by and an insight
wider and deeper than the sea.

There are four actors in this drama, and the first one is The Boy
Who Went Away. His spirit is understandable, and it is hardly too
much to suggest that a prodigal boy is a sign of our time. Certainly
he is a good symbol of America, whose aggressive spirit has led
its sons far from home. We shall not understand the reactions of
Asia, if we forget that for them we have been an aggressive civilization threatening their ways and values.

When I went around the world hurriedly a few years ago, one
great impression fixed on my mind was that the West has been in-
invading the East for a long time. When Commodore Perry finished
his treaty negotiations with the Japanese in 1854, no one could

26

pretend that it was primarily Japan's idea. We learned in the Second World War that the Japanese had appropriated our worst and not our best. The whole relationship between the West and China was a one-sided pressure for special privilege and trade advantage, with the exception of the Christian missionary enterprise.

It may be true that the British took over India in a fit of absent-mindedness, as has been suggested. But take it over they did, and the marks of that great colonizing nation can never be erased from India. Mustafa Kemal Pasha transformed Turkey into a modern, Western state after the First World War as a means of self-preservation. To survive, old cultures have had to mold their ways more into our likeness. Around the world we have been like the Prodigal, going into far places and too often wasting our substance in riotous living.

The spirit of science has a restlessness that is characteristic of the young brother. It does not emphasize respect for the past nor does it encourage contentment with the familiar. It is all for trying the untried and breaking loose from past authority. So under its inspiration, we have craved the new and we have been attracted by experimentation. This is not a bad thing, until we lose our perspective as has been the case with too much of our life. This divine restlessness can lead to greatness, but when it lacks a proper respect for the eternal and unchanging, it can lead to disaster.

The younger boy awakened one morning to the realization that he had exhausted his resources. It had never occurred to him that there was a limit to what he could spend and use. Like many a son of an indulgent father, he assumed that food, clothing, entertainment, all came freely and automatically like the sunshine. But the time came when he had to face the fact that someone had been providing these things and he had cut himself off from the provider. We cannot forever take out of the treasury unless somebody is putting something back into it.

We are learning that same lesson the hard way. As a people we have had a great reservoir of good will around the world, provided for the most part by Christian missionaries. We have been draining it away at a terrific rate and now we must consider the problem of replenishment. Of what good is power if everybody hates us? For friendship is more precious than gold and every nation and every man stands soon or late dependent on the good will of other men. Those who give us their companionship because we have something they want, will not hold us up when we are in need.

Let the younger boy who went away stand for all of us who have received so much and wasted so much. Let his condition be a warning to us that we have to contribute to the treasury if we are to find its resources available when we need them. By all means, let the spirit of adventure lead us into new places and new situations, but let us not forget that freedom is not license. Remember the little girl who said to the teacher, "I do too know how to spell *banana*. I just don't know when to stop." Like the Prodigal Son, too often we do not seem to know when to stop and face the responsibilities which God lets neither man nor society ignore forever.

The second actor in this drama is The Boy Who Stayed Home. He does not appear in a good light, and there is meanness and jealousy in him. Yet, and I confess this with some shame, I understand him and even sympathize with him, for I was an elder brother. If there is a family that does not put more responsibility on the elder than on the younger, it is most unusual. Automatically we expect the elder to be more dependable and steadier. Believe me, it gets to be an old story.

I remember walking barefooted with my brother over a hot path when we were both small boys. He began to cry because his feet burned and although mine were burning too, it never occurred to me that there was anything to do but pick him up and carry him. You may have seen a Community Chest poster showing a little boy carrying a smaller one, with this caption: "He ain't heavy. He's my brother." Don't you believe it! I can still remember that although he was my brother, he was still heavy.

This sort of thing gets tiresome. It does something to the thinking of the older brother, sometimes making him more serious than he ought to be. He gets security-minded and perhaps too calculating. He may tend to frown on all carefree behavior and become suspicious of simple joy. Church members are particularly susceptible to this elder brother attitude. Jesus was so much aware of this tendency that he seems to have leaned over backward in criticizing the Pharisee and showing sympathy for the sinner.

What really happens to the boys who stay home is so subtle that they are unaware of it. If you have ever had the delightful experience of being with people who are seasick and you are not, you will understand something of this temptation. We crossed the Atlantic Ocean a few years ago, and encountered especially severe storms. Our party became ill and for some strange reason, I was the only one who felt fine. Now I have been seasick, and that memory should have been enough to stimulate sympathy. But I had a hard time in not being obviously proud of my superiority and feeling an evil pride in not being as other men.

I was once on the budget committee of the Community Chest and president of the Council of Social Agencies at the same time. This was being caught in the middle with a vengeance, a not unusual position for me to be in. The budget men saw the laziness of people who would not provide for their children, and their cost to the community. The social worker saw only the need of innocent children. What taxpayer does not rebel in his heart at being forced to provide for people who ought to provide for themselves? Why must the community take care of the improvident and the slovenly? The answer, of course, is that helpless people are caught in this poverty trap too, and there is a level below which no community can afford to let anyone live. But the citizen who pays for these projects gladly is most unusual.

What man among us does not feel superior to a vast number of other people? It is difficult to walk in the city slums and not thank God for our own virtue. The man who can see the drunk in the gutter, or the woman who can behold the harlot in the doorway, and can look upon them with eyes full of compassion instead of disgust, must be a citizen of the kingdom indeed. For it is hard to believe that these people have not deliberately wasted their heritage and so deserve all that a righteous judgment may decree. Not many of us find it easy to say, "There but for the grace of God go I."

It is only the Christian Gospel that makes clear this unlovely tendency of elder brothers to be angry when the prodigal brother returns. Only in Christ are we able to see how badly the ones who stay at home let the father down. It is a terrible thing when jealousy takes the place of understanding, and when we fail to see that oftentimes our reward is to be unrewarded. The only protection against this sad failure is to stay so close to the Father that something of His love rubs off on us.

You may remember that Lefty Gomez who held the World Series' pitching record (six wins, no losses) was asked the secret of his success. He replied: "Clean living and a fast outfield." No pitcher gets a no-hitter without some miracle catches up against the fence. For every achievement noted on our records, there are the people who helped us up. There is very little room for pride or superiority in the man who has even a faint perception of what he owes to others. In the humility a man catches from Christ, there is the cleansing of his heart. And without this humility, God never has a chance to fill us with the joy of our relationship with Him and our brethren. The boy who stays at home needs the Father's love and forgiveness as much as if not more than the boy who goes away into the far country.

Now the third actor in the drama is not seen and is difficult to define. Let us speak about The Moral Law. Law always implies freedom and judgment and in these two elements there is summed up the relationship between man and God. The covenant between Israel and God proclaimed that Israel was free and that Israel was under judgment. We must look first of all at freedom.

No one will get into any trouble in America by talking about freedom, and most of our present-day orators bring it in sooner or later. It is a sure hit. For everyone assumes that freedom is a very good thing, indeed, and everyone thinks he is in favor of it. It seems to be almost a cliché that everybody wants freedom and no one is against it.

Yet in one school of existential philosophy, it is admitted that men are free but this is not accepted gladly. We are doomed to freedom, is the way it is put, and this terrible burden has been thrust upon us. These thinkers would discard it if they could. Let a man stop and consider what being free really means, and he will never take it lightly even if he does take it willingly. The nineteenth-century scientist Huxley said he would trade it for predestined goodness in a moment.

Whether we take our freedom gladly or reluctantly, still, we must take it. I remember serving on a committee to interview candidates for Rhodes Scholarships a few years ago. There was one boy from West Point and another who had spent one year in an English university before graduating from an American college. The West Point boy told of the strict regulations—grade levels to be maintained—certain hours in study—indeed, it was a military life applied to college.

The other boy related some experiences in the English university. No one called the roll and no one checked or seemed to care what the student did. Of course there came a time when an examination would reveal how the student had been putting in his time, but in the meantime, he was free to do pretty much as he pleased. It came to me that God has ordained that our life shall be more in the nature of an English university than like West Point. We are given a vast amount of freedom. We can postpone our duty for a considerable time; we can follow our own desires and impulses for a time. This, I believe, is the wrath of God which Paul speaks about in Romans. Certainly, it is not something to be taken lightly or easily.

Now the second element in the moral law is judgment. We begin with freedom, but we always come to judgment. The Prodigal Son had to pay for the abuse of his liberty, and there is nothing cheap or trivial in the cost. In the moment when the boy had to face the fact of a wasted heritage, a ruined life and a hopeless future, he was facing judgment. A man's life may strike this depth finally, and then he knows what hell is.

The horrible moment of awakening to reality has often been minimized in the story. It is made to seem so simple and sentimental, as we move rapidly from the boy gone wrong to the boy come home. But in between there was suffering and agony. Even when the boy started homeward, he did not go with any hope that for him there could be forgiveness or restoration. He went with the firm expectation he might become a slave, if he were fortunate, but it never seemed possible that he might be a son again.

There is a story, quite possibly apocryphal, about the philosopher John Dewey walking with his little boy on a wet, cold, windy day. The youngster had no rubbers on his feet and he was splashing around in a puddle. A friend coming by said, "You had better get that boy out of the water. He will get pneumonia." "I know it," the philosopher replied, "but I am trying to find a way to make him want to get out of the water."

Now some of us take a rather dim view of some theories of progressive education. But we must admit that God seems to deal with us more along those lines than with a big stick. Until we come to ourselves—until we want to go home, we must flounder about in the far country. In the meantime, the moral law is inexorable, and as Clement of Alexandria said in the second century, God gives us the Law as a tutor to bring us to Christ.

Finally, let us consider The Father. We must come ultimately to consider God and His character. This is the final reality to which life brings us at last. Jesus brings us to the God Who is revealed in His own life and teaching, and here we find the foundation for all of our life.

We, like the Prodigal, find that God forgives. Now this is a terrifying experience, for it is an awful thing to be forgiven. The man who regards it lightly has never truly experienced it. Voltaire

31

said one time that God would forgive him for that was His business. It was a sure sign that the witty Frenchman had never had the experience on any deep level.

If there is a man who has sinned against his marriage vows and then been forgiven, he will know something of what the runaway boy experienced. When a wife does more than just promise to forget it, but forgives the sin against her, no man will ever be the same again. He is stripped of all his pride and his defense has crumbled. He knows a cleansing of the spirit that changes his life and restores his soul. It creates humility and cracks the hard veneer of his smugness.

If there is a man who has betrayed a friendship and been forgiven by his friend, he will know something of what Jesus is telling us in this story. The shame of our act is made all the more apparent to ourselves when we are confronted by one whose friendship can withstand even our unworthiness. We almost wish he would seek revenge rather than forgive us. This changes our whole concept of personal relationship and we are never the same again in our attitude toward others and toward ourselves. The disturbing quality of forgiveness was summed up a little flippantly in the words: "Love your enemy. It will drive him crazy."

John Newton after years of wandering and sin came home to become a minister in the Church of England. He could never forget the way God saved him from shipwreck, from moral disaster, and from despair. A neighboring curate who drank too much set the curtains of his home on fire while drunk, and was burned to death. Newton heard about the tragedy and wrote this prayer: "Lord may I remember thy patience towards me when I drank down iniquity. Why was I not surprised in my sins and hurried to judgment?" This was the man who wrote a great hymn which best describes my experience:

> Amazing grace! how sweet the sound,
> That saved a wretch like me!
> I once was lost, but now am found,
> Was blind, but now I see.

We are redeemed by God's forgiveness, for we are filled with a great new hope and expectation. When Adlai Stevenson returned from travels in Asia, he said that a "revolution of expectation" was taking place in the world. It is a fine phrase and it describes the new hope in the hearts of millions of people today. They believe that a better life is possible for them and for their children. They no longer accept as final their condition of hunger, poverty and disease. No statesman can lead us on the path to a better world, unless he understands this fundamental quality of the struggle.

There is a sense in which Christ stirred up a revolution of expectation. He proclaimed that no man is hopeless and no human situation is beyond redemption. He comes to a man who has lost faith in himself, and makes him believe that bad as he knows he is, there is healing and mercy with the Lord.

While we are yet afar off, God comes to meet us, and this is the heart of the good news. We are not forced to hammer down the door, but we learn that before we were aware of our need, God sought us. As is usually the case, Paul says it perfectly: "But God shows his love for us in that while we were yet sinners Christ died for us" (Romans 5:8, R.S.V.).

There was an old Methodist circuit rider in the South many years ago. He had two boys, and as he used to say, one was always good, and one was most always bad. The bad boy would run away when his father was gone, but he could always be found at the nearest circus. The father would find him and without any scolding would simply say, "Ed, come home." This went on intermittently for several years. Then one day when the preacher came home Ed was gone and the only circus was two states away. So the old man got on a train and rode the day coach for a day and a night to the circus town. Sure enough, there was Ed. "Come home, son," said his father. "Dad," demanded the boy, "how did you find me way out here?" "Why Ed," said his father, "God always tells me where you are. I will always find you." That broke the boy's stubborn willfulness. "You win," he said. So he went home, attended school and prepared himself for the ministry. Today he is one of the South's respected preachers.

The Gospel Jesus brought to the world tells us that whether we are the boy who went away or the boy who stayed home, we cannot escape our Father's love and concern. The moment we turn homeward, He is there before us to receive us. Beyond all worldly optimism or happiness which men may find here, there is the experience of coming home to God.

The Unseen Presence

Reverend Robert James McCracken, D.D., S.T.D., L.H.D.

MINISTER, THE RIVERSIDE CHURCH, NEW YORK, NEW YORK.

In "The Unseen Presence" Dr. McCracken reaches new heights of excellence in his distinguished preaching at the Riverside Church. Drawing on the biblical story in the third chapter of the Book of Daniel, he shows the source of courage and virtue and confidence, of a life that can reach true fulfillment. It is a sermon worthy to stand with the greatest he has preached since coming to Riverside on October 2, 1946.

In the years he has been in New York, Dr. McCracken has steadily won an increasing following by the soundness of his theology, the power of his sermons and the leadership and friendship he has given the people of his church.

He was born in Motherwell, Scotland, grew up in a Scotch Presbyterian home, went to the local school, and in 1918 became a member of the Baptist Church in Motherwell. He graduated from Glasgow University and became minister of Marshall Street Baptist Church in Edinburgh; in 1933 he became lecturer in Systematic Theology at the Baptist Theological College of Scotland. This made him both preacher and teacher. In 1937 he was called to teach theology and the philosophy of religion in McMaster University, Ontario, Canada, and became closely allied to Canadian church work.

He took a year of special study at Cambridge University to prepare himself for his work at McMaster, then assumed his chair there in 1938. In 1945 and 1946 he was president of the Baptist Convention of Ontario and Quebec and attracted such favorable attention that he was called to the Riverside Church to succeed Dr. Harry Emerson Fosdick in 1946. He holds the honorary D.D. from McMaster, Bucknell, Glasgow, Colgate, Denison, the University of Vermont and Princeton; the S.T.D. from Columbia; and the L.H.D. from Bates College and Shurtleff College.

Dr. McCracken is lecturer in Practical Theology at Union Theological Seminary, New York, and has held special lectureships at Andover Newton, Yale, Texas Christian University, Princeton, Southern Baptist Theological Seminary, and Union Seminary in Rich-

34

mond, Virginia. *He has earned the reputation of having something significant to say and of saying it with brilliance and insight. He is heard over the National Radio Pulpit on Sundays. Among his books are* QUESTIONS PEOPLE ASK, THE MAKING OF THE SERMON *and a collection of his own sermons. In 1957 he traveled to Japan at the invitation of the Japan Committee for Intellectual Interchange. While in the Far East he also visited Hong Kong, the Philippines, Thailand, Burma, India and Pakistan. He saw the U.N. at work and visited missionaries, State Department officials, and leaders in education and religion.*

SERMON FIVE

EARLY IN THIS YEAR a friend told me what his most unforgettable experience had been in 1956. He had listened to a recording made by Charles Laughton. He had heard the great actor read from the Bible the story of the three Hebrew youths, Shadrach, Meshach and Abednego, who at the bidding of Nebuchadnezzar, the dictator, were cast into the burning, fiery furnace. For my friend the supreme moment in the reading had been when Laughton came to the lines: "Then Nebuchadnezzar the king was astonished, and rose up in haste, and spake, and said unto his counsellors, Did we not cast three men bound into the midst of the fire? They answered and said unto the king, True, O king. He answered and said, Lo, I see four men loose, walking in the midst of the fire, and they have no hurt; and the form of the fourth is like the Son of God."

That night when I got home I picked up my Bible, turned to the third chapter of Daniel, and read the story for myself. It must surely rank as one of the best short stories in the world's literature. I wondered why I hadn't read it oftener and why I had never made it the subject of a sermon. Those three Hebrew youths were stalwart nonconformists. They stood up for their freedom and their faith in the face of terrific pressure. There was iron in their blood. They would neither bend nor bow. Why? Because they had robust convictions. Because they were able to draw on superhuman resources. Because their strength and stamina were derived from God. My friend was right. The supreme moment in the story is reached with the words: "Lo, I see four men loose, walking in the midst of the fire, and they have no hurt; and the form of the fourth is like the Son of God."

35

But, somebody may be saying, you are treating a fabulous story, shot through with miracle, as literal, historical fact. I do not treat it as literal, historical fact. I consider that it has a basis in fact. Nebuchadnezzar the dictator was real enough. There were Hebrew youths who had to reckon with him and his policies as in our day Hebrew youths had to reckon with Hitler. Buchenwald was for many a youth, Jew and Gentile, a burning, fiery furnace, but read the letters of Paul Schneider, the young Protestant pastor imprisoned there, and you will learn how in the midst of the fire there walked the Son of God. I regard Daniel's story as a superb parable for all generations of men. Its meaning is that life demands courage as the very foundation of all virtue. Its meaning is that safety is something that life, with sin and death in it, does not offer, and playing for safety is a slavish practice, a symptom of moral arteriosclerosis. Its meaning is that the ultimate security is spiritual, that we are not alone, that God is with us, the Abiding Presence, the Unseen Leader, that if only our eyes could be opened and we could see how real and near and strong God is, our fears would be allayed and our hearts would be brave again and our arms strong.

That is the lesson I deduce from Daniel's unforgettable story. The cumulative evidence, the personal testimonies supporting it, are striking. I think of what Mahomet whispered to his one remaining follower in a terribly dark hour when all seemed lost and the pursuers were closing in on them: "Not so; we are not two, but three. For God is with us." I think of Sir Ernest Shackleton's description of the journey he and his companions made over the icy wastes of the Antarctic. "When I look back on those days with all their anxiety and peril," he wrote, "I cannot doubt that our party of three was divinely guided both over the ice and across the storm-swept sea. I know that during the long and racking march of thirty-six hours over the unnamed mountains and glaciers of South Georgia it seemed to me often that we were not three but four. I said nothing to my companions on the point, but afterwards Worsley said to me, 'Boss, I had a curious feeling on the march that there was another Person with us.' "

In the end all came out happily for Shackleton and his companions. On the other hand, Paul Schneider did not come out of Buchenwald alive. All the more on that account note his testimony in this letter addressed to his wife. "How lovely it would be if we could meet again. But as we have done, we shall leave all in God's hands, trusting Him with patience and courage. From Him alone can we expect all good things. Him shall we love with all our heart and Him alone shall we reverence and worship. So shall God be with us and our hope will not make us ashamed. Be of good cheer, be true and fear not. I hold you fast in my heart. In God we are not divided. Thank you for all the love you have given me. We shall give thanks for this time of preparation, making us ready for new trials. New sufferings will bring us new experiences of our God. Christ said, 'Lo, I am with you alway.'"

Testimonies like those are a powerful support to our Christian faith. They are part of the strength we derive from our membership in the universal Church. We are in a great succession. When doubts assail us and our convictions fade, when the light in our own souls fails, we can look back and see it shining clear and strong along the road that heroic souls have traveled in the company of God. People of all ages and nations and temperaments have borne witness to an experience of the Presence of God that has inspired them to face life and all that life can bring in sickness or suffering, hardship or death, with steady eyes. These divine resources are not confined to a few choice souls, a spiritual elite, men and women gifted with a mystical nature. They are available for us all, and they can come to us—I emphasize this—in all the staple human experiences of life, not only in storm and stress and crisis but when we walk in the sunshine and the sky above our heads has not a suggestion of a cloud in it. At all times, in cloud and sunshine, we are surrounded by a love and a grace which keep seeking for openings into our lives. God is "the Presence that disturbs us with the joy of elevated thoughts" as we walk through the natural world. He is the spiritual power which, working through human agents, has produced all that is great in music and art and literature. He is the source and inspiration of lovers' love and mothers' love. It is He whom seekers after truth are really seeking. He is not far from any of us and indeed has been near us all our days. We are all capable of responding to Him, some in one way and some in another. There are times when we flee from Him.

> I fled Him, down the nights and down the days;
> I fled Him, down the arches of the years;
> I fled Him, down the labyrinthine ways
> Of my own mind; and in the midst of tears
> I hid from Him, and under running laughter . . . .
> From those strong Feet, that followed, followed after.

But we really need Him, and really want Him. Life is not so much a record of man's search for God as of God's search for man. That is why we are here and what we are made for. God is a living, ever-present, inescapable Reality, and we are only real in so far as we are in His order, and He in us.

We learn especially from Christ that God is never far from any one of us but close at hand to support and sustain, that He is always incomparably better than the best we can think of Him, that He is far kinder to every one of us than any of us ever deserves, that He is always seeking a deeper intimacy of trust and affection with every human being. Such teaching seems too good to be true. There is so much in life and history that appears flatly to contradict it. In some ways, in some moods, it is easier to fall back on the assumption that the whole system of things about us, if not heartless and godless, is neutral. And then we are up against an inexorable trilemma. Was Christ Himself deceived, deluded, the victim of wishful thinking? Or was He a deceiver, an imposter, a fraud? Or has He taken us right to the heart of reality? How do you solve that trilemma?

I keep coming back to what the Gospels report Him as saying. Surrounding us every day of our lives is an abiding Presence. If we see the evil of our ways, that is God warning us. If we break from our sins, that is His hand laid on us; if the Unseen and the Eternal become vivid and real to us, that is His voice reaching us through all the haste and tumult of our lives. And, in the Gospels, there is His own unconquerable faith. He sees God everywhere, in nature, in people, in the march of events. The road ahead of Him darkens. What does He do? He turns to His Father, speaks not to One far away but very close at hand. The crowds turn their backs on Him, His dearest friends desert Him, yet He says: "I am not alone: the Father is with Me." And He goes on His way undaunted and invincible. Always confronting us in our deepest moments stands Christ. And ever since the Galilean days there have been the people of all nations and temperaments who have borne witness to an experience of the Presence of God that has inspired them to face life with steady eyes. When David Cairns had retired from teaching and was writing his autobiography he had this to say, and I quote him, not because what he said is singular; but because it is typical of Christian experience for sixty generations: "Life has led me to lay more and more emphasis, not on man but on the grace of God. Today I can pray from the very center of my life—

> Let me no more my comfort draw
> From my frail hold on Thee;
> In this alone rejoice with awe,
> Thy mighty grasp on me."

To have faith of this sort means *an end of loneliness,* the deeper loneliness, loneliness of soul, the loneliness that comes with separation, bereavement, misunderstanding, the struggle with fears, doubts, temptations that create a solitude in the heart into which no earthly friend can come. The faith about which I am speaking puts an end to that. It begets an assurance that encompassing us always there is a Presence to strengthen us, a Love to hearten us, a hand reached out to help us up on the steep places of the journey. In the Old Testament a Psalmist says, "Lord, Thou hast been our home." In the New Testament Paul says, "All men forsook me," and we, knowing how such an experience can make the heart a wilderness, wait for the inevitable cry of weariness, but it does not come—"All men forsook me, nevertheless, the Lord stood by me and strengthened me." David Livingstone on his return from sixteen years spent in Africa, gaunt after twenty-seven fevers, an arm hanging useless from a lion's bite, asked the students of Glasgow University, "Shall I tell you what sustained me amidst the toil, and hardship, and loneliness of my exiled life? It was the promise, 'Lo, I am with you always, even unto the end.'" If only our eyes could be opened and we could see, as others have seen, how real and near and gracious God is, we would never be afraid in the old ways or cowardly with the old cowardice, for we would know with an invincible certitude that we are not alone.

And there is this to be said further. The faith about which I am speaking provides *unfailing resources of stamina and power.* I have noticed here in the church how much we are all given to speaking of the amount of work we have to do and of the difficulty of the tasks entrusted to us—raising the budget, building up the membership, ministering to the needs of the community and the city. In our committees and discussion groups there is one word that keeps cropping up. It is the word "problems." It impresses me increasingly and challenges me in my own heart, to find that the word "problems," or the thing for which it stands, has no prominence in the New Testament. And the reason is plain. Look at your New Testament. Bethlehem, Calvary, Easter Morning, Pentecost opened the eyes of the apostles to the immensity of their resources in Christ. Listen to them. "He is able to succour them that are tempted." "He is able to keep you from falling." "He is able to supply all your need." "He is able to do exceeding abundantly above all that we ask or think." "He is able to save to the uttermost." "He is able to subdue all things unto Himself." "We are *more than* conquerors through Him that loved us." Doesn't that impress and challenge you?

John Ruskin remarks that there is evidence of ease about the great works of nature. When we look at them we don't say, "There is great effort here," but "There is great power here." Is that what people say when they look at The Riverside Church? Is that what they say when they look at our individual lives? Do they look at our strained faces and say, "There is great effort here"? Or do they see something about us which makes them say, "There is great power here"? When the people saw the radiance on the face of Moses they knew that He had been in communion with God. When their opponents looked on the faces of the apostles they "recognized that they had been with Jesus." Oughtn't we to think a bit less about statistics and give less time to organization and promotion, and instead get into closer touch with God? It is not money the Church needs most today. It is not organization. It is not social idealism. It is not intellectual acumen. It is power. And there is no way to power except through a deepened spiritual experience. We cannot stand out against the impotence which is one of the curses of modern life, civic, ecclesiastical, national and international, unless we dwell more often in the company of God's greatness. The bigness that makes Christians adequate for their tasks develops in no other way than through intimacy with the Infinite. If we are worried instead of being serene, confused instead of clear-sighted, busybodies rather than busy, nervous and fidgety when we should be steady and calm, it is because we are out of touch with the unseen Presence, aware of the immensities of the world's problems but forgetful of the immensity of our resources in Christ.

There is an old legend to the effect that Satan was once asked what he missed most since he had fallen from his former high estate in heaven. "I miss most," he answered, "the sound of the trumpets in the morning." The sound of the trumpets in the morning! What does that suggest to you? Vigor! Vitality! Alertness! Resourcefulness! Adequacy! Have we got them in our church life? Have we got them in our personal lives? Do we know where to go to get them?

Well, I have traveled a long way from Charles Laughton and his recording of the story of the three Hebrew youths. Before the day is over make a point of reading the story. You will find it in the third chapter of Daniel. If you make a point of reading it, linger over its climactic passage. "Then Nebuchadnezzar was astonished, and rose up in haste, and spake, and said unto his counsellors, Did we not cast three men bound into the midst of the fire? They answered and said unto the king, True, O king. He answered and said, Lo, I see four men loose, walking in the midst of the fire, and they have no hurt; and the form of the fourth is like the Son of God."

CHRISTIAN LIFE

On the Moving Edge of Time

Reverend Paul E. Scherer, D.D., Litt.D., LL.D.[1]

A MINISTER OF THE EVANGELICAL LUTHERAN CHURCH AND BROWN PROFESSOR OF HOMILETICS, UNION THEOLOGICAL SEMINARY, NEW YORK, NEW YORK

Each year Paul Scherer's reputation and following increase. In this sermon, "On the Moving Edge of Time," Dr. Scherer forcefully discusses God's part and place in history and in human lives. It is a sermon that sings as he preaches it.

Dr. Scherer loves to phrase religion in new, fresh language to capture and hold interest. With his mastery of words he could have been a great novelist; instead, he uses his ability for great preaching. He himself insists that the preparation of each sermon is mostly a matter of hard work. Other preachers find inspiration in his lectures and sermons, and he is in constant demand as a speaker for city-wide groups during Lent and all the year. He is increasingly sought as a speaker and preacher for universities, summer conferences, and church services.

Born in Mt. Holly Springs, Pennsylvania, in 1892, Dr. Scherer studied for his B.D. at the Lutheran Theological Seminary, Mt. Airy, Philadelphia, and was ordained a minister of the Lutheran Church at Allentown, Pennsylvania, in 1916. During 1918 and 1919 he was assistant pastor of Holy Trinity Church, Buffalo, New York. He taught at Mt. Airy Seminary from 1919 to 1929 and was pastor of Holy Trinity Lutheran Church, New York, from 1929 to 1945. In addition, he has preached frequently at colleges and universities along the Eastern seaboard, in England, and on NBC's Sunday Vespers program. At the August Conference in Northfield he has served as vice-chairman since 1937 and as a dean since 1942.

He is the author of a number of stimulating books, including WHEN GOD HIDES (*sermons*), FACTS THAT UNDERGIRD LIFE, THE PLACE

[1] Sermons by members of the Advisory Committee were contributed at the special request of the editor and are included on his responsibility.

41

WHERE THOU STANDEST, EVENT IN ETERNITY, FOR WE HAVE THIS TREAS-URE (*the Lyman Beecher lectures for 1943*), *and* THE PLIGHT OF FREEDOM. *In the recent edition of the* INTERPRETER'S BIBLE, *he contributed the expositions of Job and of the last six chapters of Luke.*

A great preacher, he now gives most of his time to training ministers and young men who attend Union Theological Seminary. His emphasis is upon preaching methods, sermon construction, expository and doctrinal preaching, written sermon manuscripts, lively delivery of the sermons, and criticisms directed toward constructive development. His work with them is sure to be shown in improved preaching throughout the country during the coming years.

SERMON SIX

"Then Samuel took a stone and set it up . . . ," I Samuel 7:12, R.S.V.

Thou hast brought us to this place, O God, by all our several ways, ever keeping faith with us, for all our unfaithfulness. Go before us still, we beseech Thee, by Thy Word and Spirit, leading us from this day forth where it shall please Thee; through Jesus Christ, our Lord. Amen.

THEN SAMUEL TOOK A STONE and set it up . . . and called its name Ebenezer, for he said, "Hitherto the Lord hath helped us."

For him, that was the key which unlocked the meaning of history. If you will have it, it will unlock the meaning of your history. And that, I suppose, without question is really the basic, prophetic function of all true religion. The scene is laid out on the hills of Canaan, three thousand years ago. Yet all at once you have on your hands a moment which seems to stand beyond the reach of change, where the passing centuries can't get at it. One might say of it that it belongs on life's only perpetual frontier. Certainly you can locate it wherever you like, quite at haphazard, in the Old Testament or in the New. From generation to generation, on this moving edge of time which we call the present, gone before you can finish a sentence about it—always this "hitherto," as some man confidently reads God into the past, and just as confidently, if not so explicitly, reads Him therefore into the future: "Hitherto hath the Lord helped us." It's everywhere equally at home. And always there are those who hearing it set their faces toward the unknown, sure that what has been true of that unfailing Presence will go on being true for-ever. Some of them have to toil desperately—but no matter; others march as if they were listening to music, and nothing but the music were important!

Yet the moment you begin to look a little more closely into this business of reading God into the past, that moment you begin to wonder if perhaps it isn't a thoroughly arbitrary thing for anybody to do: as if you were saying to yourself, "Go to now, I will put together the picture-puzzle of these years that are gone, and I will put it together as I like. I will make it spell out for me what I want it to spell out. I will see in it the hand of God." The skeptic will tell you that's what faith is. And it makes no sense. He's right about that. It makes no more sense than one of Camus' characters makes in *The Plague*—indeed not as much! He has just looked on at the agonized death of a little child, and he says, "I will never love any scheme of things which permits that."

Observe, however, as a matter of some significance surely, what a strange sort of noise those words would make on Calvary. "And when they were come to the place . . . there they crucified him, and the malefactors, one on the right hand, and the other on the left." Now let's try it: "I will never love any scheme of things which permits that." And observe too that the Christian doesn't love a scheme of things. Moreover, what loving he does, he doesn't do because he has scraped together all the evidence he could find in favor of it, and chucked out the rest. You don't fall in love that way. Nobody on this earth ever has. Shakespeare in one place seems to try it on for size. He's talking about the uses of adversity, which he forthwith compares to a toad, ugly and venomous, but wearing a precious jewel in its head; so may this our life, says he, "find tongues in trees"—and what if they fall on you?—"books in the running brooks"—but suppose you slip and drown!—"sermons in stones"—Goliath would have had a little difficulty there!—"and good in every-thing." I say you don't dare talk to me like that! I can throw enough at you to turn it into a maniac's laughter!

First you've got to make sure that I can listen with a knowledge of God in my heart which was already there when you started—knowledge of a God Who can't say anything or do anything in such a way as to be recognized by anybody who doesn't know Him. That occurred to me just the other day when I was taking a walk by the river, and I haven't yet seen anything the matter with it! This God of the Bible in His own way must first have laid His compelling hand on my life and taken it captive, as He laid His hand on those wandering tribes that struggled up at His touch out of their bondage, sending them His prophets, holding so steadily to His purpose, in such bitter loving-kindness, coming among them finally in a man out of Nazareth, only to have a spectacle made of His love, but never quitting! He hasn't quit with me. I could scarcely blame Him if He had! In the Bible you don't look around to see what you can make of life, and then look up. When Moses "looked around" he killed a man! You look up; then you look around!

"Samuel took a stone and set it up." It may not have been quite so arbitrary as you think. When we find ourselves unable to look up and then look back and say "God," it will not be because we haven't heard enough or seen enough or read enough or studied enough or thought enough. It will be because for one reason or another we have never been anywhere that mattered in His company! There used to be a program on TV, perhaps there still is, called "You Were There": when they captured Major André, or when Commodore Dewey steamed into Manila Bay—it was usually fighting of some sort! But no matter how often the announcer kept saying "You were there," he could never quite bring it off! God does. You read the first few chapters of Genesis, and you know very well you were there in Eden. That's where we too were shut out of Paradise, you and I, because we took things into our own hands and set out to be God our very selves. It's the most real place of all the places on earth. And now we want it back, and look for it everywhere, as Auden says, and find nowhere that is not a kind of desert. Then we see that our way like Israel's lies across that desert, as does the way of all human history, every stage of the journey, Exodus, Kingdom, Exile, along toward Calvary. And there, far out of earshot on the street, or at some party, but you hear it, the old Negro spiritual keeps asking, "Were you there when they crucified my Lord?" And in your heart of hearts you know that that is exactly where you were!

Then let somebody rush in and try to wipe out the past which has become your past. Let him tell you it means nothing—it would all have been the same if there had been no God; not one iota, not one jot or tittle of it would have been different. The world wags on as if He didn't exist. So that even the language which says He does has no content. Instead of being afraid to admit that, we'd better insist on it. The language which says He does exist has another kind of content: it doesn't terminate in a fact; it terminates in a relationship which interprets the facts. A relationship which sees

44

the very hiddenness of God's purpose, its silent concealments in a world where nature and history alike say both Yes and No to Him, and with equal vehemence; sees them all as the ceaseless beckoning of One Who refuses to write out His name so that you can't betray Him or deny Him, and makes no other arrangement except that when you contradict Him, with His love He will contradict you. His only compulsion is "the compulsion of a truth" which plays havoc with all our preconceived ideas of meaning, a truth that doesn't derive from what has been called "the inevitable consent of the reasoning mind"; it derives from "the leap of the suddenly illumined heart." And you will not keep that from saying "God" where many a man would say no God is!

In *The Visit*, a play taken from the German of Deurrenmatt the Swiss playwright, a vengeful woman, for a wrong he had done her, brings down ruin on a respected member of a little community; and he cannot be dissuaded from facing it, cost what it will. He knows that his guilt was the guilt of his youth, and that what is happening is out of all proportion to it. There is no justice being done in the death which his neighbors arrange for him; but he will go through with it to save them—as it turns out!—from a desolation not nearly so great as that which they bring on themselves by having the life choked out of him. And that's the end of it. One critic whose criticism I read could see in it nothing but unrelieved darkness: from beginning to end it was to him only one more mordant commentary on human life. And the only mordant comment it made was on the human life where no grace is because it isn't having any, thank you very much! While in the darkness that broods over it, for anybody who has brought with him the memory of what God has done, there would seem to brood the thicker darkness which settled down one day over Calvary. Only when you have heard that answer, have you looked into the abyss of that bitter vengeance as far as it is given a man to look.

"Samuel took a stone and set it up." He didn't do it merely to boast of a fleeting victory over the Philistines, or because somebody had reminded him when he was discouraged of how it was with Abraham or Moses! He did it in order to say something profounder than any of that, not just about part of the past, about all of it, far and near; something inside of him, at "the very marrow of his being": and he chose to do it precisely on the spot where Israel not long before had lost to her enemies the ark of God's convenant, that visible sign of His Presence in the midst of her! "And he called

45

its name Ebenezer, for he said, 'Hitherto the Lord hath helped us.' "
And that "hitherto" didn't leave out anything!

But this explicit reading of God into the past reads Him by implication into the future as well. The "hitherto" looks up, leaves out nothing, and then looks both ways—back and forward! Though indeed it seems to me considerably more disquieting as it looks forward than it is when it looks back. I do not understand what grounds we have for thinking so comfortably of the prospect, now that we are Christians. It was of course quite the reverse in New Testament times. Nobody then would have found it easy to suppose that God was somehow engaged to reduce the strain on their lives, perhaps even by whittling down His demands, making them a little less severe at any rate. We do have such a friend in Jesus. Why may we not expect Him to provide us with a few straight answers to a few difficult questions? Did He not Himself call His Spirit the Comforter? And multitudes beyond any man's counting go on being disillusioned, simply because they have never been taught, it has never been hammered at them relentlessly, that you don't read the riddles out by reading God in. Whoever learns from looking up and looking back will gird up his loins when he turns around—or as The Revised Standard Version would have it, will tighten his belt!

That doesn't seem to have come as clear by any means as it should have come by this time in the history of God's dealing with His people. Still in prayers and in sermons we are promised more than He ever has been able on His own terms to manage. And it makes no sense. It makes no sense even when we do it blatantly enough in our churches to guarantee standing room only. On a recent Saturday morning *The New York Times* announced that one visiting divine would preach the next day on "Getting What You Want." Maybe he lampooned it. I don't know. It's incredible that anybody should seriously set about hawking such a luxury item, as if civilization had nothing more the matter with it than a bad case of the sniffles! George Jean Nathan once remarked of a certain actress that she was the only Camille he had ever seen who had died of catarrh! It isn't so much a question now of getting what we want as it is a question of finding out how to want what we get! To get God may mean to get hurt! You may have to limp into the future when it happens. Jacob did.

There is that kind of double talk running all through the Bible. Men can't live without God, but who can live with Him? These chapters of Samuel I dare say were not intended to be humorous;

but they are. They are the story of how thoroughly embarrassed the Philistines were once they had actually laid their hands on the ark of the covenant. Wherever they put it down a plague broke out, and all the lords of the people said, "What shall we do with it?" It was too "hot" for anybody to keep! From city to city they moved it: three times, and every time the local politicians wanted to know, "How shall we get rid of it?" Until they sent it back where it came from; and even there it stirred up trouble!

Holiness does just that in our kind of world. When God quits having you on His hands and you start having Him on yours, you'll find out how difficult He is! Instead of letting you count your many blessings, He'll begin asking you questions about what you're going to do with them! That's how you'll know He's somewhere in the neighborhood! As Paul Lehman once suggested, the elect in God's kingdom are not the elite: we can't afford to get our sociology and our theology mixed up! The elect are the uneasy ones, with the broken crust!

The scribes and Pharisees I suppose never came so near the kingdom as on that day when they had taken a woman in adultery. Never had they felt so secure—that's the time to look out—and never were they less so! They had dressed up for the occasion in all the piety they could find, whole layers of it: otherwise they could never have invented such exquisite torture as this, jerking her out into the light of day, and flinging her down there in the temple court. She couldn't look at anybody: her very being alive must have hurt! And Jesus didn't say anything. How could He? He stooped and wrote with His finger on the ground. What else was there to do in the presence of that grim outrage, that enormous iniquity which these good men had manufactured! Then he straightened Himself for as long as He could stand their leering faces and said, "He that is without sin among you, let him first cast a stone at her." And after that He stooped again. I think never was the invitation into the kingdom of God put in such heartbreaking terms. And they which heard it went out. It's the most hopeful thing ever written of them in the Gospel. They went out one by one, beginning at the eldest: maybe because the years had worn their crust a little thinner; as I grow older I like to think that. Anyhow they went out, as you and I have to go out from before Him, and every man, one by one, on God's bare mercy, defenseless and alone! When that comes home to you, He's not far away. In any event, you won't just go on smiling, will you, as you read Him into the future?

And yet this we may know: that through it all He means intensely, and He means good. Can we get that into the record too and keep it there against the odds, as Samuel did? "Hitherto hath the Lord helped us." And there in front of him to look forward to was nothing, it would appear, but more of the same that lay behind him: a little peace perhaps, but still those scattered tribes in a land of promise where the promise hadn't yet come true! How on earth could anybody be sure it would? A thousand years later Paul got it into the record again, the God Who in all things works together for good with them that love Him—in stripes and rods and stones and shipwreck!

But why shouldn't Paul be sure? "I am persuaded, that neither death, nor life, nor angels, nor principalities, nor powers, nor things present, nor things to come, nor height, nor depth, nor any other creature, shall be able to separate us from the love of God, which is in Christ Jesus our Lord." Why? Because he was a man now "scoured on the side facing eternity"! He had been thrown out of what God had done into what God was doing! The long past of all the long centuries, Israel's past, was his past; but now that one event toward which it had been moving had become his present, and with it the very deliverance from bondage which he had once thought he was only remembering! Everything which through those centuries had made God God and kept Him God had for Paul broken into the world again!

Once you understand that, you will understand why the stripes and the rods and the stones have so little to do with it. What if the end itself should be the kind of completion "which at the beginning would have seemed the ruin"? "Safety and danger" have got them now a different meaning. Who wants to use religion any longer in order to stockpile a few more promises at a discount? Who's keeping books? Whatever happens, let it happen! Maybe we know the score well enough at last to play it by ear!

On a memorable evening not too long ago Toscanini walked over to the podium for his final concert. He was over eighty, and they had built a slender railing for him. He touched it lightly with the fingers of one hand. Then he raised his baton. A student of mine was there and wrote of it: of how the orchestra seemed to steal softly as one man into the first quiet movement of the great symphony; and of how after a while, as the volume grew, first one and then another, the first violin, viola, 'cello, bass, lifted his eyes from the notes and fastened them on the maestro there, with the wistful little smile on his lips. And all the music they had in them swept up toward that face!

Prayer: Now unto Him Who is able to do exceeding abundantly above all that we can ask or think, according to the power that worketh in us, unto Him be glory in the church throughout all ages, world without end. And the peace of God, which passeth all understanding, shall keep your hearts and minds through Christ Jesus. Amen.

CHRISTIAN LIFE

The Golden Calf: 1959-1960

Reverend Clayton Williams, D.D.[1]

MINISTER, THE AMERICAN CHURCH IN PARIS, PARIS, FRANCE

Clayton Williams preaches to Americans who live in Paris, visitors and French people who belong to his church and like his preaching. He is scholarly without being narrow, evangelical without being dogmatic. His ability to see new light in the Christian story is revealed in his sermons Sunday after Sunday. He prepares and delivers his sermons with great care.

In this distinguished sermon, Dr. Williams takes the old story of Moses and the golden calf and shows that its implications for life today are as great as they were when Moses destroyed the idol of gold his brother Aaron made for the Israelites traveling to "the Holy Land."

Dr. Williams, a native of Illinois, attended Butler College and the University of Pittsburgh. He spent 1917 and 1918 in France as a YMCA Secretary, and then joined the United States Air Service as an officer from 1918 to 1919. He studied at the University of Paris, and did special social work at Chateau-Thierry in 1921. Later that year he returned to the United States and became assistant pastor at the First Presbyterian Church in Indianapolis. Feeling the need to study theology, he attended Western Theological Seminary for four years, graduating in 1925. He went to Poughkeepsie, New York, where he was assistant pastor in 1925 and 1926.

He was invited to return to Paris as assistant minister of the famous American Church under Dr. Joseph Wilson Cochran. He

[1] Sermons by members of the Advisory Committee were contributed at the special request of the editor and are included on his responsibility.

directed young people's work and religious education there until 1933, when Dr. Cochran resigned and he was asked to become minister. He has been there ever since, except when he was forced to leave during the Nazi occupation.

He was pastor of the Seventh Presbyterian Church in Cincinnati, Ohio, from 1941 to 1945. As soon as the war was over and he could return to France, he did so and instituted a program that keeps the church busy from morning to night seven days a week.

SERMON SEVEN

"And it came to pass, as soon as he came nigh unto the camp, that he saw the calf, and the dancing: and Moses' anger waxed hot. . . . And he took the calf which they had made, and burnt it in the fire, and ground it to powder, and strewed it upon the water, and made the children of Israel to drink of it," Exodus 32:19, 20.

MOSES HAD TAKEN the leadership of the Israelites on a mandate from Yahweh, the God Whom he had encountered at the burning bush of Mt. Sinai, and his faith was based upon a personal experience with a God of Whose power and will he was convinced, but this was not the case with most of the people. They had accepted Yahweh on Moses' authority, largely because he offered them the hope of freedom from the yoke of Egyptian oppression. Their allegiance was almost entirely a matter of expediency. Men often give their allegiance to what they can get the most from, and religion often suffers from this tendency.

Yahweh was an exacting God and He had never really been enthroned in the personal lives of the people. Their faith in Him was not based upon their own experience of His Lordship, but was dependent on the vigor, vision and influence of their leader Moses.

That in itself is not unusual. Great movements have very often depended upon the personal power and conviction of some great personality. It was that way with Washington and the American Revolution, and with Lincoln and the cause of the Negro, and with Jefferson and the Federal Union of the states, and with Woodrow Wilson and the League of Nations. All too often the faith of men is based not on their personal conviction and inner commitment but upon the courage and character of another. In religion this can be fatal!

50

So this band of undisciplined and heterogeneous fugitives from bondage had taken advantage of Moses' insurrection against Pharaoh and had trailed along after him both physically and spiritually, capitalizing upon the dynamic faith and courageous initiative of their leader but never appropriating his faith for themselves. They weren't willing to make the spiritual effort necessary.

Moses' loyalty was to a religion of the spirit that centered its life on allegiance to a God Who required obedience rather than obeisance, righteousness rather than ritual, and sanctity rather than ceremony; Whose essential holiness lay not so much in the sanctions of taboo as in His inexorably righteous law and its appeal to the human conscience—but the people had never accepted this. Moses had spoken of visions which they had not seen and of an authority which they did not know, and now that he was gone from their midst they found that their faith was not equal to the occasion. Without Moses and without an adequate faith within themselves they were confronted with a spiritual crisis!

And in consequence they did what religion often does when its faith is too demanding: they sought a lesser way out and demanded a religion which was more congenial to their way of living.

When they could not measure up to the demands of a faith in a god who could not be seen or heard, they demanded a god who could; when the religion of Moses made uncomfortable and challenging spiritual demands upon them, they reduced their religion to one which they could more easily be at home in and adjust themselves to. They felt that they would be very much more comfortable in their faith with a god that they could localize in something which they could see and be sure of. They wanted to put their trust in something practical, something tangible, something that was born of the world in which they lived and was part of their own life; an earth-born and earth-centered god.

I am not sure that they were a great deal different from the rest of us. We ourselves, in our day, often have more faith in what we can hear and see and handle than we have in life's unseen world and resources, more faith in the world that we have made than in God's spiritual world.

A group of Oxford dons were once discussing the relative powers of prelates and judges: and one of them said: "The bishop is more powerful, for the judge can only say, 'You be hanged' while the bishop can say, 'You be damned.'"

"Ah," replied another, "but when the judge says, 'You be hanged,' you *are* hanged!" That ended the discussion. You see, we have more faith in the reality of hanging than damning! We are not very sure that we may be damned, but we are very sure that we may be starved or bombed or bankrupted if we are not careful. And so we put most of our effort and energy and faith into programs and political setups and business projects and put our trust in them, and we give them a great deal more concern and attention and cultivation than we give to the serious cultivation of our religion, for all of our churches and religious programs.

And that is what the Israelites did, only they called it religion. And because they had originally attached themselves to Yahweh for practical purposes, they attached themselves to this new form of religion for the same reason.

Now Aaron was too practical and clever a man to let the situation slip through his fingers. He felt the force of their desire. It was reasonable and realistic. But he was also an idealist and he did what well-intentioned leaders have often done; he discovered a rationalization which made an excellent compromise. But like all compromises in religion, it was a failure.

However, he set himself to exploit the situation, and I fancy that he thought that his solution was both expedient and idealistic. He would give them what they wanted and yet give it a semblance, at least, of spirituality. How many religions have done this! How many religions seek to give men spirituality without making demands upon them or confronting them with a cross! That is the essential difference between Christ's religion and all others.

And so Aaron set about creating a religion which the people would find satisfactory. They wanted a god that they could understand, whose standards were their standards; he would give it to them but he would incorporate the best that they knew into this religion. He would take the riches of their culture and their civilization and devote them to the making of their god. It was a subtle and appealing solution, the work of a shrewd but unprincipled mind.

And so he proposed a god who would be at once more tangible and less exacting, and to give this god a certain visible prestige he required the consecration of their richest and finest possessions for his creation. They were to devote the best that they had. This god was to be no ordinary god, but the best that they could produce!

It was the inspiration of an intensely practical man, but it is worth noting that Aaron's decision was taken, not as a result of hours of mountain-top meditation upon God and His will for the people, but as a result of consideration of what practical measures would best suit the situation. He came into being not through revelation but through man's desire, like Hitler's Nordic God.

The new god and the new religion were born of expediency, not of divine inspiration or revelation. It was the old story: "*Vox populi, vox Dei,*" the easy way out!

And so Aaron said to the people: "Bring your best gold, the finest you have, and we shall make better use of it. It has been used for your adornment, it shall be used to adorn God. Consecrate it to God and we shall make His image of it."

That sounds laudable, doesn't it? It has captured the imagination of more than one leader! And so they brought their golden ornaments, their earrings and their bracelets and their necklaces and their gold pieces, and they were all melted down. Then Aaron put their finest craftsmen to work making a model, beautifully tooled and skillfully worked, to produce the finest piece of art that their culture could bring into being: a golden bullock, an ancient Hebrew form of God. The result was a god born of their own making.

Afterward, when he was making his excuses to Moses, he said that he had simply poured in the ornaments and poured out the gold and there had come out this golden calf, as though he and the people had had no part in it.

"This bull calf had come forth of itself. It had formed itself." But if he meant this to absolve him of any responsibility, he failed, for there was more truth in that than he realized.

Events do follow in sequences. They are tied together one after another. Set the stage and things happen accordingly. Consequences follow circumstances. Outlooks, attitudes and desires find their expression almost automatically.

That to which one's thought and life are devoted becomes one's god, eventually. It's bound to come out, if not in one way, then another. So it's not surprising that the golden bullock came out. It was integral and congenial to their life.

It represented the god of brute force and stubborn ease that they had secretly worshiped in their hearts. The fruit of their own hands. The thing in which their faith ultimately reposed. The result was earth-born and earth-bound. There was no high aspiration behind it, no vibrant life in it, no spark of the divine to vitalize it, no touch of heaven and no authority save that which they, themselves, gave it. It was the product of their own conception.

The pull of pragmatism is always a strong one. We tend to worship the thing which works, the person who succeeds—to make accomplishment the object of our admiration and devotion, forgetful of the possibility that the thing which works may work because it is in a little scheme of things, while the failure may be the failure of high aim and great vision!

The ugly duckling may be ugly because it is a swan, the misfit a misfit because he is bigger than the role for which we have cast him, the vision visionary because of the littleness of our horizon, the prophet repudiated because he belongs to the eternal scheme of things.

Ah, the danger is that we should cramp our thought of religion into the framework of our own making and twist its meaning to suit our ideas and turn it to our purposes, not God's. That's what Aaron did!

"This is your God, Oh Israel," he cried, "Who brought you out of the land of Egypt."

That's the temptation of secularism. Not only to offer men a visible project in which to put their faith, but to insist that all progress has been of man's own making in the use of these things.

"This god, which you have made with your hands and bought with your gold, has saved you." Your own skill and cleverness and wisdom and sacrifice have brought you your freedom.

Our clever tanks and atomic bombs and expert organization, our science and our industry will be our salvation. Our skill and our learning will bring us the kingdom of heaven. This god which we have made has brought us up out of the land of bondage.

That's the danger of secularism! It makes us identify the kingdom of success and material progress with the kingdom of God. But see what it does to life. Having set up this golden bullock in the place for sacred things, they began to dance about it in the celebration of their worship!

Two things which are intrinsic to this act are worth noting. One is the very evident relief they experienced in having a god they could see. It does put a strain upon one's faith to have a god that cannot be seen! It requires a heroic faith to maintain a spiritual religion that centers its trust in the intangible values of the heart, the seemingly impractical goodness of a Sermon on the Mount!

Moreover, they also found relief in having a god who imposed no restrictions and challenged no practices. Their religion was so completely oriented in the world of their day and conformed so perfectly to its conventions, reflecting, as secularism always does, the attitudes and thoughts of the people, that it never confronted them with any new challenge.

54

Spiritual religion always has to struggle, not only with the desire of men to focus it in some material form: a mass, a shrine, a sanctuary or a creed; but also with the tendency to let it degenerate into the cult of an indulgent and indifferent god who makes no demands, stirs no conscience, requires no repentance and troubles no hearts.

And second, an earth-bound god required only an earth-centered religion and so it never rose to any heights. Their worship was the mere circling of dancing feet, a mere matter of repetition, round and round, on and on, in the same steps, a sort of vicious circle, leading nowhere.

Despite all our conveniences and all our inventions, life is just an aimless going-on if it has no eternal reference and no eternal goal, and all our effort and all our sacrifice is futile. That is the lesson here.

Then came the day of reckoning. Moses came down from the mountain top with the law of God in his hand! And against that inexorable, divine law, with its divine imperative, the poverty of their religion of expediency was glaringly apparent.

It was a day of judgment. Taking the golden bullock, scorning its careful craft and cultivated beauty, on which they had set such store, Moses cast it into the fire and ground its gold to powder and strewed it upon the water and made the people to drink of their folly.

It was the inevitable consequence. The object of their faith brought its own judgment upon them, as it always does whenever we put our trust in our own contriving rather than in obedience to the purposes of a sovereign God; whenever we make our things, however fine, the objects of our faith, rather than the instruments of God's purposes.

Therein lies the great apostasy of our own age and day. The providence of God has provided our age with an abundance of gifts and powers, far beyond any other, and the great temptation, the essential nature of selfishness, is to put our faith in these things which we have achieved.

The great danger inherent in the discovery of atomic energy lies not alone or essentially in the fact, so often pointed out, that our physical power has outstripped our moral power, but in the danger that the pride of power may lead us utterly to destroy ourselves, both physically and spiritually. For atomic force not only gives satanic power to evil purpose; it threatens us with the destruction that pride's perversion produces.

The pretentious, optimistic self-sufficiency of the secular religion of our day can only issue in our drinking of the dregs of futile humanism. We have seen that these past few decades, when we too have been beguiled into worshiping the fruit of our hands and minds.

"Come," said our leaders, in all sincerity, "come bring the best that you have: your skill, your knowledge, your talents and your wealth and we shall build a heaven upon earth! Bring your money and your cleverness and your leadership, your science and your organizing ability and your inventive genius and your skilled labor and pour it all in and we shall have a new world order." And we did, and out came not a new world order but the old order confirmed in its imperialistic selfishness.

And that is the repeated testimony of history! The sands of history are strewn with the wreckage of nations that have risen to prominence only to destroy themselves.

Dwight Eisenhower is right in insisting that no nation can survive without a strong religious faith, but unless that faith is constantly oriented in and corrected by a genuine contact with the sovereign God and a sensitiveness to His will, it will lead us to tragedy.

Please don't mistake me. Don't think for a moment that I am cynical about human effort! We must never give up, or give less than the best that we have, but we dare not build if the prayer upon our lips and in our hearts is not: "Thy kingdom come, Thy will be done." For we face the dreadful judgment that always issues in frustration when the dominating motive of our life is the will to create our own world and to make our own standards and label them "the kingdom of God."

We must realize that the city of heart's desire, for which man has been seeking, is one whose builder and maker is God, not man: "That except God build the house, they labor in vain who build."

Secular history can never fulfill itself until it becomes divine history, until the grace of God enters into history and redeems human wills and hearts, and cleanses and empowers human efforts by bringing them into submission to the eternal will and eternal power which we know through Christ. Only then can life find its consummation, "For we are not sufficient of ourselves," as St. Paul says in II Corinthians; despite all our science and knowledge and skill and atomic energy, "Our sufficiency is of God"!

The city will be built but by the grace of God. For behind it all, there still stands the unseen God Whose finger has written His law, unchanging, unchallenged, uncompromised! The Master of the destiny of men and nations, the Ruler of this universe, in which we, after all, are but creatures!

And all our skill, all our effort, all our cleverness, yes and all our idealism, will only serve to create a world which will totter and fall and come to naught, if we do not put Him and His purpose first! All our efforts, however clever, are futile, utterly futile, if we humble not ourselves before God and seek His will, as it was revealed to us in Christ, with sincerity of heart.

For only as we humble ourselves before His Holy will, and in humility seek His word for us, shall we ever find the kingdom of Heaven!

CHRISTIAN LIFE

Long Day's Journey into Light

Reverend James. T. Cleland, D.D.

DEAN OF THE CHAPEL AND JAMES B. DUKE PROFESSOR OF PREACH-
ING IN THE DIVINITY SCHOOL OF DUKE UNIVERSITY, DURHAM, NORTH
CAROLINA; A MINISTER OF THE PRESBYTERIAN CHURCH.

Born in Glasgow, Scotland, in 1903, James T. Cleland attended school in Glasgow, graduated from Glasgow University in 1924, and served as assistant in three parishes of the Church of Scotland during his theological training. He was graduated from Glasgow University Divinity Hall in 1927, gaining distinction in ecclesiastical history, after which he came to America.

Dr. Cleland was appointed to the Jarvie Fellowship at Union Theological Seminary in New York, then returned to Scotland on the Black Fellowship at Divinity Hall, Glasgow University; from 1929 to 1931 he was Faulds Teaching Fellow at the University. In 1931 Amherst College called him to its department of religion.

On May 23, 1938, he was ordained a minister of the Presbyterian Church, U.S.A., and spent 1938 and 1939 on leave of absence in Europe and the Near East. In 1944–45 he did graduate work at Union, and in 1945 he was appointed Preacher to the University and Professor of Preaching in the Divinity School at Duke University, Durham, North Carolina. In the summers of 1948 and 1955 he was guest Professor of Homiletics at Union Theological Seminary. In 1954 he earned the Th.D. degree from Union. He delivered the Frederic Rogers Kellogg Lectures, Episcopal Theological School, Cambridge, Massachusetts, in 1953, which were published as THE

TRUE AND LIVELY WORD. *He has contributed three expositions to* THE INTERPRETER'S BIBLE *and writes a bimonthly article for* THE CHAPLAIN *under the heading "Preacher's Clinic."*

During the winter months Professor Cleland preaches in many of the preparatory schools, colleges, and universities on the Eastern seaboard. Among his enthusiasms are the Scottish poet Robert Burns, and the collecting of religious poetry. In Scotland he played soccer, and at Amherst and Duke has had a hand, as assistant coach, in turning out consistently successful soccer teams. His preaching shows a fine understanding of the problems of man, a kindly sense of humor, and an ability to say the right word in the right place.

"Long Day's Journey into Light" is one of the most unusual sermons of recent years. It was preached on February 9, 1957, at the Duke University Chapel.

SERMON EIGHT

(II Corinthians 11:23–31)

RECENTLY A COLLEAGUE GAVE ME A COPY of Eugene O'Neill's *Long Day's Journey Into Night*,[1] first published in 1956. I have now read it twice, and I have also seen the play. Let me share my experience with you.

Long Day's Journey Into Night is located, through all four acts, in the living room of a summer home in New London, Connecticut, from the beginning until the close of an August day in 1912. It is one long day's journey into night, with its four acts timed at 8:30, 12:45, 6:30, midnight. The playwright thus preserves two of the Aristotelian unities—place and time: one set, one day.

In that living room a father and mother and two sons—the Tyrones—talk and talk and talk about themselves: each about himself; each about the others: their relationship to one another; their loving hatred of one another; their angry affection for one another. There is no action in the play; but there is talk—three and a half hours of it. Bitterness is succeeded by regret which, in turn, leads to renewed bitterness and subsequent real, but ineffective, apologies. Lies are told that deceive no one, lies which are spoken in a mixture of family love and self-justification. The play is a four-handed

[1] Quotations from Eugene O'Neill are used by special permission of Yale University Press.

58

game of confessional solitaire, in which there is neither expiation nor atonement.

The characters cannot be painted in black or white; the color would be closer to battleship gray, with purple patches. If I were to use adjectives to describe that day's life with the Tyrones, I would have to employ them in three different categories: vivid, repetitive, unforgettable, haunting; bitter, twisted, harrowing, impotent; compassionate, appealing, pitiful and pathetic. It is a poetic drama, where moods clash and change because no character understands himself as a whole person. The endless conversation is set in an atmosphere of fuddled garrulousness and drug-addiction. When the play ends, all is quiet—but no one is saved. The curtain is rung down on the drunken, drugged sleep of the damned. The members of the family know one another a little better; but tomorrow is going to be another day like yesterday. So the audience goes home, forgiving—but frustrated. There is some pity for the Tyrones, but little admiration. There is no classical catharsis, no purification for the watcher.

❄ ❄ ❄ ❄ ❄

It isn't enough to say: "Don't worry. This is typically Irish, and the Tyrones, like O'Neill, are Irish." Yes, but we are all Irish, to some extent, because we are all mortal men and women. This play is that old Irish epitaph come to life: "An Irishman doesn't know what he wants, and he won't be content till he gets it." Therefore, he lives ineffectually; and *he* is some of us. So let us look at the four characters, one by one, and try to find what is driving them to Hell, here and hereafter. Let me thumbnail-sketch them.

James Tyrone, sixty-five years old, is an actor who gave up the chance to be a great actor by accepting one popular and perennial role which brought him money and more money. Remembering the poverty-stricken days of his childhood, he has become a penny-pincher and is now a petty, mean, bullying, inebriated miser, with undertones of loyalty, humility and remorse.

His wife, Mary, age fifty-four, was reared in a convent school and expected to become a nun before she married. She has lost one child, through her own neglect (so she blames herself), and has become a drug-addict, because of careless medical prescription in the illness following the birth of her third child. She loves her man and her boys, but looks back with regret on the years of hotel-living, as she followed her husband's company around the country.

59

Jamie, the elder son, age thirty-three, is an embittered drunkard and a dissatisfied libertine, who is shot through with a jealousy which caused him to effect the death of one brother and makes him long for the destruction of the other. He loathes the life which has him under its spell and detests himself when he is drunk enough to be honest about himself—*in vino veritas*.

Edmund, the youngest child, age twenty-three, is a drinking consumptive, with a doubting desire to write. He is on the surface like Jamie, an alcoholic and a roué. But, inside, there are yearnings for beauty and for peace.

A servant girl, also Irish, completes the cast.

There are four main characters, then. Yet, that is not true. There are really eight. Each has what the Germans call a *Doppelgänger*, a second self, and the conversation is penetrated and permeated with this everlasting duality: blame and pity; rage and apology; failure and yearning. There is a double self constantly before us: the what "is," and the what "might-have-been," and, in the mother's case, the what "was."

It is an exhausting encounter to sit through this play. I do not recommend it for relaxation.

Is it possible to get behind the symptoms to causes? What gave rise to all this money-grabbing and drug-addiction and unhappy drinking and unsatisfactory lechery? One can point casually to the death of the second child, in which all four are involved. The father caused it by insisting that his wife be with him on the road, though the child needed her. Mary caused it by choosing to be a wife rather than a mother. Jamie caused it by making sure that the child caught measles from him, and so died, because of his jealousy. And the unborn Edmund was involved, because he was brought into the world to replace the dead baby, and made his mother so ill than an unskilled doctor prescribed morphine and started her on the way to be a dope addict. There is the obvious cause. Yet, we know families which have wept and worked and prayed their way through similar calamities, and emerged, bloody but unbowed.

Other causal factors are involved: James Tyrone's fear of poverty and his longing to be a great actor rather than a popular stage-idol; Mary's yearning for a real home, and her pathetic return to her childhood dream of being a nun; Jamie's guilt, not merely because he deliberately gave the baby measles, but because of his efforts to ruin Edmund morally; Edmund's terror at the thought of tuberculosis and his desire to write and to write well, instead of the stammering stuff he produces. But, even then, the real causes are not here.

Each seeks to escape himself, and none can find a dominating larger self to which he may give himself. They have no internal, inviolable center of loyalty; they have no invisible means of support. If a man is not self-sufficient—and few of us are—then God or Satan, the spiritual or the demonic, takes over the direction of a person's life. God is peripheral in this play; spiritual values are prominent by their absence. The demonic is enthusiastically present in the unbalanced love of money, the false satisfaction of drugs, the unhappy dependence on alcohol, and the unrewarding bed of the prostitute. This is a little saga of the effectively damned. It is a day in the life of a family on the brink of oblivion, because in not one of them is there any basic personal security.

* * * * *

Then, there is no cure, no balm in Gilead? There is none in the play. It ends with the mother recalling in a sad, wakeful dream her days in the convent; with the father stirring in the chair where he slouches drunk; with Jamie and Edmund "motionless." Yet there are hints at the possibility of healing, given by each of the characters, except Jamie.

Mary says to her husband: "James! We've loved each other! We always will! Let's remember only that, and not try to understand what we cannot understand, or help things that cannot be helped —the things life has done to us we cannot excuse or explain."

She says to him again: "I know you love me, James, in spite of everything." He answers: "Yes! As God is my judge! Always and forever, Mary!" She replies: "And I love you, dear, in spite of everything."

She says to Edmund: "You must try to understand and forgive him [your Father], too, and not feel contempt. . . ."

The father says to Edmund: "When you deny God, you deny hope. . . . When you deny God, you deny sanity!"

Edmund says to his father: ". . . you have to make allowances in this damned family or go nuts."

He talks again, in an amazing monologue, of "belonging to something greater than my own life, or the life of Man, to Life itself! To God, if you want to put it that way." He refers to "peace, the end of the quest, the last harbor, the joy of belonging to a fulfillment

beyond men's lousy, pitiful, greedy fears and hopes and dreams!
. . . Like a saint's vision of beatitude."

Love and God. Forgiveness and peace. Belonging and beatitude.
Haven't you heard it all before? Isn't it the refrain of the Bible,
from beginning to end? Isn't God the invisible means of support,
who quickens love in us, so that on earth we may have peace, that
lack of worry at the heart, which creates blessedness? Let me recall
it to you:

> Surely goodness and mercy shall follow me
>   all the days of my life;
> And I shall dwell in the house of the Lord
>   for ever.   (Psalm 23:6, R.S.V.)

> When Israel was a child, I loved him,
>   and out of Egypt I called my son. . . .
> Yet it was I who taught Ephraim to walk,
>   I took them up in my arms; . . .
> I led them with cords of compassion,
>   with the bands of love,
> and I became to them as one
>   who eases the yoke on their jaws,
>   and I bent down to them and fed them.
>   (Hosea 11:1, 3–4, R.S.V.)

If you, then, who are evil, know how to give good gifts to your children,
how much more will your Father who is in heaven give good gifts to
those who ask him?   (Matt. 7:11, R.S.V.)

Beloved, let us love one another; for love is of God, and he who loves
is born of God and knows God. He who does not love does not know
God; for God is love. . . . In this is love, not that we loved God but that
he loved us and sent his Son . . . Beloved, if God so loved us, we also
ought to love one another. No man has ever seen God; if we love one
another, God abides in us and his love is perfected in us.
                          (I John 4:7, 8, 10–12, R.S.V.)

Let Paul interpret all this for us. "Paul, you certainly went through
Hell and high water on earth, judging from your autobiography
(II Corinthians 11:23–31). How did you do it?" Can you hear his
answer? "I discovered that God loved me even before I became
aware of it. That did something to me. I yielded myself to that
almost unbelievable fact—that the great God loves me, wants me
as His companion on earth. Now, I just have to love others as He

loved me and nothing can stop it—'Hell or high water on earth,' as you put it. I go through these afflictions I listed because He loves me and, as a consequence, I love my fellows."

Love and God. Love, which according to John, is God. Love, through which we know God, the groundwork of life. That's what the Tyrones were groping for. In that is their hope of salvation, their hope of spiritual health. This is the invisible means of support which the demonic, obviously, did not supply. This is the remedy: the committing of self to the more than self, which reëstablishes the self by giving it the dignity of "son, daughter of God," and then seeks to work, in love, through it. Thus, a person is given back his soul, redeemed, then made perfect by the exercise of love, which is the continual expression of God, and, therefore, the renewed revelation of Himself.

If we don't believe it, how do we account for Paul, and Augustine, and Wesley, and Kagawa, and Schweitzer, and for the people we ourselves know who live like this? If we do believe it, how do we set about getting the Tyrones and our parents and our students and our roommates to see it? Granted that this is the remedy, what is the mode of treatment?

* * * * *

Let us be honest: They may first need medical, psychiatric help. What is obvious to the Tyrones, under the influences of drink or drugs, had better become obvious and accepted when they are cold sober. And it will take the skill of an expert to make them cold sober. During that treatment, and steadily after it, they must be loved. They must be loved, not because they are lovely, but because they need love.

The psychiatrist may do that; it depends on his "world view." We, as Christians, must do it. We must love them, not to make the Tyrones Christian, not to make them lovely, not to influence them and make them our friends, but because they need love, as we need love and as we received it from God, and from His disciples. They will need to know humble, understanding, humorous Christians who go out to them in perpetual good will, despite their misunderstanding, their self-assertion, their impatience, their backslidings, their hostility. That may call for more than one Christian—it will be an exhausting job.

Here is where the Church comes in, the Church which goes to them, the Church to which they come. It needs Christians, proficient, not only in personal relations, but in doctrine. Because the Tyrones will ask questions—how they will ask questions! It means knowledge, a capacity for elucidation, a grasp of books to be read, studied and digested. It requires a Christian who is expert in the faith, in its life and work, in its beliefs and their exposition.

Following that, it requires that the Tyrones try out this belief in practice. Alcoholics Anonymous has taught us this, that, in order to keep from slipping back, one keeps others from slipping back.

It is a long process but the steps are clear: action, interpretation, incitement to action—that is the Christian procedure.

* * * * *

You say that won't work with the Tyrones? It did—with one of them. *Long Day's Journey Into Night* is autobiographical. Eugene O'Neill was the youngest Tyrone, Edmund. He wrote this play in 1941 (fifteen years before it was published) and dedicated it to his wife, on their twelfth wedding anniversary. Do you know why? Because *she loved* him back to life and light. She exorcised his demon; she washed away his guilt, even his suffering. She gave him dignity and peace and exhilaration.

If I were producing that play, I would read the dedication *after* the fall of the final curtain. Or, is that "bad theater," even if it is homiletically sound? Let me try again. I would print the dedication in the program. Why? Because it explains the reason for the writing of the play, and it offers the catharsis, the purifying and the elevating of the emotions, which the play, per se, does not seem to give. Let me read the dedication:

For Carlotta, on our 12th Wedding Anniversary

Dearest: I give you the original script of this play of old sorrow, written in tears and blood. A sadly inappropriate gift, it would seem, for a day celebrating happiness. But you will understand. I mean it as a tribute to your love and tenderness which gave me the faith in love that enabled me to face my dead at last and write this play—write it with deep pity and understanding and forgiveness for *all* the four haunted Tyrones. These twelve years, Beloved One, have been a Journey into Light—into love. You know my gratitude. And my love!

Gene

Tao House
July 22, 1941

This expression of Eugene O'Neill's is within the Christian "world view," because it understood the catharsis and the impelling force of love. It was a long day's journey into—light.

O God,
Who art love and who dost work continually in love;
Grant us to know that Thou art love, and grant us to live in love;
That Thy saving health may be known, and Thy love lived by us;
Through Jesus Christ, Thy love incarnate, Thy Son and our Lord.

Amen.

CHRISTIAN LIFE

When God Hides

Reverend Joseph R. Sizoo, D.D., Litt.D., S.T.D., LL.D.[1]

A MINISTER OF THE REFORMED CHURCH AND PROFESSOR OF RELI-
GION AND DIRECTOR OF THE CHAPEL AT GEORGE WASHINGTON UNI-
VERSITY, WASHINGTON, D.C.

*Dr. Sizoo takes an old theme and preaches a magnificent sermon
on Job, suffering, questions that disturb men, the paradoxes of life,
and the answers the Christian faith gives to men for living.*

*Born in the Netherlands, he was brought to the United States
by his parents. He graduated from Hope College and New Brunswick Theological Seminary, was a missionary in South India in
1910 and 1911, and was minister of churches in Malden, New York,
and Somerville, New Jersey. In the summer of 1923 he was Minister
of the American Church at the Hague.*

*He rose to prominence as minister of the famous New York
Avenue Presbyterian Church in Washington, D.C., from 1924 to
1936, where presidents, senators, and distinguished men and women
from all walks of life crowded to hear him Sunday after Sunday.
In 1936 St. Nicholas Collegiate Church in New York called him to
be its minister and his preaching attracted full congregations. In
1947 he became president of the New Brunswick Theological Seminary. He was appointed as Professor of Religion and Director of
the chapel at George Washington University in 1952.*

*In 1942 he was president of the General Synod of the Reformed
Church in America, and he has been president of The Greater New
York Federation of Churches. His books have won him a wide
following, especially* ON GUARD, NOT ALONE, MAKE LIFE WORTH LIVING,

---

[1] Sermons by members of the advisory committee were contributed at the
request of the editor and are included on his responsibility.

65

PREACHING UNASHAMED, AND I BELIEVE IN THE BIBLE. *During the Second World War he traveled extensively to visit Army and Navy bases, talking with chaplains and enlisted men, and later he made a special tour to Korea to address the men on the fighting front. He was voted "Clergy Churchman of the Year 1958" by the Religious Heritage of America, Inc.*

His work has been recognized with the honorary doctorate by Hope College, Columbia University, Rutgers University, and George Washington University.

SERMON NINE

UNTOLD CENTURIES AGO, long before the birth of the Christian Era, in the land of Uz, perhaps a mythical Shangri-La, there lived a man who was affluent, prosperous and God-fearing. His name was Job. He was rich in lands, his harvests were abundant, his barns bulged, his family setting was happy, his cattle multiplied, his wealth increased and his reputation grew. He became the first citizen of all that land. Suddenly, without rhyme or reason, without warning or premonition, the whole universe tumbled in on him. He was stripped of his wealth, his harvests were destroyed, his family fell apart, his barns were burned, his cattle were stolen, his wealth vanished, his sons died in a drunken brawl, his reputation withered, his wife cursed him and he was smitten with a dire disease.

What was so unreasoning and unreasonable was that it came to pass through no fault of transgression on his part. Sometimes men fall apart because of some secret sin which they carry as Rachel carried a hidden idol in the saddlebag. But there was no stain upon his escutcheon, no skeleton in his closet. He had done nothing untoward. He lived with a conscience void of offense before God and man. But there it was. His universe tumbled in. So out of the dim and muffled past there came this poignant cry: "I waited for the light, but thou sendest darkness. I called unto thee, but thou answerest not. Wherefore hidest thou thy face?"

That old-world story is not so old. It is relived and repeated a thousand times in every generation and land. Job is not so much a personality as a representative, not so much an individual as a type of all humanity. You do not have to travel far or live long to discover that there are occasions when we stand by that bewildered man who was staggered by the events of life and stumbled into my study crying, "It is easier to believe in no God than to believe in a God who lets things like this happen."

Sometimes God hides Himself. We seek Him, but He withdraws. We call to Him, but the only answer is the echo of our own voice. Sometimes life seems a vast Calvary over which there hangs a cloud as it hung two thousand years ago for three eternity-long hours over Golgotha. There are times when the whole universe smells of blood, brain washing, and browbeatings. Behind the heartbreaks that embitter, the sorrows that are never assuaged, the tears that do not dry, and the loneliness that has no healing is the fear that God has hid from us.

The person is not normal who is not sometimes staggered, whose soul is not sometimes chilled by events which tear at his being as a fox gnaws at a foot caught in the jaws of a steel trap. There are occasions when life does not make sense.

Here is that embittered soldier I met on Heartbreak Ridge in Korea with whom I had been talking about the events of life. He looked at me sharply and broke out with, "I'll tell you what's the matter with the world; your God has let us down." There is that university student who had come to the end of his academic career. He had made a brilliant record, won every prize, earned and carried away every honor. The following week there was awaiting him a promising and lucrative position. The next morning he was to be married to his childhood sweetheart. Then on his way to commencement he was killed. Here are two godly people whom I know very well. They fell in love, were married and set up a Christian home. Then they prayed long, long hours for a little child and at last when the child was born, it was Mongoloid. I am thinking of that man whom I visited often in the hospital. He had had thirteen operations and thirty-nine blood transfusions. One day he said to me, "I do not complain, but sometimes things do not make sense. I know all this will end in death. I want it, but it won't come." There is that British sea captain, Sir John Hawkins, who sailed his ship along the African coast kidnapping Negroes to sell to the slave trade. When he captured them, he chained them to the deck of his ship. And then he christened his ship "The Jesus," and God did nothing.

Was Nietzsche right when he said, "God is dead. He spoke to us but is silent now. All we touch is a corpse"? What can you make of all that? Has the Christian faith any answer to this dilemma? How can one face life on the basis of, "Wherefore hidest thou thy face?"

* * * * *

The Christian faith affirms it is true. It never glosses over unpleasant facts. It does not deny it. You do not answer the question of Job by refusing to recognize it. It is a cheap thing to run up the white flag and say it is only a figment of the imagination. You may say that suffering, pain and disillusionment are only bedtime stories, but when you tell that to the marines charging up Iwo Jima, or to a group of university students with their history books open before them, do not try to take up a collection.

You cannot answer the question of Job by running away from life and seeking refuge in retreats, where well-fed people sleep in little cubicles on foam mattresses, with Persian rugs on the floor, and a psychiatric couch in the corner, while an attendant feeds them pink pills of living positively.

You cannot answer the question of Job by the popular philosophy of Sartre's existentialism: "Man exists only for himself. What need have we of God? The only God is creative self-interest. Get rid of the idea, emancipate yourself, God is dead. Be a man."

But that is not the answer. The blunt fact is, if you will take time to read the Bible you will discover that God is both self-revealing and self-concealing. Man searches for God, God hides from man: that is the eternal dilemma and the eternal torment of life. There came a time when Mary had to say, "Why hast thou dealt thus with us?" There was an occasion when the disciples said to Jesus, as He was sleeping on a pillow in the stern of a little ship about to be capsized by the storm, "Master, carest thou not that we perish?" There was an hour when Jesus cried out, "My God, my God, why hast thou forsaken me?" Over the hills of time there still comes the voice of the prophet saying, "My thoughts are not your thoughts, neither are your ways my ways." The apostle Paul spoke for all when he wrote, "His ways are past finding out." Jesus warned His disciples with, "It is not for you to know the times or the seasons."

There are areas of life forever closed to us. Some things we will never know. There are divine roadblocks in life, before which God stands saying, "So far, but no farther." This whole modern attitude to miracles is built on the assumption that finite man can dictate the terms and the procedures by which God must govern the universe which He has made; it is as unworthy as it is impossible.

There are times when God goes into hiding. So is life tested. Just as the photographer carries his sensitive films into a darkroom to develop them, so man is tested in the dark hours of disillusionment and suffering that the angels of his better self may get their chance.

You cannot have starlight without the night; you cannot have courage without peril; you cannot have sympathy without suffering; you cannot have tenderness without pain.

* * * * *

The Christian faith has a second answer. It is the contradiction of everything I have said so far. But after all, life is a paradox. The Christian faith affirms it isn't true. At best it is only a half-truth. The hiding of God is set in the framework of a divine love. Because you cannot see Him is no reason to suppose He is not there. Because you do not hear Him is no reason to conclude He has not spoken. When God hides, the only thing you really can say is that you have lost contact with Him. In reality He is as much in the one as in the other. God is the Creator of both; He made both the light and the darkness. God does not come to us with the dawn and bow out of the universe when light closes in. Darkness and light are both alike to Him.

You cannot square life to the narrow margin of human understanding. It is always a hazardous thing to carry the little lamp of reason into the dark and say, "He is not there." We need to hear again a voice that spoke long ago to a bewildered people, "Be still and know that I am God." Believe me, His hand is stronger than you think, His wisdom is deeper than you know, and His love is broader than you dream. Not the denial of mystery, but the acceptance of it makes for great living.

Some time ago in Arlington Cemetery in Washington they buried the mortal remains of one of the most gallant men who ever slept under the stars, Admiral Richard E. Byrd. To those who knew him his going has left a hole in the sky. I recall his telling a group about an experience he had on one of his later journeys to the South Pole. You will recall in that expedition to the Antarctic he set up an advance base some two hundred miles beyond the main depot, where he lived alone for scientific and psychological research. While there he was overcome by monoxide poisoning and almost came to the end of the road. He wrote about it later. Let me quote from his book: "About three o'clock on the morning of June third I had another lucid phase. I tried without success to force my body into sleep. The sleeping pills were on the shelf. The flashlight fingered the bottle. I reached for the bottle, but then I stopped. It was impossible to go on like this. I found a match and lighted a candle. An unused sheet of paper lay on the bunk. I wrote, 'The universe is not dead. Therefore there is an intelligence there, and it is all-pervading. Though I am cut off from human beings I am not alone.' Dousing the candle I slipped into the bag and repeated the sentiments over and over again. Sleep came." Men and women, when the lamps go out and the lights begin to flicker; when it is touch and go; when hope no longer sees a star, and love no longer hears the rustling of the leaves, you may say, "I am not alone." "The mountains shall depart, and the hills be removed, but my kindness shall not depart from thee, neither shall the convenant of my peace be broken saith the Lord that hath mercy on thee."

* * * * *

The Christian faith has a third answer. The issue of man's search for God and God's hiding from man is resolved in Jesus Christ. Christ brought God out of hiding. When men saw Him, they called Him Immanuel, God with us. If ever you wonder where He is or if He is, turn the pages of the Book all the way back until you hear Him say, "He that hath seen me hath seen the father also"; "I and the father are one"; "I am the way, the truth, and the life, no man cometh unto the father but by me." In Christ you see the eternal God in time, the invisible God in the flesh, the omnipotent God in history, and the infinite God in space.

There is a significant and often forgotten incident in the recorded story of the Crucifixion. You read, "And when He gave up the Ghost, the veil of the temple was rent in twain from the bottom to the top." God came out of hiding on Calvary and stood before the ages saying, "Lo I am with you always even unto the end of time."

Francis Thompson in the nineteenth century wrote a moving poem, "The Hound of Heaven." He concluded it with these lines:

> All which I took from thee, I did but take
> Not for thy harms,
> But just that thou mightest seek it in My arms.
> All which thy child's mistake
> Fancies as lost, I have stored for thee at home:
> Rise, clasp My hand and come!

Christ on the Margins of Life

Reverend Carl F. H. Henry, Th.D., Ph.D.

A MINISTER OF THE AMERICAN BAPTIST CHURCH, PROFESSOR OF
THEOLOGY AND CHRISTIAN PHILOSOPHY AT FULLER THEOLOGICAL
SEMINARY, AND EDITOR OF *Christianity Today*, WASHINGTON, D.C.,
AND PASADENA, CALIFORNIA

Carl Henry is distinguished as an author, teacher, and preacher. He preaches in some of America's best-known pulpits and has appeared on the summer programs of numerous Bible conferences. He is Professor of Theology and Christian Philosophy at Fuller Theological Seminary in Pasadena, California, and editor of the magazine CHRISTIANITY TODAY.

Dr. Henry was formerly chairman of the Department of Philosophy of Religion at Northern Baptist Theological Seminary, Chicago. He has served as Visiting Professor of Theology at Wheaton College, Illinois, Gordon Divinity School in Boston, and Winona Lake Summer School of Theology. He studied at Wheaton College, took his B.D. and Th.D. from Northern Baptist Seminary, and his Ph.D. from Boston University. He did research at New College, Edinburgh, Scotland.

Among his books are REMAKING THE MODERN WORLD, THE PROTESTANT DILEMMA, NOTES ON THE DOCTRINE OF GOD, FIFTY YEARS OF PROTESTANT THEOLOGY, THE DRIFT OF WESTERN THOUGHT *and* CHRISTIAN PERSONAL ETHICS. *Evangelical Books recently distributed the compilation,* CONTEMPORARY EVANGELICAL THOUGHT, *of which he was general editor and author of the chapter "Religion and Science."*

Formerly a Long Island newspaperman, he once edited THE SMITHTOWN STAR *and the* PORT JEFFERSON TIMES-ECHO, *both Long Island weeklies, and has served as suburban correspondent for the New York* HERALD TRIBUNE, THE NEW YORK TIMES, STANDARD NEWS ASSOCIATION *and the* CHICAGO TRIBUNE. *He has written a book on* SUCCESSFUL CHURCH PUBLICITY *and in 1950 spearheaded the Mid-Century Rose Bowl Rally in Pasadena, attended by fifty thousand persons—the largest Christian rally in the history of the West. He served several years as chairman or cochairman of the annual Rose Bowl Easter Sunrise Service. From 1945 to 1952 Dr. Henry was literary editor of* UNITED EVANGELICAL ACTION, *and is a frequent contributor to religious periodicals.*

He has served on a National Association of Evangelicals committee for the formulation of a Christian philosophy of education, was long chairman of that organization's Commission of Evangelical Social Action, and has twice served on its Board of Administration.

When Fuller Theological Seminary was begun in 1947, he became during its first year the school's acting dean. In 1951 he delivered the initial series of W. B. Riley Memorial Lectures at Northwestern Schools; in 1952, a course of lectures at Central Baptist Seminary, Toronto; and in 1957, the Wilkinson Lectures at Northern Baptist Seminary, Chicago.

In the summer of 1952 Dr. Henry was one of four American professors who accompanied a "flying seminar" of sixty-five students to Europe and the Near East under the sponsorship of Winona Lake School of Theology. His book, GLIMPSES OF A SACRED LAND, *stemmed from that trip.*

SERMON TEN

> ". . . Let us alone; what have we to do with thee, thou Jesus of Nazareth? Art thou come to destroy us? I know thee who thou art; the Holy One of God," Luke 4:34.

THAT STARTLING CRY broke the sacred stillness of the Capernaum synagogue one Sabbath day. And from those words, in the language of dread, one can write much of the biography of this man, just as one can read between the lines on a young widow's face, between the scars and bruises on a laboring man's hands, between the gleam and glare of a lunatic's eyes. *Let us alone; what have we to do with thee, thou Jesus of Nazareth?* A sudden, unpremeditated outburst, at an unexpected meeting face to face with Jesus.

Because the outlook of this man touches at so many interesting points the life and experience of the average Western man today, I want to single out three strands of his story as the framework in which to set our meditation of the morning. His story has a point of contact, I say, especially with the man of the West, the man of Europe and the Americas; not the Oriental man, whose plight is that he has never heard the preaching of the Gospel, and who does not know that Jesus Christ came to save sinners, but the Western

72

man, who shows the marks of his revolt against Jesus Christ written over almost everything he does.

I ask you to notice: (1) How much this man knows about Jesus Christ; (2) that the knowledge this man has of Jesus serves as an instrument of his condemnation, rather than as an instrument of salvation; (3) that only the healing and redemptive touch of Jesus Christ restored him to usefulness to God and to himself and to society again, even as the touch of Christ alone can spare us from our doom today and restore us to usefulness again.

First, notice *how much this man knows about Jesus.*

He calls him Jesus of Nazareth, the name by which Jesus was familiarly known as the worker of mighty wonders and the man of miracles from Galilee. In the fourth chapter of Luke it is too early for this demon-possessed man in Capernaum to have known all about the mighty works of Jesus. But something had reached him of the impact of that One Who healed the sick, Who cleansed the lepers—those miserable creatures who whenever they met their townspeople on the streets called out "Unclean! Unclean! Unclean!" —Who gave the blind sight to see, Who raised the dead, Who never knew what it was to look upon sickness and suffering without being able rightly to relate it to the power and justice and mercy of God. And I ask you, isn't it enough, to come one day into the very presence of Jesus of Nazareth, during the days of His earthly ministry—when a public sign was being given that in Him God was come in the flesh, that the day must inevitably come when neither sickness nor death nor demons nor Satan could withstand His power—isn't it enough, to come face to face with Jesus of Nazareth (every man with his own thorn in the flesh, this man with his demons), and to want nothing to do with Him? *I know thee who thou art . . . Jesus of Nazareth.* How much this man knew about Jesus.

But he knows more about Jesus than that. He calls him not only Jesus of Nazareth, but he calls him *the Holy One.* And again I ask, isn't it enough, in view of every man's case history of sin and shame —the days and the months and the years of moral failure and loss, the whole of it known to God, every deed, every word, every thought and motive—isn't it enough one day to stand with the whole accumulation of transgression and scandal in the Presence of the Holy One—Who never knew what it was to be sorry for anything that ever He did, of Whom the Heavenly Father could say, "This is my beloved Son; hear ye him," and Who could Himself say, "I do always the things that please him,"—isn't it enough, to stand one day face to face with the One Who knew in His own being the answer to the problem of sin and guilt that overwhelms the rest of us—and to want nothing to do with Him? Isn't that enough? *Jesus of Nazareth . . . the Holy One;* how much this man knew about Him.

Yet he knows even more about Jesus than that. For he calls Him not simply the Holy One, but *the Holy One of God: I know thee who thou art: the Holy One of God.* Now, it would be too much to suggest that by that prepositional phrase *of God* this man in the Capernaum synagogue intends all that John the Baptist meant, for example, when the Baptist—brought up in a priestly family, schooled in the inner meaning of the Old Testament Scriptures—cried out: "Behold the Lamb of God, who taketh away the sin of the world." But who knows how much insight this man in Capernaum may have had into the Messianic significance of Jesus Christ, into His redemptive significance—here in the synagogue, where he would hear passages speaking not only of the righteousness and holiness of God ("Thou art holy, O thou that inhabitest the praises of Israel," Psalm 22:3), but he would learn also of the mercy and grace of God ("He was wounded for our transgressions, he was bruised for our iniquities; the chastisement of our peace was upon him, and with his stripes we are healed," Isaiah 53:5). *I know thee who thou art: the Holy One of God.* How much this man knew about Jesus.

Second, notice that this man is a symbol of the average Western man today because he holds his knowledge in the way of rebellion; *the knowledge that he has serves as an instrument of his condemnation rather than of his salvation.* His problem is exactly our problem throughout the Western world today; he has light, but it is not acted upon; he knows enough about Jesus even in the course of rebellion that a chance meeting face to face hurls his conscience to the very threshold of divine judgment: *Art thou come to destroy us?* is a quite intelligible question on the unrepentant sinner's lips. Today the cross casts its shadow over every city and hamlet of Europe and the Americas. You can scarcely find a community that is unpopulated by a church. And however inadequate and confused the average man's knowledge of Jesus Christ may be, he has light enough a hundred times over to send him scampering to Calvary for the forgiveness of his sins. You who listen this morning without God's forgiveness are not without light; God has opened a door and has charted a path for you a hundred times over, but you have not come.

And the knowledge which you have, if unappropriated, condemns you. How often I met with a sincere company of people Sunday morning after Sunday morning, repeating the words: "I believe in God the Father Almighty, maker of heaven and earth

74

. . . etc." And I find no fault with those words. I am not suggesting that creeds are unimportant. It makes a lot of difference what you believe. But if that's all that you have—a set of speculative beliefs, a series of propositions to which you give mental assent—that never becomes the instrument of a personal acceptance of Jesus Christ as Saviour and Lord; if you do not know what Jesus meant when He said "Except a man be born again, he cannot see the kingdom of God" (John 3:3); if you don't know what Paul meant when he said, "If any man be in Christ, he is a new creature; old things are passed away; behold, all things are become new" (II Corinthians 5:17); if you think there is no great difference between merely a speculative knowledge of these things and a personal experience in which Jesus Christ becomes Saviour and Lord of the whole man—the mind, the will, the emotions—then leave this man, this demon-possessed man, in the Capernaum synagogue, leave him with his demons and with his knowledge about Jesus, and never let the healing touch of Christ flow through his veins. How much he knew about Jesus, and yet his unappropriated knowledge condemned Him!

Notice how, for all his knowledge, he pleads for voluntary exile from Christ. The light in his soul had led him that day to the synagogue. I wonder why he came to the house of worship that day. Could he perhaps have thought that here, this very day, he might be restored to usefulness again—usefulness to himself, to his family, to society, to God? One day during our Lord's incarnation, he was privileged in the providence of God to be closer to Jesus of Nazareth during His earthly ministry than some of us are this morning. All the noblest longings in his shackled frame must have conspired to-gether for a high hour. But at the crucial moment when he could have had the water of life for the mere drinking, when he could have had bread from heaven for the mere taking, he cried out: *Let us alone; what have we to do with thee, thou Jesus of Nazareth? . . . I know thee who thou art: the Holy One of God.* It was a prayer against mercy. The Revised Standard Version translates the Greek as an interjection of despair: *Ah, what have we to do with thee . . . ?* But he draws a circle around his life, and shuts Christ out. He makes of his heart a cell that Christ is forbidden to enter. He prefers isolation with himself and with demons, isolation in his sins and his suffering. In our vernacular, he cries out, "Keep your hands off my life!" And I tell you that human life must be an awful mess when the only relief one can find is to get away from Christ. It must be a hell of hells, when one is driven to nurture a heart estranged from God, untenanted by the Holy Spirit, frequented only with demons, unvisited by godly influences, forlorn and desolate of spiritual things.

And that is where we seem to be driven more and more by the secular and profane drift of Western culture today. We push Jesus Christ more and more to the very margin of modern life. In politics, we hold our war and peace conferences without any intimation that it is any longer significant for human life that God made peace by the blood of the cross in A.D. 30. Away with You, Jesus; what have we to do with You! In education, we have swept the Living God and His commandments and the Bible out of our public schoolrooms, and comfort ourselves with prattle about moral and spiritual values. Away with You, Jesus; what have we to do with You! In science, we have enthroned an evolutionary philosophy that reduced to seeming irrelevance the revealed account of Creation and the miracles of the Hebrew-Christian religion, including the supernatural birth and Resurrection of Christ. Away with You, Jesus; what have we to do with You! In labor, we have lost the meaning of work, the sense of divine vocation, and multitudes hunger only for materialistic gain. Away with You, Jesus; what have we to do with You! In recreation, we have allowed Hollywood and the bestsellers to exalt a scale of values that often runs directly counter to the formula for blessedness that Jesus gave in the Beatitudes. Away with You, Jesus; what have we to do with You! We have moved Jesus to the very periphery of modern life and culture, and we cannot hope to gain by losing Him. The knowledge that we have will condemn us. In the terrible events of our times—the shadows of global war, the rise of world tyrants, the interstellar power that has fallen into the hands of the Russians, the weakening of the democracies, the widening of the pagan religions—the rebellious conscience of man, who has light that he spurns, stands condemned by Jesus of Nazareth, the Holy One of God, and in his conscience modern man is secretly driven to ask: "Art thou come to destroy us?" And He will, unless we repent. For the knowledge we have, if not an instrument in our salvation, becomes an instrument of condemnation.

Notice finally that *only the healing touch of Christ upon human life and culture can free it from the bondage and penalty and guilt of sin,* even as the touch of Christ alone restored this demon-possessed man to usefulness again.

You are waiting, some of you, for me to say something about these demons. And I shall. They are the undetected false gods of our modern idolatrous culture and living. Modernist scholars hardly knew what to do with them; if the world gets better and better, as they thought, demons must be consigned to the past; better yet, get rid of them as superstition and myth. This same modernist scholarship, however, emphasized at least that Jesus is the best example of right religious insight and adjustment. But Jesus Himself believed in the reality of Satan and demons. This was not a matter merely of accommodation on His part to the temper of the times, for he corrected the prevailing theological errors of His contemporaries. If He merely pretended to cast out demons, can He be defended against the charge of pretension and deception? He spent forty days in the wilderness, tempted of Satan and victorious over him; indeed, He represented His whole ministry as the rout and doom of Satan and his hosts, and He cast demons out by the power of His word. Under the pressures of the time in which we live, men speak against wide areas of the demonic in modern life, although they shy away from the reality of Satan and demons. Jesus reminds us that the world is under the sway of Satan and his hosts, and that we need supernatural rescue. In the Western world, invaded for centuries by the Gospel and its power, actual demon possession may be a relatively rare phenomenon, although the subtleties of the world of evil are such that even here we may be in for great surprise. Cultures prone to deny the realities of evil are most likely already victimized by them. This much is clear—if Christ is not Lord of your life, even you are courting idols and false gods, and your soul is swayed by other spirits than the Holy Spirit.

Now the great tragedy today is that even men and women who name the name of Christ, and who have made some elemental beginning in the Christian life, are prone to frustrate the work of Christ in their lives. They have passed through an experience in which they have pleaded, "Into my heart, Into my heart,/Come into my heart, Lord Jesus;/Come in today, Come in to stay,/Come into my heart, Lord Jesus." Now the temptation to backslide, of course, is with us always, and the Christian victory needs to be won again and again, day after day, hour after hour. But today our churches are full of members who would rather be possessed by some filthy habit than to be possessed by Christ Jesus. Christianity in the world today is embarrassed by the hordes who will go "only so far" with Jesus; beyond that point they cry out, "Let me alone; what have I to do with thee, thou Jesus of Nazareth?" They bear the scars of hardness and spiritual insensitivity. For it leaves scars in the life of love to profess that Jesus Christ is "the sweetest name" that one has ever heard, and then to live through years of spiritual experience in which Christ's nearness is a source of annoyance, anxiety, irritation, vexation and misery of soul. For some, the compromise of our Lord's power in their lives is not a matter of fleshly and carnal sin, but of unconsecrated means. They gladly give their lives to Christ, but not their money. I wonder whether you know that in 1929, in the stock market crash, Christians—those whose names were on Protestant church rolls—lost enough money in speculation to have paid the debt on all the Protestant churches in the United States? Now I want to be careful what I say about this, for I am a firm believer in free enterprise and find no warrant for collectivism and socialism in the Scriptures. But it may have been in some instances the judgment of God upon money that was withheld from Jesus. And one of the marks of our materialistic age is that the redemptive touch of Christ upon modern life and society is impeded by the lack of consecrated gifts for foreign missions, for new churches, for Christian education, and for the whole enterprise of evangelical effort. Then again, some others think that giving their lives to Christ is simply a matter of avoiding a given catalogue of sins, and of tithing their money, but they have no conception of Christian vocation as such. They think that full-time Christian service is something intended only for ministers and missionaries, or they shy away from the notion of a specific dedication of their talents to Christ and from the conception of one's daily job as a divine calling. In 1943, in the Plaza Hotel in Chicago, I spent almost half an hour with the great evangelist Gypsy Smith, who had crossed the Atlantic five times, knocking on the door of America for revival. Those were the days before Billy Graham's ministry had come to prominence. I asked Gypsy Smith why revival had not come to America. His answer is still significant. "Revival has not come to America," he said, "because when the Holy Spirit puts His hand upon some young life in this land for a consecrated and dedicated work, the average young person tends to say, like the demon-possessed man in the Gospels, 'Let me alone; what have I to do with thee, thou Jesus of Nazareth?'"

The healing touch of Christ upon your life and mine, the redemptive touch of Christ upon modern life and society, that is our great hope for casting out the false gods and for breaking every idol down. Jesus comes today to a society quite aware that "his word

78

was with power," but which also prefers to evade the spiritual decisions He would urge upon it. He comes to fill the vacuum in your life, to heal its witheredness. Let His command quiet the fury of your life this day. Hear Him speak peace to your turbulent soul. Greet Him as the worker of wonders from Nazareth, ready to transform your tangled being; as the Holy One, ready to show you to moral victory; as the Redeemer of your soul, ready to deliver you from sin and death. Let the fame of Him surge through your life, through your home, through your street, through your city. Why send Him on—on to some neighbor's heart, when your own is so empty? Why shunt Him to a neighbor's home, when yours is Christless? Why send Him to another street, when your own needs His visit and work and Presence? Why send Him to another city, to another land, through your neglect, when through your response and obedience His fame can go through every place of our own region round about?

CHRISTMAS

The Humble Crib and the Heavenly Wonder

Reverend Johnstone G. Patrick, Litt D.

MINISTER, FIRST PRESBYTERIAN CHURCH, SAYRE, PENNSYLVANIA

This sermon combines in a most unusual manner the glory of Christmas and the eternal power of Easter. It is worth reading the entire sermon to feel the truth of his statement: "If there had been no Easter, there would be no Christmas festival today."

Dr. Patrick was born and brought up in the rolling Scottish countryside north of the Firth of Forth and a stone's throw from the world-famed golfing center, St. Andrews, Fifeshire. After his schooling in Scotland, he attended Cliff College, Sheffield, England, and Spurgeon's Theological College, London, England, and was ordained to holy orders in 1944. Shortly after he assumed his first ministerial charge, his London church was "blitzed" by a flying bomb—one of the last to fall on the city. Since then, his ministerial duties have taken him to St. Peter Port, Guernsey, Channel Islands, to Ontario, Canada, and finally to the United States.

79

He came here in 1955 to assume his duties as minister of the First Presbyterian Church, Sayre, Pennsylvania. Dr. Patrick is the author of the book, ABOVE THE THORN, and his literary offerings have been published in periodicals on both sides of the Atlantic. Over fifty of his sermons have been published in THE CHRISTIAN CENTURY PULPIT, PULPIT DIGEST, PULPIT PREACHING, THE CHRISTIAN WORLD, THE CHRISTIAN WORLD PULPIT, THE CHRISTIAN HERALD, etc.

Dr. Patrick's sermon prose sings. He has a fluency with words and a dramatic style in his rhetoric which could help many young ministers as they work to perfect their sermonic style and content.

SERMON ELEVEN

> "And the Word was made flesh, and dwelt among us, (and we beheld his glory, the glory as of the only begotten son of the Father,) full of grace and truth," John 1:14

A SERMON ON CHRISTMAS; what could be easier? The subject is shot through and through with color; the theme is throbbing with romance. It conjures up for us a crowded gallery of cheerful pictures, all limned from childhood memories—carols and snow and Christmas stockings and tiny trees abloom with toys; brightly printed cards on the mantelpiece or piano, holly and mistletoe; plum puddings alight, family fun and games. The season possesses overtones and undertones of meaning that would require an uncountable number of sermons to exhaust.

There is a subtle something abroad in the air at Christmastide that warms hearts, opens purse strings, and makes tired mouths to smile; something that sets streams of surreptitious sympathy overflowing, that fills and floods the mind with "thoughts so sudden, that they seem the revelations of a dream"; something that exercises a delightful spell over the imagination and unloads on our doorsteps a freight of friendship fraught "with the fragrance of home-dwelling joys"; something that clings with cherishing fondness about all small children, that helps to hush the world's sighing and swell its singing, and enkindles new purpose and inspiration; something that lights lovely little colored candles, to quote the farrier in George Eliot's great novel, *Silas Marner,* "i' the dark and i' the lone places" of this life. Indeed, the very word Christmas itself is magical; it falls on the ear like the tinkle of merry bells.

I

But to get behind the tinsel and the formalities and to preach about the reality is not so easy. It is never easy to preach about Christ, and Christmas without Christ is shorn of all its sublime significance, robbed of its rhyme and reason, and bleached of its best colors. Any Christmas celebration in which the Christ Child is conspicuously absent is like a frame without a picture; like a life lacking in love; like a feast without food. Christmas without Christ in it is a brief boom of hectic gaiety and forced friendliness, followed all too frequently and fleet-footedly by a bitter slump.

It is true that Christmas is not the liturgical season for lamentations: it is the time to say "Merry Christmas" and mean it honestly, kindly and expansively. But once we forget the Good News, "the glorious tidings of great joy," the Christmas season begins to pall on us. The Good News is that God came down into this world on the first Christmas morning. In His cosmic-sweeping mercy the infinite, everlasting God—not just a moral reformer, a religious poet, a gentleman of absolute integrity—broke into human history. He stooped beneath the lowest and least inviting roof in Bethlehem, and clothed Himself in the garment of our own frail flesh. It is not so astounding that God came down to earth; had He not visited "this vale of tears," spiritually, many times before? Of course He had! He once filled a desert shrub with the perfume of His Presence and glory and it flamed with fire. On another occasion He entered a great mountain and it quivered and quaked with His Presence. But the amazing fact is that "in the fullness of time" He shrank to the size of a small son of man and limited Himself to the loveliest of all earth's languages—the language of a new-born baby's cry! "The Word was made flesh, and dwelt among us, . . . full of grace and truth."

Eric Gill, an exquisite English artist, who did more than his "little bit" towards reintegrating bed and board, the small farm and the workshop, the home and the school, earth and heaven, has called the Incarnation "the greatest of all rhetorical acts"—an act of *utterance*. Christ was God's greatest and gentlest message, the Word by which He communicated with the world.

II

Let us loose the reins of our imagination a little and look at the straw-strewn manger over there: at the young country girl in her 'teens, that middle-aged man approaching the shady side of fifty, and at that Baby only a few hours old! Suppose we had actually gone, in company with some horny-handed herdsmen and some star-led sages from the East, into that cobweb-covered cattle-cave, all those long years ago; would we have seen any difference between that Baby and the baby we have—or used to have—at home? I think not. He would have felt the cold of that winter's night and have cried, too.

It is marvelous in our mind's eye to see Him, "who keeps Israel," sleeping *in* a manger. But can any man measure, count, imagine all that has come *out* of a manger? A vast society of God's friends, churches, chapels, monasteries, abbeys, ministers, missionaries, cathedrals, schools and colleges, paintings and poems, songs and hymns, oratorios, plays, orphanages, hospitals, political liberties and institutions, millions of books, thoughts and deeds, "faith, hope and charity"—all these, and very much more besides, emerged from a mean manger! The marvel of the Manger is just that!

"I should go so far as to say that, spiritually speaking, everything which is gigantic is spiritually suspect." Gabriel Marcel, a truly fine French philosopher, uttered these words. And Lancelot Andrewes, the sixteenth-century son of English piety and ordered loveliness, in a Christmas sermon, sums up the immortal message of the manager: "The great lesson is to be little, seeing this day infinite greatness become so little. Eternity a child, the rays of glory wrapped in rags, Heaven crowded into the corner of a stable, and He that is everywhere want a room."

III

Let us transport ourselves in thought to the straggling, sleepy street of old-world Nazareth on to which opens the door of the village carpenter's workshop. See, He is sitting with His feet in wood-shavings, behind His father, with a hammer and some nails and a bit of waste wood. Do you think He ever hit His finger? Of course He did, and howled when He did it. "In all things like to us" is the manner in which an ancient writer put it, "excepting sin." His growth was a man's, and His heart was a man's. "The word was made flesh, and dwelt among us, . . . full of grace and truth."

Allow some twenty or thirty years of our Lord's earthly life to slip away, and let us look again. On a low hill outside an old city wall, a little crowd is swaying. You can almost hear the hard breathing of someone in excruciating pain, and mocking laughter, and the dull thud of a hammer. Suddenly the crowd swirls back, and over its shifting edge a forbidding black outline gradually rises against the eastern sky. A grisly cross sways, hesitates, and finally settles into its socket. There is a muffled cheer, and then silence through which sounds a voice, so tired, so patient, so loving. "Father, forgive . . ." That is all: the most universal pair of words in human language, the most instinctive feelings in the human heart. "The Word was made flesh, and dwelt among us, . . . full of grace and truth."

Behind the majesty and mystery, the glory and grandeur, of God made man, within His very divinity there beats a human heart, a heart with all the emotions and sympathies of a man. All that we suffer, He has endured in His own flesh, and far more than that. All the trials, even the temptations, of mind and heart and body He has undergone like us. He, if anyone in the whole universe, understands and knows. He knows every fiber of our frail flesh; He follows every vagrant thought; He thrills to every throbbing of our hearts. Surely in Him—and in Him alone—we shall find the succor and sympathy and salvation we seek. That is the threefold lesson of the crib, the carpenter's bench, and the cross—the astounding and tremendous truth that we are, at Christmas time, so apt to forget.

The life of Him whose birth Christians commemorate each Christmastide was all of one piece, like the seamless garment He wore. At the end of that life, the loveliest and lowliest and lordliest ever lived out under these ordinary skies, stands a cross. Bethlehem and Calvary must never be separated in meaning or in time. It took the crudest of all cribs, a life saturated with service and sacrifice, and the grisliest of all gibbets to defeat death, shatter sin's soul-destroying power, dispel the darkness of doubt and leave behind an empty tomb in Joseph's garden. Not only by His humble birth in the stable, but by His bloody sweat and suffering, by His toil and tears, by His death and resurrection, is He the Saviour of the world.

Jean Burden, a little-known present-day American poetess, in her poem *Christmas* spells out so well the truth we do well to harbor in our hearts at this holy, happy time:

> Because the cross
>   became a tree,
> because the rock
>   became a door,
> we celebrate
>   return to birth,
> we kneel upon
>   the humble floor.

<blockquote>
For this our shepherds
    sing their hymns,
for this our Wise Men
    travel far:
because the cross
    became a tree;
because the stone
    became a star.
</blockquote>

If there had been no Easter, there would be no Christmas festival today.

We are assured, since "the Word was made flesh, and dwelt among us," that sin will not be allowed to have the last word in our world. The fire of divine love our Heavenly Father sent His Son to kindle on the hearth of the human heart will not be blown out. Even though it may be very late in the eleventh hour of human history, it is not too late for us to turn back to Bethlehem—the "Bethlehem beyond despair"—where the victorious way of the cross begins. We have only to go and give Him the trust of our tarnished lives, to believe in Him enough to obey Him, and to receive from Him the Christmas gift of eternal life.

"The Word" that became flesh in our world on that far-off first Christmas morning will "become flesh" in us when we accept the challenge of Christmastide. With all the glittering guile and glory of a goodly gold, His Star once again is beckoning. Follow the gleam!

THE CHURCH

On Earth Is Not His Equal

Reverend William O. Byrd
MINISTER, FIRST METHODIST CHURCH, PINE BLUFF, ARKANSAS

This sermon on the Church and preaching today, on what makes a man preach Sunday after Sunday and what the Church stands for, deserves to be read and preached in many places. It was preached on October 27, 1957.

William O. Byrd is a native of Meridian, Mississippi, and a graduate of Louisiana Polytechnic Institute, Ruston, Louisiana, and of Southern Methodist University.

He has been pastor of Methodist churches in Bonita, Farmers-

ville, and of the University Methodist Church in Lake Charles, Louisiana. He served three years as an Army chaplain, eighteen months overseas, part of the time with the 82nd Airborne Division as Parachute Infantry Chaplain. On his return, he was pastor of First Methodist Church, Arkadelphia, Arkansas and is now in his fourth year at First Methodist Church, Pine Bluff, Arkansas.

SERMON TWELVE

> ". . . But whom say ye that I am? . . . Thou art the Christ, the Son of the living God. . . . upon this rock I will build my church; and the gates of hell shall not prevail against it," Matthew 16:15–18

"WHY IN THE WORLD DO YOU DO IT? Why do you stand up there, Sunday after Sunday, and preach your heart out—when you *know* very well that not one in a thousand will really notice or long remember what you say, much less let it change their lives? Why do you do it?"

This rather searching question came from a brilliant mind, a young man wrestling with the deeper meaning of life. He came to me after I had preached one of my so-called "controversial" sermons, something about race and brotherhood. Then after talking about his personal questions, he asked: "Why do you do it—Sunday after Sunday?"

He hit me at a difficult time. I had just passed a birthday and I was looking back on all the years I had wasted. And I thought of the thousands of sermons I had preached and the other thousands that my people had heard from other ministers and from me, and with so little apparent results through the years.

It was quite a question—why? And to top it off, I had been looking through the records of this church for the past thirty years, reading the minutes of official meetings of the Board. Time after time, almost as a theme song, great issues were raised, great plans formulated, and then at the bottom of the minutes this phrase: "After much discussion—no action was taken!"

And I looked back at the missed opportunities of this, and of so many other churches, because people were not willing to pay the price of total commitment to the dreams they themselves had of greatness for their church.

So the question stood, and I remembered, and couldn't beg the question. It had just enough truth in it to hurt—the absurdities of so many activities in the church, so much of it irrevelant to life as it ought to be lived, the cowardice of silence on vital issues, the simple inertia of this and other churches, all these keeping this and other churches from moving forward "like a mighty army." And I could sympathize with a fellow minister when he was asked: "And how many people do you have in your church?" He replied, "Oh, about three hundred souls—and a few heels!"

Call me a disillusioned preacher if you like, but you can't ignore the question. Not and be honest at all. We have to admit that after the years of our lives we still find the same problems in the church —and the same "problem people." From the human point of view the Church *is* a failure. And, if you try to justify it there alone, then the haunting "Why keep on?" will go unanswered.

But, you see, the point is that the Church *admits* its failure. It is a magnificent failure. In fact, the Church is the *one* institution in society whose sole requirement for membership is that the person applying admits his own unworthiness—admits that he or she is not equal to the battle of life alone. Now, that's not so in any other group. You cannot join any other organization on that basis. Yet the Church of the Living God insists that every last and least one of us can say: "I do not believe that I am worthy of what God has done for me, and because I *am* unworthy, I want to be part of the Church to serve Him better."

Only the true church—the Holy, Catholic Church—the Divine Fellowship—takes us as we *are* in order to help us to *become* what He would have us be. Here is the true nature of the Church. When we realize it, we will quit apologizing for the human failures within it and proclaim the Divine throughout it. *The greatness of the Church is not in its membership but in its Lord.*

Yes, we admit that when judged by the mind of her Master, the Church must bow in contrition, but thanks be to God that it is still true that:

Where the spirit of the Lord is, there is the one true Church, Apostolic and Universal, whose Holy Faith we—Sunday after Sunday—do reverently declare.

Here is our hope in a world wherein we fight against powers and principalities, against spiritual wickedness in high places; where we know that nothing on earth can be evil's equal but the Man of God, our Lord, Christ Jesus is His name.

Here, then, is the greater question—and it contains the answer to my young friend's "why?" and to my own heart. The question is *not* what you think of the Church and its members or ministers. The question is: "What do *you* think of her Lord, Jesus Christ?" *He* is the One Whom we seek, and find, and follow. *He is why* I preach and *why* we worship Sunday after Sunday, even though deeply conscious of the failure of the Church and my own shortcomings.

Oh, it would be easy to spend the rest of this hour pointing out the failures of the Church, to quibble over its useless fights and quarrels and denominations. But our need is not a re-statement of what the Church does or does not do, but a re-affirmation of our faith that the Church exists as the Body of Christ. And Christ is so searching a fact that soon or late every last and least one of us must come to grips with Him. We must decide, we must respond.

We must say with Peter, "Thou art the Christ, the son of the living God!" Or we must say that He was a visionary, an idealist who spoke beautiful but impractical words, a fool, a historical figure, a dead Jew—and that's all. But, the moment you so dismiss Him, you leave yourself wide open to another question: "What shall *I become* in life?" and you can't escape His relationship to that "becoming."

No, you can't take it or leave it. You can ignore the Church, even laugh at it, but you can't ignore the insistent Christ. You must live by some faith—or *unfaith*—in Him.

> "What think ye of Christ," friend? "When all's done and said?
> Like you this Christianity or not?
> It may be false, but will you wish it true?
> Has it your vote to be so if it can be?"
> —Robert Browning, *Bishop Blougram's Apology*

That is the soul-arresting question that we face every time we walk into a church. No matter what the subject for the day, if it is a Christian church you and I must make some kind of decision about a Galilean carpenter named Jesus. Born in obscurity, He left the world few words, no writings. He held no political office, He led no army, He wrote no music. The historians of His day for the most part thought Him unworthy of mention, yet His spirit is *the* inescapable *fact* of history.

And, Where the Spirit of the Lord Is, There Is the One True Church! If we could see *that* Church, and follow as did the disciples at risk and cost, *then* we would find the Power and the Glory. For upon *this* rock—the simple faith of a fisherman following on, *this* lightning flash in the darkness of time, *this* heartbeat of the eternal, is built the Church. Here is God's thrust into our world and time to provide fellowship with Him for all eternity. Here is God becoming real for you and for me. Now, what think ye of Christ?

Look—See the Church as the Body of Christ. Strengthened, empowered, triumphant, confident in the soul's invincible surmise that Christ is her Lord—The Church—beyond the corrosion of the years, beyond "the world's slow stain," beyond the mortality of all mortal men, beyond all powers and principalities, the Church stands "a mighty fortress" and the gates of hell have not—shall not—prevail against her.

Kingdoms may topple, ideologies pass, cities crumble, yet the Church endures. Why? Why does it—Sunday after Sunday—endure? Not the caricature that we make of the Church: a kind of second-rate debating club where "controversial" issues are never, never mentioned; just another social club for the company of the comfortable, instead of the fellowship of the concerned. That church we go to because, well, the family always did go, or it's expected of one in our social standing to attend, or, just for the heck of it. No, *that* church will fail and should fail. There is the human equation.

But the Church does not consist of a Book of Numbers, wherein some nice parson wrote our name. The Church of the living Christ is the Book of the Acts of the Spirit of God wherein we meet a Person. The Church is not a creed—but the life breath of the Living God, the very blood of life, coursing through the veins of those who would see beyond themselves. This is a far cry from the silly little club we've made of it.

But if we could ever grasp the reality of *the* Church. It does not belong to us, we belong to it! Only then shall we begin to understand the high calling of Christ. Yes, like a mighty army would move the Church of God, if we would quit whining in the rear ranks, refusing to pay the price of combat for Christ. Yes, *churches* shall fail—but *the* Church, the Body of Christ, keeps on, Sunday after Sunday, century after century, until the kingdoms of this world shall become the kingdom of our Lord.

And So We Keep on, Sunday After Sunday. Why? To proclaim again that only Christ can equal anything this world may hurl against us. To remind us, and the world, that if it were not for the Church we would never have heard of this Master. Think a moment—beyond the brief oral traditions, there was a vast gap in history and if it were not for the Church we may have lost His redemptive words and

Presence. Someone has defined the Church as "the community that remembers Jesus." If it were not for this remembering you and I would not this day be enjoying what we call a Christian culture.

I grow a little weary of these people who so glibly proclaim: "Oh, you don't have to belong to the church, to believe—just live by the golden rule." Where did you get that golden rule? If it were not for the Church no one would be bothered by a golden rule. Without the continuing Church there would be no Sermon on the Mount, no basis for a culture as Christian as ours, even pagan though it be at times. The Church has kept alive that endless line of splendor for those who enjoy a first-hand fellowship rather than a second-hand morality.

And this second-hand morality is our grave danger in America today—not a Russian satellite or the threat of Communist troops. All this talk about a better world, or even the American way of life, is silly unless we remember that the church is the social soil in which grow the roots of greatness for America. We sing about the "Faith of our Fathers" but we haven't made it our own.

You can't escape that—you can laugh at the church, belittle it all you want—and then you have to admit that the very ideals which you yourself say ought to be followed are alive today because of the Church. In spite of the littleness of its ministers and members, it is the sacred ark that has kept America great.

I am tired of attending civic clubs where member after member speaks out "agin" Communism and its threat to America. Yet too often the one speaking loudest never darkens the door of a Church. I believe with all of my heart that no individual has the right to complain and shout about the threat of Communism or any other "ism" to destroy America who is not a praying, paying, active member of some local church. For it is the Church that holds the ultimate weapon against Communism.

That is why, Sunday after Sunday, we preach—and worship. These morally proud people who can be good enough without the Church—you've met these wise fools, as "good as any church member," they brag. If bothered at all, it is from having their self-made haloes too tight. Self-styled intellectuals, they laugh at the wisdom of God.

You cannot name a single area in all your life that does not owe a debt of gratitude to the church. Are *you* a scholar, a teacher? Then the Church, in spite of notable exceptions, has historically been the mother of learning, keeping alive the flickering torch of knowledge. Are *you* a laborer? Then the Church, in the Spirit of her Lord, has led the fight for a living wage and the dignity of honest toil. Especially am I proud to be a Methodist in this area—for Methodism was born with John Wesley going into the mines of Wales to insist that those grubby men were children of God and therefore had a right to a living wage—to stand tall. Are *you* a woman? Then the Church, following after her Lord, has insisted that you are an individual, not chattel property to be used. Are *you* a child? Even here the Church, echoing her Master, has insisted upon your right to an adequate childhood, without sweatshop labor.

Why, out of simple gratitude, even if I doubted her, I would have to belong to the Church. Theoretically there may have been other ways to keep the Spirit of Jesus alive in each generation, but the historical fact is that the Church did it. And every last one of us is indebted for our Christian heritage. Norman Pittenger reminded us: "The New Testament knows nothing of a Christian outside of the fellowship of the Church." That is why, Sunday after Sunday, I must be a part of it.

In the Final Analysis, We Go Sunday After Sunday Because We Instinctively Know That We Are Not Good Enough Alone. There is relationship to life—and we seek a togetherness. Hypocrites in the Church? Of course, but come on in, there is always room for one more. But, in the fellowship of the risen Lord, beyond the hypocrisy of little people, there is the living relationship with those who would be better than they are. It is here that the Lord helps us to channel what little goodness we achieve. And goodness must be organized. In such a day when countless organizations, councils, etc., are being formed to vomit out hate, can the individual who would count for good be satisfied to stand *alone*, sitting back and saying "somebody ought to do something"? R. H. Tawney, the English sociologist, reminds us that if you seek God apart from your fellows you will not find God but the devil, and he will bear a striking resemblance to your own countenance. Aye, so is it.

The Church calls you to yourself and out of yourself into greatness. There is a togetherness in the Church that is beyond our own strength. There is a sense of belonging, of importance beyond self-importance. The Church reminds us that with her Lord there is no unimportant person. Each of us is highly responsible for our world, for good or ill. Even Pogo, of funny-paper fame, has a lengthy discussion about satellites and such, only to turn to the more immediate problem: "What do you think causes juvenile delinquents?"

And the turtle replies, "Adult delinquents, naturally—and after all, us adults have some seniority rights." And the turtle is right. In God's kind of world, *you* are of tremendous importance for the next generation. In such a world as this, nothing is lost. Every action may have eternal significance.

You think your little life not important? The other day I read that a man received a Ph.D from Oxford University. The thesis for his degree was titled: "The influence of the Motion of Fish's Tails Upon the Tides of the Ocean." That's right! And he proved, to his satisfaction at least, that the great tides of the world *are* influenced by the motion of fish's tails. You who think your life doesn't count —are not ye of much more value than many fish's tails? Do you think for one moment that the God Who created such a universe in which every movement has meaning can overlook *you*, a person for whom His only Son died? And in Whose fellowship you may live forever?

That's Why We Keep On, Sunday After Sunday. To remind us of the fellowship that would redeem our life from mediocrity, to transform our *Worship into Worth-Ship.* It isn't a question of why more people are not changed. The miracle is that some *are* changed. You can't get away from it. You can see them all around you. They have met Him.

And He is Whom you seek. Not a building, nor people, nor an impatient parson—but a *Person.* And so Sunday after Sunday you follow the Spiritual Quest until there will come a time when He breaks through all the trappings, the petty little people, even your own littleness and doubt, and *you meet Him.* And in this Divine Encounter, this adoration of God in Christ, you will give yourself to Him.

This Is What Matters. This is *all* that matters. This total self-commitment to Him. And I do not know how you or I, or anyone else, can share in that high moment, unless we are willing to have patience and humility enough to sit down in a congregation of like-minded people, that we, like the disciples, "might be *with* Him." So say, "I am not worthy—but God has loved me so much, that He *wants me* with Him."

Here is the ultimate reason, the only answer to my young friend, and to my own doubts. This is why we keep on, Sunday after Sunday. For the Church, beyond all its failures, is the mystical Body of our Lord. And the Master Himself promised: "Where two or three are gathered in my Name, there will I be also."

So, my vocation, and yours, is to keep that rendezvous with Christ.

What think ye of Christ? Nothing on earth can be the equal of your problems, your burdens, and your possibilities. Nothing—but Christ. What do *you* think?

The Necessity of Commitment

Reverend Calvin De Vries, Minister
SHERWOOD PRESBYTERIAN CHURCH, WASHINGTON, D.C.

Calvin De Vries was born in the Middle West, attended North-western Junior College and Hope College, where he took honors in philosophy, then attended New Brunswick Theological Seminary, graduating in 1947. For ten years he was one of the ministers of Fourth Presbyterian Church in Chicago, and since 1957 has been pastor of Sherwood Church in Washington.

He has lectured on Christian Education at McCormick Theological Seminary for ministers' conferences and speaks on various college campuses during Religion-in-Life Week. His father was a minister of the Reformed Church and he has two brothers in the Presbyterian ministry.

This sermon emphasizes the need for personal commitment to Christ rather than a mere intellectual or theoretical association. It is brave, forthright preaching.

SERMON THIRTEEN

THE GERMAN ARTIST of a century past, Hoffman, has a well known painting, "Christ and the Rich Young Ruler," in which is dramatized the dominant demand of the Christian life: commitment. A young man, character and intelligence in his pensive face, stands before Jesus. He has come to ask Jesus what he should do to inherit eternal life, or in our vernacular, what he must do to qualify for the Christian life. Jesus reminds him of the commandments, and the young man replies with simple candor that he has always obeyed these. According to ostensible standards he was a deeply religious person. He came from a fine family, grew up in the church, was intelligent, moral and concerned. Unless we understand this we shall miss the full force of the story. Jesus then asks him to sell all that he has, give it to the poor and follow him. At this point Hoffman catches the scene. Here stands the young man. He cannot look into Jesus' searching eyes for he will not meet this demand, and he leaves with deep dejection.

This is not a story about a share-the-wealth plan. Either poverty or wealth can pose problems for the Christian. The real issue here is one of commitment. What was asked of the young man was a total commitment, a total engagement of his life by Jesus Christ. Is it startling to realize that Jesus Christ asks no less from any one of us who would be a Christian?

The young man, like many persons and communities today, would have been appalled at the suggestion that his religion was superficial and that in a radical sense he was deeply irreligious. Nevertheless, precisely this is the position of the Bible. To be a profoundly religious person in the biblical sense is not in the first place to be very moral or to know all about the Bible. If this were true there could be no way in which, for instance, David or Peter could be described as "religious." Both were impulsive persons, capable of bald disloyalties, with lives of considerable moral ambiguity. Yet both stand as mountain peaks on the horizon of the Bible. Both, for all their disloyalties, were profoundly religious persons for they were deeply committed persons. This is the most searching test of religious depth and earnestness.

Take the razor edge of this test and see how it exposes the superficiality of much that passes for religion today. Many of us, with restrained pride, speak of the communities in which we live as religious. In them we find a high concern for the arts, for world affairs, for charitable and social service work. Religious cynics we have with us always. But for the most part our communities not only tolerate religious faith; in a detached and sophisticated way they consider themselves religious. Predestination and psychoanalysis are raised in the same evening. Modern theologians such as Niebuhr and Tillich are often quoted by the presumed patrons of religion. Above all else, religion is often discussed. However, to speak of a personal and searching commitment to Jesus Christ as Lord and Saviour would be regarded as rather vulgar.

It is exactly in this sense that many of our communities are irreligious from a Biblical perspective. Persons assiduously avoid soul-shaking commitments by their detached talk about religion. Few of them care about God in a gripping way. One suspects that the most deeply irreligious people are not always the cynics but rather those who can speak charmingly about religion and yet refuse to be engaged by it. This mood often passes for the virtue of tolerance. It is not tolerance but rather pervasive skepticism. No one has the right to be called tolerant unless he cares about something so deeply he would die for it, still granting the right of opposing points of view and really listening to them.

When the Apostle Paul came to Athens and spoke at the famed Areopagus he found just such a disengaged audience. His chronicler puts it somewhat cynically, "Now all the Athenians . . . spent their time in nothing except telling or hearing something new." And Paul, tongue in cheek one suspects, begins by saying, "I perceive that in every way you are very religious." Paul was not successful in Athens. It wasn't that these people were opposed to religion. They didn't care enough. They were against any position that was articulate and probing and certain. The Areopagus was, no doubt, the same court which four hundred and fifty years earlier had charged Socrates with "corrupting young men and not recognizing the gods whom the city recognized."

It is an interesting commentary on Greek civilization, the greatest intellectual culture the world has known, that it never came to a clear-cut and deeply felt monotheistic faith, as did the late Old Testament prophets. Isn't the reason obvious? The discovery of truth is dependent not only upon intellectual abilities but much more upon willingness to be engaged by the truth. It depends upon commitment. The deeply committed person often understands truth more deeply simply because he gives himself to it, than does the more intelligent person whose skepticism sometimes prevents any meaningful participation in truth.

What I have been saying would be quite misunderstood if taken merely as critical moralism directed to others. Eventually we must turn the focus of this matter upon our own lives. All of our thinking and talking about the Christian faith, all of our church attendance and our prim righteousness, are meaningless apart from a deep and determining commitment to Jesus Christ. For biblical faith is not so much concerned with religious ideas or morals as it is concerned with man's ultimate allegiance, his complete commitment to God's will and way for his life.

To be committed to Jesus Christ is not a mystical or highly emotional experience. Rather, it means that we are so captured, so grasped by God in Jesus Christ that this becomes the creative center of all we are and do and think. This commitment is the final ground for every decision we make. By and through it all lesser values are determined. Its field of application is the whole of one's experience, from race relations to our clothes budget. It is the most intense experience of which a person is capable.

Consider how inescapable such a commitment becomes when we expose our lives to Jesus Christ. He comes to us in the strange world of the Bible, with its ideas and assumptions, many of which we can no longer accept. Yet there is in the Bible a central core which we must either accept or reject; we cannot evade it. This core is the offer of a relationship with God through Jesus Christ. To accept it and be grasped by it completely is to be a Christian.

Human nature being what it is, Jesus Christ will not let us rest. He is disturbing. We give him wonderful names but he comes back and says, "If any man come to me and hate not his father, and mother, and wife, and children, and brethren, and sisters, yea, and his own life also, he cannot be my disciple." He himself shatters all of our sentimental and idealized images of what he asks to remind us that words come easy but total commitment is everything.

Something incendiary about Jesus Christ calls for decisions whenever we really confront him. We are haunted by His ways, which are beyond us. Over against the hostilities of our lives stands His depthless love. Against our duplicities and deceits is His purity. His offer of wholeness and healing cries out to our deep needs. His revelation of God's forgiveness confronts our sin and attendant guilt. His victory over death echoes down the corridors of human existence whenever we face the nothingness of death. To respond is to become committed, and to be committed is to be so grasped by him that he becomes inescapable.

Complementing Jesus' demand for commitment is the inescapable need for commitment to something in every human life. Is someone here thinking that he should prefer doing as he pleases? This strikes you as real freedom. But I put it to you that actually nothing is so hazardous and so limiting. Who would think of a great ocean liner as free if its rudders were useless? It would be at the mercy of nature's destructive powers. To have no commitment, no gripping loyalty, is to experience meaninglessness. No clergyman but rather a prominent New York psychotherapist wrote in one of his books, "The chief problem of people in the middle decade of the twentieth century is emptiness . . ."

The matter is not faced by saying, "I can get along without

Jesus Christ." Of course one can; but it reminds us of Hermann Hagedorn's lines from "The Heart of Youth,"

> "Where men with blinkered eyes and hobbled feet
> Grope down a narrow gorge and call it life."

One can get along without education too, crimp through life without friendships, without medical science, without meaningful work. It is a question of what Jesus Christ can do with your life and add to it, enlarging, deepening, directing and redeeming it. We can be smug and self-satisfied on the outside, wistfully empty on the inside. Or we can be captured by the highest and the best that human existence knows, Jesus Christ. He can fulfill life. He can light the lamp that no darkness can ever put out.

If a decision for or against Jesus becomes inescapable when we honestly confront him, then think how commitment to him wonderfully changes a central concern of us all: that of being morally whole and good. How many of us live with distressing guilt, feeling that we are not really good persons! We have deep levels of anger without wanting them. Our sincerest resolves to be better persons crumple like thin dikes under the beating of the restless sea of our emotions. A small child put her finger on the issue: "The harder I try the worser I am."

In just the same way we suppose that one can be good by knowing the right and having a strong enough sense of duty to follow it. I doubt that there is a more crippling illusion, whether fostered by religion or irreligion, than the idea that duty and the aggressive self-will are the way to virtue. Clearly there are times when duty is a necessary discipline. Duty has held many a marriage together until something more creative could enter and redeem the relationship. But think how inadequate duty is as a word to describe the relationship between husband and wife. Only love is adequate, such a deep commitment to each other that even troubles become creative for the relationship.

This is what the Bible says about goodness. There is another way to virtue, an easier way if you will, than the strong-arm methods of sheer duty. It is to be so changed and healed and redeemed within that goodness becomes the spontaneous by-product. Precisely this is what commitment to Jesus Christ offers us. Think of the difference! On the one hand are persons whose goodness is labored and rigid, pervaded by a sense of hostility to life. Their goodness often becomes a form of badness. They remind one of the boy at a piano recital who has been compelled to practice the piano when he actually loathed it; and now he stumbles through his selection to the discomfort of everyone present. Over against him is the child whose parents have taught him to love music. He is grasped by it. He has never been forced to play the piano, but listen now to the feeling and meaning he puts into the music. And so there are people who are good because something has happened inside their minds and feelings and wills. Their goodness is natural and infectious. They demonstrate the title of a great sermon, "The Explosive Power of a New Affection." Just so Jesus Christ and commitment to him change the matter of moral goodness.

Suppose we were to say to the Apostle Paul: "What a will power you must have had, Paul, starting out as a persecutor and ending up as a saint!" He would have come back with deep feeling, "It was not my will power. Rather, my will was taken hold of and captured. What the law and duty could not do, human nature being what it is, that God did for me in Jesus Christ." Here is the key to the whole Christian life, its joy and freedom and wholeness. "A good tree brings forth good fruit" said Jesus. A self that has been changed and healed within, in an ever more deepening way, is spontaneously good. Jesus Christ saves us from a prim virtue that is always preening itself. He saves us from within, through commitment to himself, so that our goodness arises not from a slavish conscience but rather from purity of heart.

Consider one more benefit of such an absorbing commitment as Jesus Christ calls for. Such a commitment enlarges and enriches life. Do not many of us raise fundamental doubts about that? In earlier days, going through an intellectual struggle with the Christian faith, I was certain that commitment meant giving up one's intelligence, sacrificing one's inner self in a way that was essentially unrealistic and destructive. Commitment had overtones of confinement, of rigidity and puritanism. The whole experience of my life has been that when one commits one's life to Jesus Christ there are indeed sacrifices, often of things deeply cherished. But one always receives them back again, profoundly enriched and enlarged.

We need, all of us, to lift commitment to Jesus Christ out of a narrow parochialism. Commitment does not force us into a kind of prefabricated personality. Commitment is choice of direction. It is a living loyalty, an enlarging trust, a saving love. One cannot make one's Christian life over in the image of another or it will be false. It is erroneous to think that commitment must be identified with conversion experiences, as redemptive as they can be. But commitment must be real, specific and personal. When it is one can be as intelligent as one wishes, as fun-loving as another, having lost nothing but having gained "Someone" for whom we would not trade the whole world.

Have you ever had the experience of being forced to do something for a friend, give something to another? Perhaps you felt cheated and sorry for yourself. Then one day the other person repaid you a thousand times over. What began with feelings of forced sacrifice ended up with enlargement. How often commitment to Jesus Christ is like that. We thought we would be confined when actually we were set free. We expected to pay a fine but found instead that we were receiving dividends.

Belonging to Jesus Christ is always a wonderfully redeeming experience. It means that although in our finest virtues there lurks unrighteousness, that although in our highest faith stands despair, that although in every moment of life is the threat of death, still we belong to another who is able to do for us far more than we are either able to ask or to think. For it is to God that we ultimately belong, and our commitment to him, through Jesus Christ, is merely our confirmation of the most irrevocable truth of our existence.

Bending over a cradle a mother whispers to her child, "Baby, you're mine. I loved you into life." Soon, however, the years gather their momentum and the infant is a child, claimed by the uninhibited joys of life's morning. One day the child is a youth, thinking about his future. He chooses a vocation and it claims his mind and heart, seeming to say, "You belong to me. I will make you great." The years move on, and one day his hand is taken by another's hand, who whispers, "Lover, you are mine. We were meant for one another." Yet how restlessly the river of life moves on into the strong, middle years of life with the claims of parenthood, of work and of friends, the siren claims of pleasure and social eminence. But the years refuse to linger and life's river becomes fuller and deeper and slower. One day this life slips through the narrows of death into eternity's ocean. There in the depthlessness of God and His love, the life hears the whisper, "my child, you are Mine. You have always been Mine. It was I Who gave you life. It was I Who drew you irresistibly back to Myself through all other lesser claims, by the love of Jesus Christ. From Me you came and to Me you return. Only I can say that you really and wholly belong to Me."

The Tragic Sense of Life

Reverend Paul Waitman Hoon, Ph.D., S.T.D.

A METHODIST MINISTER AND HENRY SLOANE COFFIN PROFESSOR OF
PASTORAL THEOLOGY AT UNION THEOLOGICAL SEMINARY, NEW YORK

*After years as a successful pastor and preacher, Dr. Hoon was
invited in 1953 to become Professor of Pastoral Theology at Union
Theological Seminary, New York, to teach other men how to make
their ministry in the Christian Church effective today.*

*Paul Hoon was born in Chicago on February 11, 1910. He studied
at the University of Cincinnati, and took his bachelor's degree at
Yale and his B.D. at Union Theological Seminary in 1934. He studied
at Marburg, Germany, in the same year, at Cambridge, England,
in 1935, and took his Ph.D. at the University at Edinburgh in 1936.*

*His ministry began as student assistant minister at Madison
Avenue Presbyterian Church, New York, in 1931 and 1932; he was
next assistant minister at Chester Hill Methodist Church, Mount
Vernon, New York, from 1932 to 1934. He was ordained a Methodist
minister in 1933, and appointed minister at New Milford, Connecticut, where he served from 1936 to 1938. He served at Sum-
merfield Methodist Church, Bridgeport, Connecticut, from 1938 to
1941; at First Methodist Church, Germantown, Pennsylvania, from
1943 to 1953. He was a lecturer at Drew Theological Seminary in
1949 and 1950, and has been Professor of Pastoral Theology at
Union Seminary since 1953. He has written the exposition of the
epistles of Saint John for* THE INTERPRETER'S BIBLE, *and several articles in religious journals. Ursinus College conferred the honorary
S.T.D. upon him in 1948.*

SERMON FOURTEEN

"Woman, why weepest thou?" John 20:15

THE QUESTION Jesus addresses to Mary in the passage read as
part of our lesson is a question that searches the meaning of our

devotion as we contemplate Jesus moving through the last days of His life to the cross. Mary, you remember, is pictured as standing before the empty tomb weeping—"the New Testament's classic figure of sorrow," she has been called. She does not know until the final moment that Jesus is risen. She is still thinking and feeling in terms of His death. She is still in Lent, as it were; she is not yet in Easter. And as she stands weeping, Jesus draws near and speaks to her, and asks: "Woman, why weepest thou?"

Is not that a question that the contemplation of Jesus' Passion sets for us, too, not in the sense of tender rebuke with which Jesus addresses it to Mary, but rather in a searching, piercing sense that inquires into the depths of our devotion and remembrance? Here are the lines, for example, of Faber's familiar hymn of the Passion:

O come and mourn with me awhile;
O come ye to the Saviour's side.
A broken heart, a fount of tears,
Ask, and they will not be denied.

What is it for us as people of faith really to mourn? What is this broken heart, this fount of tears of which faith sings? Why do we weep, really? Is our mourning something we manufacture, something not quite authentic or real? Is our mourning only convention, a turning to the Passion only because the calendar brings it again before our minds? Or is mourning for others of us a kind of contemplation of great drama? The Greeks used to speak of the effect of dramatic tragedy as *therapeia psyches,* as a cleansing of the soul. And as one goes to the theater to see great tragedy on the stage—Oedipus, Hamlet or Othello—, so many people, you feel, turn to the cross as spectators watching a tragic drama, fascinated, enrapt, temporarily feeling that they have been made better men.

Just to say these things is to pronounce upon them their own judgment, isn't it? Clearly, for the Christian man this question of Jesus, "Why weepest thou?" goes far beyond them. Indeed, in its deepest meaning this question has to do with more than Lent or Holy Week, with more even than our contemplation of the cross. It has to do with the very springs of our living, with our basic attitudes toward life, with our insight and compassion or our lack of them. For would not part of our answer to this question at our best be that the sorrow of the cross is part of that larger sorrow that for the earnest and sensitive man is always an essential dimension of life? That indeed unless you know the meaning of tears as the

Gospel interprets them, you cannot know the meaning of life itself or the answer that faith makes to life's tears? The fact is, the New Testament would long ago have been a forgotten book if there were not a cross in it and tears at the heart of it. "The power of a religion," Söderblom once wrote, "is not to be judged by its hymns of praise but by its experience of the misery and blackness of life. And Christianity has gone down into the depths." So it is! The Gospel speaks to human life with reality and authority because it knows so profoundly that men weep. And Mary's tears are of the same tears that all men weep who know the tragic sense of life and try to comprehend it. For thoughtful people, our world is always in one sense a Lenten world. There are always tears in it. Jan Masaryk said of Dostoevski that as he looked at life's folly and pathos, ". . . he smiled, but he smiled with tears in his eyes." There *are* tears in our eyes when we read life truly. It is as if tears make clean our vision and help us to see as we could not before: "Woman, why weepest thou?"

* * * * *

But it is not only that Mary weeps. It is above all Jesus' question, "*Why* weepest thou?" that most matters here. For Mary's tears are Christian tears and Jesus' question is a Christian question, if I may so put it. They are set within the Christian Gospel, and they are bounded on the one hand by the cross and on the other by the open tomb. This is the Christ speaking! It is Christian faith, not philosophy or ethics or drama that asks: "Why weepest thou?" The Gospel has always known, as man's best thought has always known, the tragic sense of life. But the Gospel uniquely comprehends tragedy by locating its meaning not merely in the fact that men weep but in the things that make them weep: "Woman, *why* weepest thou?" The sources of our happiness, we often say, reveal what we are. But the Gospel declares that the opposite is even more true, that the things that make us weep best reveal what we are. Our tears are the index to our character. They disclose our deepest insight. They show what we really care about. They reveal how we understand or fail to understand the essential sorrow of life: "Woman, why weepest thou?"

Do we weep only for ourselves, for example? Do we self-centeredly magnify life's little vexations and disappointments into tragedy? Some people weep because they are not invited somewhere they want to be invited. Some people weep because they cannot go where they want to go on their vacation. Some people weep because they do not get a new dress or a new car. You see, when we answer honestly the question, "Why weepest thou?" we can begin to know how mature or childish, how Christian or unchristian we are in our sorrow.

But there are some things in life worth weeping about, and the tears we shed measure our understanding of them. I said a moment ago that the New Testament would long ago have been a forgotten book if there were not tears in it. Do you remember Peter as St. Luke describes him on that last night of Jesus' life? Only a few hours before, Peter had sworn that he would go through suffering and through death with Jesus. But then came the fateful hour in the high priest's palace, and the oaths and the betrayal, and the heart-clutching cry of the cock crowing as Jesus had foretold, and the look on Jesus' face as Jesus turned toward him. No wonder that Luke wrote at the end of it all: "Peter went out, and wept bitterly."

Or there are the tears that Mary herself had shed once before, on that day she had knelt at Jesus' feet in the house of Simon the Pharisee. A woman of the city, a sinner, she had been; but somewhere, somehow she had met Jesus, and found in Him the love and purity her woman's soul had craved. And as He sat at meat, she knelt and kissed His feet, and bathed them with her tears and wiped them with her hair. Such tears tell us something! Our sins, and what Jesus means to us in our sins, these are worth weeping about. A prayer of one of the saints has come down to us through the centuries: "O God, grant unto me tears of penitence, tears of yearning, tears of salvation to cleanse my soul and make me wholly pure." "Woman, why weepest thou?"

Or, there is Jesus Himself. Twice in His life He is described as weeping. There was that day when He came to Bethany after Lazarus had died, and He stood before Lazarus' tomb. As the awfulness of death and the grief of Lazarus' loved ones mingled with His own, it was too much for Jesus. And John wrote simply: "Jesus wept." Why did Jesus weep? In part, I think, simply because He loved Lazarus and Martha and Mary, and sometimes that is why we weep, and there is nothing wrong about that. To weep because you love is why God weeps, too. But Jesus wept more, I think, because evil in the black hour of death again confronted Him. Jesus knew disease and death. He was at war with them all the time. But there, somehow, evil struck through to the depths of His soul. There it was, stark and awful in the dead, decaying body of what had once been a living man. Jesus wept because He saw evil and felt it, because of what evil was doing to man's life and man's world.

And then Jesus wept on Palm Sunday, you remember, when the triumphal procession came round a crest in the road to Jerusalem, and suddenly the spires and minarets of the city and of the temple flashed in the morning light. Jesus loved His capital city. He loved His nation. He loved the temple of His faith. But these had rejected Him. They did not know the day of their salvation. "And when he was come near, he beheld the city and wept over it saying, 'O Jerusalem, Jerusalem, if thou hadst known the things that belong unto thy peace. But now are they hid from thine eyes.'" Again it was evil, and the pathos and tragedy of what evil was doing to life, that drew Jesus' tears. With a Saviour's vision He saw the masses of men misled and oppressed. He saw their poverty and pain. He saw the multitudes in their need, and the wickedness and corruption of evil men destroying them. "And when he was come near the city he wept over it . . ."

Such tears tell us something. They too tell us what is worth weeping about. Do we weep because we really feel something of what evil in its hideous malignity is doing to man and his world? Do we weep because we have grappled at first hand with disease and death? Do we weep because the cities of our world know not the things that belong unto their peace? Do we weep because of judgment that our social sins shall bring upon us? Or do we curse instead of weep? Do we laugh instead of weep? Do you remember Jesus' awful words of reversal in Luke's Gospel: "Woe unto you who laugh now, for ye shall mourn. Blessed are ye that weep now, for ye shall be comforted"?

Or, on a still deeper level, do we weep only because men suffer? The tears of those who weep for their fellow men are noble tears. But the ultimate sorrow in the Gospel, I think, is not even this sorrow. Mary wept at the tomb in part, yes, because of what had happened to another Whom she loved. There had been the horror of the cross, the seeming failure of Jesus' cause, and the final indignity—so she supposed—that Jesus' body had been taken away and she knew not where they had laid Him. But it was not only a man who had thus suffered. It was God! Evil in its malign fury had crucified God. Tragedy is seen in its full dimension, in other words, only when you see it as faith sees it, when set within a universe whose very heart is vulnerable to pain and evil. God—for the man of faith—is a tragic God. The lamb, we say, has been slain from the foundation of the world.

Yes, the things that make us weep or fail to weep, these do tell us what we are. They tell us how profoundly or shallowly we read life, and of the depth and vision with which we meet it. Our tears lay bare our soul. "Woman, why weepest thou?"

But then, there is the question: What is the issue of our weeping? "Why—to what purpose—weepest thou?" What does the contemplation of tragedy ultimately do to us—and through us—to our world? I must ask that question because just to interpret life with the dimension of sorrow is not of itself necessarily a noble thing. Some people, we know, weep only to impress other people with their weeping. Their vanity corrupts the meaning of sorrow. The trouble with the Pharisees, Jesus once remarked, was that they fasted and wore sackcloth and ashes *"to be seen of men."* So today people still weep to be seen of men. A person loses a loved one in death; but he weeps, and goes on weeping, in order to gain sympathy and recognition for himself. A politician figuratively weeps over some social evil, in order to exploit it for partisan purposes. Or a critic of our culture, sensitive to the despair and peril all about us, goes beyond sincerity to engage in what has been well called "existential screaming." Or we weep for our sins only in order to prove to ourselves that we can weep.

Again, some people weep because it is emotionally pleasurable to weep, and sorrow is corrupted because it is distorted into an experience of emotional egotism. I remember hearing Marian Anderson in a concert at the Academy of Music in Philadelphia some years ago. One of her songs was the Negro spiritual, "Nobody Knows the Trouble I've Seen." Typical of so many of the spirituals, it was a song of deep, brooding heartache, born of the immemorial sorrow of the Negro people. Hardly an eye in the vast hall was not moist with tears when she finished. But how many of those people, I wondered, really cared about the tragedy of the Negro. The tragedy of the Negro to most of them was merely something they wept about for a moment because they found emotional pleasure in Marian Anderson's singing.

No, if we weep, are we not to weep that our tears draw us to others who weep? Tragedy only ennobles when it is more than passing emotion, when somehow it initiates a man into what has been beautifully called the "Christian fraternity of pain." To the question, "Why weepest thou?" the Christian man makes more of an answer than vain words or passing emotion, an answer, rather, of life lifted out of itself and its own grief and plunged savingly into the grief of the world.

* * * * *

But is there not also this issue to our weeping—the vision that needful as the dimension of sorrow is to life, for the man of faith it is not the final dimension, and that as the tragedy of Good Friday is gathered up in Easter morning, so our human sorrow is finally gathered up in the mercy of God? Mary weeping before the tomb, I have said, is the classic figure of Christian sorrow. But is she not also the classic figure of sorrow comforted with Christian comfort? In one sense Mary stands within the dimension of Lent, yes. But she is really in Easter. She weeps for her Lord, but He for Whom she weeps has already risen. He but speaks her name and her universe changes. The ultimate foundations of life are revealed. Good is seen to underlie evil. Life proclaims its victory over death. Mary's sorrow is not the final thing, for He who asks, "Why weepest thou?" stays her tears with the vision of Himself.

Here, faith declares, is the final dimension of life, and without it man's world will always be a Lenten world. For man cannot finally comfort himself. He cannot stay his own tears. The pleasures with which man deadens his sorrow turn out to be so futile. Or the comfort of other people, even that cannot stay our tears. It can comfort us up to a point, but beyond that point we must go it alone, or with God. Or our intellects of which we are so proud, turn out to avail so little. Oswald Garrison Villard once wrote that all through his life he remembered a remark of John Dewey in a seminar on Plato at Columbia. Dewey said: "I have learned to take all my troubles back to Plato." Some men may choose to do that. But Plato could not have stayed Mary's tears, nor our tears. Nothing *human* can finally stay our tears. No, only the victory of the open tomb that matches at every point the sorrow of the cross can do that. It is finally only the God of Jesus Christ Who wipes away all tears from men's eyes. To those who trust in Him alone is it given to know how there shall be no more death, neither sorrow nor crying, that there shall be no more pain, that the former things are passed away.

"Woman, why weepest thou?"

Prayer: O God, Thou Father of all comfort, Thou Who in Christ has bared Thy heart to our grief and sin, help us to set our tears within Thy light and love. Teach us the lessons of truth and sympathy that sorrow can bring to us. Open our hearts to the woe of the world, and through it lift us unto Thee. Amen.

The Holy Place and Redemption

Reverend Chalmers Coe
A MINISTER OF THE CONGREGATIONAL CHURCH AND ASSOCIATE PRO-
FESSOR OF PRACTICS, HARTFORD THEOLOGICAL SEMINARY, HART-
FORD, CONNECTICUT.

This sermon for Good Friday touches both the Old and New Testaments as Mr. Coe presents his message of the Holy Place and Redemption, leaving the reader with much to ponder on the most important day of Holy Week, the day of the Crucifixion.

Born December 31, 1922, in Boston, Mr. Coe lived in Waterbury, Connecticut, and Oak Park, Illinois. He took his A.B. at Yale in 1943, his B.D., also at Yale, in 1945. He was minister of the Congregational Church in East Hampton, Connecticut, from 1945 to 1948; of the First Church in Amherst, Massachusetts, from 1948 to 1954; and of Mount Vernon Church in Boston from 1954 to 1956. He has been at Hartford Theological Seminary since 1956.

He was lecturer at Yale Divinity School in 1955 and is a member of the Committee on Religious Life and Study of the Yale University Council, and a delegate of the Congregational Christian Churches to the Faith and Order Study Conference at Oberlin in 1957. He is one of the promising younger men of our time.

SERMON FIFTEEN

"And the Lord said unto Moses, Speak unto Aaron thy brother, that he come not at all times into the holy place within the veil before the mercy seat, which is upon the ark; that he die not: for I will appear in the cloud upon the mercy seat. Thus shall Aaron come into the holy place: with a young bullock for a sin offering, and a ram for a burnt offering," Leviticus 16:2, 3

FOR YEARS they had carried it with them wherever they went. It was only a box of wood trimmed with gold and with two tablets of stone inside it. And yet they called it the ark of God; for the tablets had His law inscribed on them, and the box itself was decorated with crude images of cherubim—symbols of His Presence; so that they firmly believed Him to be there. On its top was a gold plate, valuable enough in itself, perhaps, but to the untutored eye only a gold plate. And yet they called that gold plate the mercy seat; for on it they dashed the blood of sacrifical animals, and knew—or thought they knew—that mercy came to them then. That was why they carried the ark over the trackless wilderness, and shoved it before them as they marched into furious battle, gave their lives to rescue it from the desecrating touch of an enemy, and even kept most of their own people from coming too near and handling it. And once in a twelvemonth—according to a later tradition—a priest of the house of Aaron went in to it dressed in his ritual garments and there obtained forgiveness for all his people. For years they had carried it with them wherever they went, or worshiped before it at Jerusalem. And they would go on doing so for years to come.

Until—and here, abruptly, we have to leap across ten centuries, at least—there came into the city of Jerusalem, and to a low hill outside the city wall, One Who forever did away with the need of any such ritual. As one of His apostles put it, a man whose name is now forgotten: "He entered in *once* into the holy place, having obtained *eternal* redemption for us." No longer once a year, but once for all time. Have you ever wondered why these ancient, barbaric verses from Leviticus seem so distasteful and so irrelevant to us now? It is not simply because they are primitive and crude and repellent, but because the things they speak of have come true, more gloriously true than their authors could possibly have known. The blood of bulls and goats? The very notion is absurd. Such is the difference which the cross of Jesus Christ has made.

Nevertheless, and as we meet here from twelve until two on Friday of Holy Week, I think that we cannot afford to be neglectful of the worship of long ago. And that for an all-important reason: the New Testament understanding of the cross has its basis in ideas supplied by the Old. And in that sense you and I are the spiritual descendants of those men who stood at a respectful distance from the ark of God, and shouted their wild songs of praise, and trembled to think of the earth-shattering events over which their priest presided.

107

I

For, first, the ark and the mercy seat were together *the place of holiness*. Not holiness as we often misconstrue it: a sort of amalgam of all the pleasant virtues, and a few not-so-pleasant virtues besides; the kind of dull and petty moralism people are praising when they sing, "Take time to be holy." Ten minutes a day to be decent! No; the holiness of the mercy seat is the mystery, the otherness, of the God before Whom men feel compelled to bow in awe and wonder. That is why the Jews burned incense; to hide with smoke the place where God was, for no man might see His face and live.

We cannot really understand Good Friday unless we are willing to affirm the holiness, the mystery, of it. No wonder the Christian Church has never tried to make one single intellectual summary of Jesus' work upon the cross binding for its members. There are things so ineffable that they beggar definition. Our minds are just too limited to comprehend them wholly, our spiritual vision too weak to see them clearly. Have you ever had someone come up to you, someone in deep trouble who for the first time, it may be, is compelled to face personal tragedy of the most horrifying kind? He says: "I know you worship regularly in a Christian church. I know your children go to Sunday School. Now, tell me, what does the cross of Jesus mean? How is it supposed to meet me in *my* crucifixion?" You are stunned, likely as not; grope back into your memory for the words of a long-forgotten catechism, or rattle off some phrases of St. Paul, or merely stand stammering and helpless. For you cannot put it into words. No one ever can do so to his satisfaction.

Doesn't Good Friday, therefore, tell us this, that the only attitude with which we can approach the mystery of Jesus' death is the attitude of awe? And precisely here American Christianity has a great deal still to learn. We have been so very friendly with God in these last years, have treated Him as though He were a kind of glorified vice-president. A syndicated authority on personal problems informs us that Jesus was the first great genius in advertising and had excellent public relations. A major league baseball player dies, and a writer comments in a newspaper that the man has entered the "clubhouse of the Great Beyond." It is all so congenial. Then we come to Good Friday, and everything is changed. Here is a God Who involved Himself in death and failure. It passes belief; or, at any rate, it passes understanding. And there is nothing for it but to take to our knees in awe.

In Kenneth Grahame's book, *The Wind in the Willows*, the Rat and the Mole approach the great god Pan on an island in the middle of a river. The light, they notice, has become almost blinding; the atmosphere is subtly different; the birds have stopped singing, and there is a stillness all around them. " 'Rat,' Mole found breath to whisper, shaking. 'Are you afraid?' 'Afraid?' murmured the Rat, his eyes shining with unutterable love. 'Afraid! Of *Him?* O, never, never! And yet—and yet—O, Mole, I am afraid!' "

That is something of what the Gospel means by the holiness of the cross. God was there; and we can only gaze on it with awe.

II

In the second place, the ark of God and the mercy seat were together *the place of loneliness*. One man, one solitary man, had the right of entrance to them. True, he carried with him the sacrifices of his fellows. True, again, he was acting as their representative. And true, he bore an exciting message with him when he emerged from the secret fastness of the shrine. For a moment, though, he was accompanied by no one, stood without a single human ally before a holiness which common men were unable to bear.

The same principle is at the heart of Christian faith. I know, of course, as you do, how precious and how priceless is our modern recovery of the notion of community. We have stopped talking in the old, patronizing way about "organized religion," as though a man's dealings with God were private first of all and only "organized" afterward—corporate by option. We are speaking more and more today of the Christian body, of that unity in Christ which is the portion of His servants. T. S. Eliot has written:

> What life have we if we have not life together?
> There is no life not in community,
> And no community not lived for God.

All of that is incontestably and marvelously true. Besides, there is the undeniable witness of the New Testament to the fact that Jesus took with Him to Calvary the burdens of an apostate, hostile world. "He bore our sins," wrote the apostle with a tremendous certainty; "he bore our sins in his body on the tree."

And yet, the cross has something about it of loneliness, the loneliness of an ancient priest before the ark of God. It is part of the grandeur of Golgotha, as well as part of the scandal which many serious and discriminating people have found in Christianity, that the death of one man can be said to have had such incalculable consequences for the world. His disciples, so the evangelists said, "Forsook him and fled." He staggered unaided over the path of sorrows. The solitary death He knew is thrown into even bolder relief by the men who perished beside Him, for they were ordinary hooligans. And, whatever it meant, that cry of His—"My God, my God, why hast thou forsaken me?"—is the ultimate in separation. Then, afterward, came the lonely grave.

What does it mean? This, in the midst of much more: there is no loneliness you will ever be called upon to endure which the Son of God has not shared. We are living in an age when men and women are desperately in search of what they call "togetherness," when "the organization man" is a goal feverishly pursued by many lost and anxious spirits. And all of these spurious forms of community are so much chaff, bare husks, compared with the community God offers you and me in the Christ Who died forsaken and alone. As Ronald Budge has reminded us, years ago the explorer Shackleton, with two friends, found himself in grave danger on the icecap of Antarctica. The snows, the wind, the bitter cold, made it a serious question whether or not they would come through to safety. When the march was over, Shackleton tells us in his diary, one of his companions—Worsley—said, "I had a curious feeling all the time that there was another Person with us." At which the explorer lifted his head, and answered, "So had I."

And Jesus Christ, upon His cross of death, meets our loneliness and conquers it.

III

The ark and the mercy seat were the place of holiness. One man, and one only, could approach the innermost sanctuary. And it was the place, too, of loneliness. Now what was the result? What, in those primitive times, did men believe to be the upshot of this strange, to us quite weird, ceremonial? Why did they go through with it? The reason is clear. For the third fact about the ark, a fact which offers further hints of Calvary's meaning, is that it was *the place of forgiveness*. Here, at God's behest, the bullock and the goat were brought. Here the offerer presented the beast he had loved, whom he had come to look upon almost as a member of his family; he placed his hands upon its head in order to identify himself with it; and then, with a sharp knife, he cut its throat and the creature's life ebbed swiftly away. Here the priest took the blood, went in-

110

side, and covered the mercy seat with it as an offering to God. And, when he returned, he brought forgiveness with him.

Well, anyone who did it now would soon find at his door representatives of the Society for the Prevention of Cruelty to Animals. And rightly so. For we have, in some respects at least, a different understanding of forgiveness. It is one thing to say that pardon involves cost. It is one thing to believe that self-love, and willfulness, and treachery against a neighbor, and gluttony, and greed—all of which, and more, we mean by sin—are offenses to the glory of an infinitely righteous God, and cry for sacrifice. It is quite another to hold that the blood of bulls and goats can accomplish what men once claimed it could. Can a faithless husband restore his wife's love and confidence by buying her a new refrigerator? Can you gain back a grossly slandered friend by the simple expedient of taking him to lunch? Can you win the affection of a cruelly beaten child by handing him a bag of gumdrops when you come in the front door at supper time? And can the blood of bulls avail to remove the guilt in which every one of us stands before heaven? The New Testament gives a ringing and defiant answer. "No!" it cries. "God alone, He Himself, must do it. And He has! He has come in Jesus Christ. He sent His Own Son, that we might find life in His Name. He is both sacrificer and sacrificed. He has paid the price no one else could pay. He has mounted the hill, has lain upon the ground, has been lifted up in agony, has seen the shadow of death pass over the land. He has cried forgiveness on His tormentors. Blessing and honor and glory and power be unto Him."

That is why we call this day Good Friday; why, for all the solemnity and hush of it, we have no other course than to sing wild songs of jubilation when the three hours of darkness are at an end, when the veil of the temple has been torn in two from the top to the bottom, and when the centurion speaks his halting words of wonder. There is a purity, a matchless and unexampled purity, which has taken the stains of our life to itself, and wiped them out forever and forever.

Give yourself to it. Hold fast to it. Remember that, in Christ, God receives you when, in your unworthiness, you did not deserve so glad a welcome.

> Say, what saw you, Man?
> And say, what heard?
> I saw, while angels sang,
> Jesus the Word.

Saw you aught else, Man?
Aught else heard you?
I saw the Son of Man,
And the wind blew.

Saw you beside, Man?
Or heard beside?
I saw, while murderers mocked,
The crucified.

Nay, what is this, Man?
And Who is He?
The holy child must die
For you and me.

Oh! what can we give, Brother!
For such a thing,
Body and soul, Brother!
To Christ the King.[1]

There Is No Death

Reverend Daniel A. Poling, LL.D., Litt.D., D.D., L.H.D.
EDITOR OF *The Christian Herald*, PRESIDENT OF WORLD'S CHRIS-
TIAN ENDEAVOR UNION, CHAPLAIN OF THE CHAPEL OF FOUR CHAP-
LAINS AND A MINISTER OF THE REFORMED CHURCH IN AMERICA.

*Dan Poling, as he is affectionately known all over the world,
has had a brilliant career as a minister, editor, political leader, author
and guide of young people. He has traveled all over the world, has
been active in government and in welfare work; he leads the Christian Endeavor groups to ever-growing programs for brotherhood
and the Christianizing of the world; and he has raised the* CHRISTIAN
HERALD *to a position of eminence.*

*As Minister of Marble Collegiate Church on Fifth Avenue, New
York, from 1922 to 1930, he popularized street preaching by having
a pulpit built at the corner of the church where Fifth Avenue and
Twenty-ninth Street meet, and five days a week crowds stopped to*

[1] From *A Diary* of Readings by John Baillie (Charles Scribner's Sons,
1955). Used by permission of the publisher.

*listen to music and a religious message by Dr. Poling or his invited
guest speakers.*

*He was pastor of the Baptist Temple, Philadelphia from 1936
to 1948; he has served as consultant to Mr. J. C. Penney in his welfare programs; he is chaplain of the interfaith memorial, the Chapel
of Four Chaplains, in Philadelphia. He was active in war work in
both World War I and II, is one of the leaders of the Boy Scouts,
and was president for two years of the Greater New York Federation of Churches. He is the author of* MOTHERS OF MEN, HUTS IN HELL,
LEARN TO LIVE, WHAT MEN NEED MOST, ADVENTURE IN EVANGELISM,
THE FURNACE *(novel),* JOHN OF OREGON *(novel),* THE HERETIC *(novel),*
BETWEEN TWO WORLDS *(novel),* TREASURY OF BEST-LOVED HYMNS, A
PREACHER LOOKS AT WAR, A TREASURY OF GREAT SERMONS *(1944),
editorials in* CHRISTIAN HERALD *and a dozen other volumes.*

*This sermon was preached at the Easter Sunrise Service in Ar-
lington National Cemetery, Washington, D.C., April 6, 1958.*

SERMON SIXTEEN

A FEW MOMENTS AGO there was darkness and silence. Now there
is light. And above the effulgent glory which presently floods the
world, in the miracle of Easter there is the greater light, "that light-
eth every man coming into the world."

Here, in another sunrise, overlooking the Potomac and at a
nation's sacred shrine, the Tomb of the Unknown Soldier, we face
the world's old, timeless question: "What is life?" Life is physical
existence, but infinitely more. Life is the beginning of death. Life
is the sum of all things; and the cynic adds, the end of all things. But
to that last we do not consent. Life is a gift—we receive it. Life
is an achievement—we make it. Life is sorrow and sickness and
sin—and life is holy. Life is doubt! Life is disillusionment. Life is
denial—and life is the greatest of all affirmations. Life is the supreme paradox of time and space, for this life is the "childhood of
our immortality."

These are the answers—or some of them—to man's question,
"What is life?" But the real question, the supreme question which
is personal and with all its poignant implications, remains unanswered: "What is *my* life?"

Perhaps never in human history before, never since records were
written on the walls of caves, has this ageless question of the ages

113

been so far from its answer. But there is an answer. It is the answer that transcends time and space, that measures doubt and denial and makes at last a bridge across the grave. It is the answer of Easter. It is the dawn most sublime. It is the sunrise of the soul. It is the answer of the Resurrection Christ, Himself: "He is thy Life!"

Once beside an open grave Robert Ingersoll stood and heard its whisper; then spoke these immortal words: "Life is a narrow veil," he said, "between the cold and barren peaks of two eternities. We cry aloud, ' 'Tis vain.' The only answer is the wailing echo of our cry. But in the night of death hope sees a star and, listening, love can hear the rustle of a wing." And at this Easter dawn we hear above the rustle of a wing the voice of One Who said that Life was Holy, and Who lifted the humblest child into a distinction higher than the tallest. He made human personality, yours and mine, without respect to race or color, the object of His love, the reason for His coming, the cause of Calvary and the triumph of the Resurrection. "I am come," He said, "that they might have life and that they might have it more abundantly." He spoke the words first to the starved of Judea and Galilee, to those who had but a bare existence. The proud Roman with his conquering spear prodded them from his path. Often they were too hopeless to dream and too weak to pray. But it is written that "they heard Him gladly." Their joy was in what He said and because they could understand what He said, since He spoke not in the unknown tongue of the Temple, but in the vernacular of the street. In their diseased bodies and broken spirits He planted the seed of hope, and the flower took root and grew. In all the years that lie between that far-off divine event which we here again commemorate, the common man, the little people, in spite of pogroms and wars, have cherished the prospect of the more abundant life because Jesus gave the promise and, though crucified, dead and buried, is the Risen Lord of its ultimate fulfillment. "I will not leave you comfortless," He said, "I will come to you. . . . Come unto me all ye that labor and are heavy laden, and I will give you rest." And today each of us may answer— "I know Whom I have believed and am persuaded that He is able to keep that which I have committed unto Him against that day."

Against this belief which through the centuries for unnumbered millions of men and women has become an experience, godless ideologies and anti-God systems beat in vain. Little men in haughty pride have sought to lift statism or racism or classism above human personality. For a little time they have prevailed against their brothers. But always truth crushed to earth rises again and freedom born of God is eternal. Human personality! The priceless worth of the individual! The inviolable human soul—for these God made the world and created all things. And for these He sent His only Son to live and serve, to die and rise again. A little child, your child and mine, and the humblest offspring of the most underprivileged family in the most remote place of the earth is to the Galilean more precious than a city or an empire, for cities and empires disappear, civilizations and cultures decay, but the soul lives forever. Life itself is the offspring of faith, while death is the child of doubt.

"Dost thou believe?" was a question Jesus once raised. "I believe; help Thou mine unbelief," is the prayer God answers first. I believe in myself not as I am, but as I may become and as I purpose to achieve. I believe in my fellows, in spite of those who may have wronged me. I believe in the essential worth of humankind, the genius of friendship, the simplicity of little children and the infinite values that repose in the humblest men. I believe in my country and that patriotism is more than a passing sentiment; more, too, than a national passion. I believe that freedom can no longer be isolated and that peace must be for all if presently it is to be at all. I believe in God and in Jesus Christ His Son the Risen Lord.

But there is one word above all others that articulates the Easter dawn: "He is thy life"; and in Him is life that shall never die. Here is the unique and infinite value of the Christian's faith. "Whosoever liveth and believeth in me," He said, "shall never die."

> The stars shall fade,
> The sun himself grow dim with age
> And nations sink in years;
> But Thou shalt flourish in immortal youth,
> Unhurt amidst the war of elements,
> The wreck of matter and the crash of worlds.

One of the last statements prepared by President Franklin Delano Roosevelt was "Man's Greatest Victory." Dictated to Robert Sherwood, it was written, at my request, for *Christian Herald*, and appeared in our Easter issue, April, 1945, where it was read after the President's death. Here is what he wrote:

Here in Washington, and across the Potomac in Virginia, we see many noble monuments to the glorious dead—to the Americans whose souls go marching on. But these monuments would be meaningless did they not symbolize something very profound within all of us and that is, faith in the eternally living spirit.

That faith becomes all the more powerful in these tragic days of war. Out of suffering comes a renewal of the life of the spirit. The men who have gallantly given their lives have turned our thoughts to religion—to a realization of man's dependence upon the Providence of God.

The story of the Resurrection is the expression of man's highest aspiration; it is the story of man's greatest victory—his triumph over death; it is a source of consolation for those whose loved ones have given their lives and a source of inspiration for all generations yet unborn.

The heart of a President's confession of personal faith is in those words: "The story of the Resurrection is the expression of man's highest aspiration; it is the story of man's greatest victory—his triumph over death." My final answer and yours must be the answer of one's personal faith and experience, as was this answer of the man who dictated it in the White House just across the river from where we now worship.

But, "How do you believe in immortality?" The question was asked by a typical university man. "As I believe in love," was my reply. "Yes?" he questioned with a rising inflection. "Yes!" I answered. "Because I have experienced it." "But," my friend continued, "I want not sentiment, not emotion, however real to you, sir, but reason, hard reason, reason to answer a hard question. I am not a child, my world is a world of realism." "And mine," I replied. "I believe in immortality as I believe in love, because I have experienced it. Because it is real. Because to otherwise conclude would be to me unreasonable."

I cannot prove love as a man proves a problem in mathematics. I cannot put its equation on a blackboard. I never yet have found it in the bottom of a crucible, nor shaken it gently in a test tube. But it is real, more real to me than houses and streets, more real than words and laughter. And it is powerful, more powerful than death, for I love beyond the grave. I believe in love because I have experienced it; because it has held me in its arms and because, when its arms have fallen lifeless, it has yet remained. Love is the essence of immortality.

I believe in immortality because neither can my reason avoid its conclusion nor my heart escape its emotion. I have never seen it with my physical eyes and yet I have seen it, have seen it as truly as I have seen love.

It was a never-to-be-forgotten morning in February, 1918. With an orderly I waited in the rain at the top of a communicating trench "somewhere in France." A platoon of men from a machine-gun company were coming out. They were a sorry sight, bedraggled, hungry and utterly weary. The first lieutenant who brought up the rear

116

stopped to inquire the way to the nearest canteen. He was sick, a fever was fairly burning him up. "Tonsillitis," he said, as he leaned on a stick he had torn from the support of a "duck board." "And trench foot," he added. Then pulling himself together, he stumbled after his men. I watched him go. It was when he had taken less than a hundred steps—I covered the distance in just that many, a little later—that a three-inch high-explosive shell "let go" in the midst of his platoon. Hearing it coming, we had flung ourselves flat in the mud. And then at the screams of agony, we had hurried over to the wounded and dead. We looked after those who still needed the little we could do for them and then we gathered together the fragments.

It was there on a red highway of France that I experienced immortality. I *knew* that the lad with the aching throat, the lad whose sick eyes had just looked into mine, the lad with whom I had just talked, was not in what I was picking up. I had not talked to that! *And I knew that he was somewhere!*

I knew that there had been authority enough to begin his life, and to carry it from his mother's womb to that shell-scarred road. Short of immortality, I had just two alternatives: either Creative Authority willed to leave that personality there in the blood and muck, willed to end it or to see it end in such a sorry fashion; or the Authority which could create was unable to continue, was helpless before the event, was without resources beyond that road in front of Toul. Either conclusion was to me unreasonable. That young lieutenant either stopped where I picked up his scattered body or he went on. I *know* that he went on.

And I know that those whose forms I touch when only their forms remain, when to my touch there can never come again a responding pressure; those "dear dead" whom I have lost, I have but "lost awhile." I know that they live and I know where to find them! I know that I shall meet them "just around the corner."

In nature nothing is ever annihilated. Forms change, patterns are altered, and I do not profess to know the form and pattern of life beyond that which we call death. I do not even attempt to anticipate the details. But to conclude that a law which operates everywhere else in life ceases to operate only in life's highest, noblest form—human personality—is unreasonable. Shall only thought and recognition and the *you* of you be destroyed? As winter comes, I watch the mother of my children put her flowers "to sleep" on the old New Hampshire farm. Buried deep under the leaf mold and then beneath the snow, they wait until their springtime. But always there is a springtime and always the flowers come again. Am I so less than these?

Life does go on. That which we know as life is by our own experience incomplete. Nothing gets done. Those who live the longest frequently leave the most that is unfinished. There isn't time enough to write the books, to paint the pictures. There isn't time enough to see our visions through. I tell you that either these earthbound years are but the beginning, or there is in creation itself a colossal immorality.

The dawn that met us here moves now from the unfathomed mysteries of the East across the vast expanses of the Western world. And as He rose from Joseph's tomb, hope springs eternal in our breasts. We will not consent to failure. We will not accept the conclusions of despair. We will not surrender our beloved dead! In Him we claim the Peace that passeth knowledge, Peace beyond the barricades of fear, the Peace of Christ. Call Him a mere man if you will, but as the Easter Sabbath stillness opens out upon the fields and market places, you will find Him on a throne of adoration, high and lifted up above all the sons of men. You will hear the singing of the waters that flow down from a spring that was opened for the healing of the nations under a skull-shaped hill long ago.

As for me, I believe the Resurrection message, the miracle of Easter. I take my stand beside the Galilean fisherman whose bugle sounds over the ages: "Thou art the Christ, the Son of the Living God."

FAITH

The Child-Mind

Reverend Henry P. Van Dusen, Ph.D., S.T.D., D.D.

A MINISTER OF THE PRESBYTERIAN CHURCH AND PRESIDENT, UNION THEOLOGICAL SEMINARY, NEW YORK, NEW YORK

This sermon emphasizes anew Christ's attitude toward children and points out the great need for understanding children and the childlike faith that accepts God as heavenly Father.

Henry P. Van Dusen is steadily becoming recognized as one of the great theological leaders of the United States today. Born in Philadelphia, Pennsylvania, in 1897, Dr. Van Dusen studied at

118

Princeton University, Union Theological Seminary, and Edinburgh University, Scotland, where he received his Ph.D. in 1932. His honorary degrees include the S.T.D. degree, from New York University, and the D.D. degree from Amherst College, Edinburgh University, Oberlin College, and Yale University, Queen's University, Ontario, and Harvard University.

He began his career as an educator as instructor at Union Theological Seminary in 1926; he was Assistant Professor of Systematic Theology and the Philosophy of Religion from 1928 to 1931, Associate Prefessor from 1931 to 1936, and has been Professor of Systematic Theology since 1936. He was Dean of Students from 1931 to 1939, and has been president of the faculty since 1945. He has also been president of the faculty of Auburn Theological Seminary since 1945.

In 1924 Dr. Van Dusen was ordained to the ministry in the Presbyterian Church. He is a trustee of Princeton University, Ginling College, Nanking Theological Seminary, Yenching University, and the Little School. He is president of the United Board for Christian Colleges in China; a member of the Board of Foreign Missions, Presbyterian Church, U.S.A.; chairman of the Study Committee, World Council of Churches; president of the Union Settlement Association; and a trustee of the Rockefeller Foundation and the General Education Board.

He has written or edited more than twenty books, among them IN QUEST OF LIFE'S MEANING, THE PLAIN MAN SEEKS FOR GOD, REALITY AND RELIGION, FOR THE HEALING OF THE NATIONS, THEY FOUND THE CHURCH THERE, WORLD CHRISTIANITY, GOD IN EDUCATION *and* SPIRIT, SON, AND FATHER.

SERMON SEVENTEEN

> "Unless you turn and become like little children, you will never enter into the Kingdom of Heaven," Matthew 18:3
> "Whoever does not receive the Kingdom of God like a child, shall never enter therein," Mark 10:15

THESE ARE TEXTS which one approaches with extreme hesitancy. For one thing, they have been so much preached upon as to have been worn thin and flat. And so much preaching on them has been merely sentimental.

119

But Jesus' attitude to childhood, while rich with humor and affection, was not sentimental. Indeed, these two most striking appeals to the child-spirit arose from the pressure of public tasks and at the heart of life's insistent business: in one case, as a direct reply to a serious and mature question about life: "Who is the greatest in the kingdom of heaven?"; in the other case, as a sharp rebuke to men and women much like ourselves: "Whoever does not receive the kingdom of God shall not enter therein."

Let there be no doubt in our minds that these words come direct from the lips of Jesus—indeed, are His most distinctive and insistent teaching. Dr. C. H. Dodd, in *The Authority of the Bible* (Harper & Brothers), cites precisely these passages as our most convincing proof of the reliability of the Gospel records.

There is no evidence that this attitude was appreciated in the early Church. For Paul and the other New Testament writers, the child suggests childishness rather than childlikeness. . . . Their faithfulness to historical memory led them to represent their Master as dealing with children . . . in a way they did not understand, but felt to be characteristic of Him.

What was it of such supreme importance for mature life that Jesus saw in the mind of childhood? The reply which leaps to our lips is—surely it is the *innocency,* the *naïveté,* the *freshness* of childhood which appealed to him. Recall childhood's portrait by Francis Thompson, himself one of the most child-minded of our poets:

Know you what it is to be a child? It is to be something very different from the man of today. It is to have a spirit yet streaming from the waters of baptism, it is to believe in love, to believe in loveliness, to believe in belief; it is to be so little that the elves can reach to whisper in your ear; it is to turn pumpkins into coaches, and mice into horses, lowness into loftiness, and nothing into everything, for each child has its fairy godmother in its own soul; it is to live in a nutshell and to count yourself the king of infinite space; it is

> To see a World in a grain of sand,
> And a heaven in a wild flower,
> Hold Infinity in the palm of your hand,
> And Eternity in an hour.

But that is sentiment, though not sentimentality. Much as we may envy childhood's innocence, it is not for us. We must look deeper for the secret to which Jesus pointed. Is it, perhaps, in two other invariable characteristics of the *child-mind:* the child's *grasp on truth* and the child's *confidence in life*—childhood's *insight* and childhood's *trust?*

We all know well the devastating character of childhood's frankness. What one of us has not had cause as a parent to suffer intense embarrassment because of that frankness; or, as a bystander, to rejoice with ill-concealed glee at the pungent and piercing acuteness of that insight? For childhood's insight is devastating not because it is frank, but because it is so often sound. And the outlook of the child-mind is important not because it is innocent and intrigues us, but because it has a unique grasp on truth and thereby shames us.

The secrets of childhood's unique insight are at least two:

(1) *The child draws his wisdom from the most familiar, commonplace facts of daily experience.* He requires no equipment to see life truly other than his own simple, direct observation.

No wonder Jesus found in it the key to all true knowing. It was from precisely the same sources and in the same manner that His own insight was derived. It is no accident that He found it natural to body forth what He had to say in figures drawn from the home, the shop, the open field, town life—the central place of widowhood in the teaching of One Whose mother had been widowed from His early youth; leaven rising in meal; the loaf baking in the oven; candles; moths; rust; the sweeping of the house; the persistent search in every corner for a single lost coin; old clothes too fragile for patching; children squabbling on the village green; and the familiar town characters: the unfortunate widow, the unjust judge, the undisciplined son.

Behind His employment of such simple and obvious material to portray ultimate truth was His assumption that His hearers could not fail to recognize the truth when it was so presented to them. Here is one of the most neglected features of Jesus' teaching—His unfailing assumption that, in the really crucial issues of life, men and women know the answers to their own questions. His task was not to convince them of this truth and to that course of action, but merely to remind them of what they already knew, to make inescapably vivid by a figure or a story of an analogy the knowledge which they already possessed. That is why there is almost wholly absent from His teaching argument or persuasion or reasoning. And it is this which gives to His teaching its overwhelming impression

121

of authority. He simply states truths. Everyone honest with himself and life must recognize them.

So, now, answering men's queries about the baffling issues of human destiny, His reply is: "Except you turn and become as little children. . . ." "Unless you seek wisdom from the sources habitually tapped by the child-mind—from the simplest, most familiar, most commonplace facts of daily life—you will never discover it."

(2) *Again, the child draws his wisdom from his immediate, unfettered response to life.* Ask a child what he thinks of someone. The reply comes back at once—spontaneous, unpremeditated. And in nine cases out of ten, true. The answer may be brutally devastating. It may be surprisingly generous. It is almost certainly uncannily sound.

Now, ask an adult his opinion of the same person. There is a moment's pause to think. And, in that moment, what are some of the considerations which quickly flit across the mind?

What is this person *supposed* to be like? What is he generally thought to be like? What am I expected to answer? How will my answer be taken? What would be a brilliant reply to the question? an amusing reply? What is the witty, the clever, the politic thing to say?

These—and a dozen other considerations. And, in that fragmentary moment, the fresh, clear reflection of that person's character in the mirror of our unspoiled wisdom has been muddied, clouded, distorted by alien considerations: the invasion into our judgment of factors of self-concern, of fear of what others will think, of ambition. What is the proper thing to do and say? What is the most likely way to make a favorable impression? Our answer, when it is given, is not our own native judgment, but an amalgam of our own thought with common opinion. In childhood, there is a direct contact of our minds with truth. In maturity, there is the intervention of worldly wisdom and self-concern. These it is which hopelessly pervert the native wisdom of men.

This is the beginning of the death of intellectual honesty, and of significant grasp on truth. But—is that not the way in which we do most of our thinking most of the time? Not merely about people, but about all the important questions of life.

There is a native capacity of the human soul for recognition of significant truth which information, education, training may sharpen and improve. Or they may fatally distort and destroy. In the final analysis, this is our most trustworthy guide. Not that it is always wholly right, but that it is the best of the many fallible guides at our disposal. Naïve insight, some would label it. So Professor Whitehead, describing the rebellion of the romantic poets, especially Wordsworth, against the prevailing materialism of the early nineteenth century, says:

Wordsworth was not bothered by any intellectual antagonism. What moved him was moral repulsion. He felt that something had been left out, and that what had been left out comprised everything that was most important.

I hold that the ultimate appeal is to naïve experience and that is why I lay such stress on the evidence of poetry.

The winning of mature wisdom is the recovery of the inherent, intuitive insight of the child-mind, the native wisdom of our mind before it has been forced into the artificial strait jacket of formal and unreal structures—confidence in the direct response of our minds to truth.

II

But there is a deeper secret of childhood's approach to life. Not only the child's insight—his grasp on truth; but also the child's confidence in life—childhood's trust.

The child is left in no uncertainty about his situation in life. He learns, early, that he stands always, a creature, and a very insignificant creature, over against a great *Other* which he has not created and cannot control, but to which he must be obedient and with which he must learn to co-operate. That *Other* is the world of nature, of parents, of other people, of the rules and customs of society, of the accumulated wisdom of mankind. Sometimes it seems a harsh and heartless world; often a kindly and loving world; always a fascinating, curious, intriguing, adventurous world. But— always it stands there: the great, immutable, implacable *Other*— the given facts to which life must be bent. Before those facts, the child must sit down in humble inquiry to discover their nature and to learn obedience.

And at the center of that *Other* is always the face of a person— Mother, Father, Teacher, Friend. Over and over again, the child has no course open to him but to place his hand in that of this person, and trust.

That is the best possible preparation for mature life. For that is precisely our situation in life, our whole life through. Childhood's perspective in life is important not because it is charming or intriguing or dutiful, but because it is true.

We do not customarily associate the child-mind with the scientific attitude. But it was one of the greatest modern scientists who gave us the classic description of the conditions for scientific discovery—to sit down before the facts like a child and follow wherever they may lead.

Here is, perhaps, the most basic vice of the contemporary mind. It has lost childhood's recognition of its own creatureliness; it has lost childhood's eager but humble expectancy before the great *Other* which determines its existence and its happiness. As a foreign observer has remarked, "The modern American has been burning incense at his own altar and his own countenance has been hidden from himself in the smoke." Outwardly his life has been marked by plenty, success, exuberant and expansive self-confidence; inwardly by deepening unreality, uncertainty and threatened disintegration. It is, of course—the whole attitude of the Modern Mind—absurd, ridiculous, ludicrous; utterly childish. There is only one possible corrective for it—that it should turn sharp about and face in precisely the opposite direction.

The beginning of all wisdom, as of true religion—the only beginning which gives to any of us promise of a successful outcome —is to recognize that we are creatures, standing like children before a great, mysterious *Reality* which determines for us the conditions of our existence. That is the true beginning, not because it is a modest or pious attitude, but for the sole and sufficient reason that it precisely corresponds with the truth of the matter. For we do stand, all of us, whenever wisdom guides our minds toward sane humility, face to face with the great Divine *Other* before Whom we must sit down as little children to learn—and to worship.

If we are wise, like the child, we discover at the heart of that vast, mysterious *Other* the Face of One Whom we may call "Father." Like the child, we have no alternative but to place confidence in Him, and trust.

In the words of one of the loveliest of the Bach chorales:

> Therefore I thank my God, and joy to do His will;
> I know, whate'er befalls, His love doth lead me still.
> So like a little child, who clasps his father's hand,
> Serene I take my way; in faith untroubled stand.

This is the final judgment of one of the wisest and noblest of our contemporaries. Albert Schweitzer, leaving his distinguished career as scholar and musician to spend his life in medical service among the fever-ridden natives of West Africa, summarized his mature judgment on life thus:

The conviction that in after life we must struggle to remain thinking as freely and feeling as deeply as we did in our youth has accompanied me on my road through life as a faithful advisor. Instinctively I have taken care not to become what is generally understood by the term a man of ripe experience. . . . We believed once in the victory of truth; but we do not now. We believed in goodness; but we do not now. We were zealous for justice; but we are not so now. We trusted in the power of kindness and peaceableness; we do not now. We were capable of enthusiasm; but we are not now.

Deeper experience of life, however, advises our inexperience differently. It exhorts us to hold fast, our whole life through, to the thoughts which inspire us. It is through the idealism of youth that man catches sight of truth, and in that idealism he possesses a wealth which he must never exchange for anything else.[1]

The most distinguished living Hindu philosopher, when asked what he regarded as the most profound religious saying, without a moment's hesitancy, replied: "Unless you turn and become as a little child, ye shall not see the Kingdom of God."

FAITH

This We Believe: The Invincible Conviction of a Protestant

Reverend David Haxton Carswell Read, D.D.
MINISTER, MADISON AVENUE PRESBYTERIAN CHURCH, NEW YORK, NEW YORK

Dr. Read discusses the basis of Protestant belief and shows the power of faith in a world torn by war, economic controversies, international misunderstanding, and personal problems. He urges a positive faith and an active religious life.
He was born on January 2, 1910, at Cupar, Fife, Scotland. He

[1] From *Memoirs of Childhood and Youth* by Albert Schweitzer (The Macmillan Company). Used by permission of the publisher.

attended Daniel Stewart's College in Edinburgh, and studied at the University of Edinburgh from 1928 to 1932, then at Montpellier, Strasbourg, and Paris (in 1932 and 1933), and at Marburg in 1934. He took his theological degree at New College, Edinburgh, and was ordained and installed at Coldstream West, Church of Scotland, in 1936. From 1939 to 1945 he was chaplain to the Forces of the British Army, and was a prisoner of war from June, 1940, to April, 1945. He is reported to have done much to keep morale high among the prisoners.

From 1939 to 1949 he was minister of Greenbank Church, Edinburgh. He was the first chaplain to the University of Edinburgh, in 1949, and was appointed chaplain to Her Majesty the Queen in Scotland in 1952. When Madison Avenue Presbyterian Church in New York City sought a minister to succeed Dr. George Buttrick, Dr. Read was called in January, 1956. He received the honorary D.D. from Edinburgh University in July, 1956.

He was Warrack Lecturer on Preaching at the University of Glasgow in 1950–51, Old Saint Andrew's Memorial Lecturer on Worship in Toronto in 1954, and George Shepard Lecturer on Preaching at Bangor Theological Seminary in 1959; he has led University Christian Missions in Scotland, Australia, Canada, and the United States. He has also had much experience in the field of radio and television.

Dr. Read has written THE SPIRIT OF LIFE, PRISONERS' QUEST (*a collection of lectures given in prisoner of war camp*), CALL IT A DAY, THE COMMUNICATION OF THE GOSPEL, *and* THE CHRISTIAN FAITH. *He has also published articles in* THE SCOTTISH JOURNAL OF THEOLOGY, THE ATLANTIC MONTHLY, THE EXPOSITORY TIMES, *and many other religious and secular journals.*

His sermons at Madison Avenue Presbyterian Church are attracting increasing attention and attendance by their quality and content. This sermon was preached on October 26, 1958.

SERMON EIGHTEEN

> "For in him dwelleth all the fulness of the Godhead bodily. And ye are complete in him, which is the head of all principality and power," Colossians 2:9, 10

EVERY SERIOUS CHRISTIAN TODAY, aware of the major struggle for the soul of man in our generation, must be troubled by the spectacle

126

of a splintered church. Nero is said to have fiddled while Rome was burning: what will a future historian have to say about Rome and Geneva and Canterbury, and the other great provinces of Christendom fiddling their respective tunes while our world is burning in the flames of materialism, nationalism and Communism? And any serious Christian who has studied the New Testament knows that this was never the will of Christ, or His apostles. The prayer of our Lord was "that they all may be one—that the world may believe that thou hast sent me." "I beseech you, brethren," said St. Paul, ". . . that ye all speak the same thing and that there be no division among you—Is Christ divided?"

If we are concerned about this situation, as we ought to be, what should we be doing about it? There are two ways of approaching the question of Christian unity and we must make up our minds which is most truly in line with the will of God.

The first we might call the way of "leveling-down." If our religious convictions are sufficiently muted or diluted it is always possible to reach a measure of agreement. This is the popular method today. Under the umbrella labeled "Inter-Faith" or "Nonsectarian" we get together—and it is good that we do. But we must not deceive ourselves. Under such an umbrella there is either a conspiracy of silence about our radical divergence of conviction, or else there is simply the watery fellowship of those who don't believe too much in anything at all. For it is always possible to reach agreement on the lowest common denominator of belief. A careless Protestant and a nonpracticing Roman Catholic would find their unity much more quickly than the Pope and the Archbishop of Canterbury. A Jew who had given up attending the synagogue could switch without difficulty to staying away from church. We have to ask ourselves whether, in fact, this "lowest common denominator" attitude does anything at all to strengthen the cause of religion in a secularized world. Modern Protestants are perhaps specially guilty of taking this easy road to agreement in the name of a tolerance which is often little more than apathy.

The other approach is totally different—and much more difficult. You could call it a "leveling-up." It means seeking not the "lowest common denominator" but the "highest common factor," and implies a passionate desire for truth. It is pursued by men and women who know what they believe, but are persuaded that there is still more to be revealed to them. They seek to meet their separated brethren not in the valleys where beliefs don't matter, but on distant mountain tops of still higher and truer faith. They believe they will get there, not by abandoning their deepest convictions, but by a firmer grasp of what they believe to be true, combined with a sure belief that in God alone will our differences be reconciled. This is why a strong, believing Protestant, and a strong believing Roman Catholic often find, in spite of deep disagreement, a spirtual unity unknown to those who practice the easy tolerance of the apathetic.

I am one of those who dislikes being an adjectival Christian, a member of an adjectival church. The Bible knows nothing of "Protestant" or "Roman Catholic" Christians, or of "Presbyterian," "Episcopal," or "Orthodox" churches. I should like to be just a Christian and a member of *the* Church. But we must face the facts. It is no more possible to avoid the adjectives today than it would be to join the United States Army and refuse to be attached to any regiment. Those who try to avoid denominations only succeed in founding another denomination. Therefore we must accept the fact that, until God shows us a better way, we are Protestant Christians and members of a Presbyterian Church. We shall not help the cause of Christianity by ignoring our tradition. And the time is surely ripe for us to think again why we are Protestants and to proclaim the truth as we see it with charity and clarity, and with confidence and vigor.

"And ye are complete in him." This is the foundation-rock of the Protestant Christian. Jesus Christ is the all-sufficient Lord and Saviour of mankind. We are *complete* in Him. Christ as the Divine Son of God *is* our salvation, and everyone and everything else in the Church is totally subordinate to Him. This we believe to be the Christian Gospel from the beginning, that we can find our true life through faith in Christ Who died for us and rose again to be our Lord, and that the Church is the community of believers, the Body of which Christ alone is Head. The Reformation brought no new religion to the world: it was simply a renewing of this central loyalty of the Church, a scrubbing away of all that tended to obscure the presence and power of the living Christ. That mistakes were made is certain. (Every husband knows how something valuable can get lost in the course of a violent housecleaning). But everyone familiar with the condition of the Medieval Church knows that some such cleansing was shouting to be done. And it must not stop there. A Protestant is not one who believes in the Reformation, but one who believes that the Church in every age needs continual reforming by the Spirit of the living Christ. "We are complete in him." Each age has its own way of obscuring that fact from the ordinary man.

There is a radical simplicity about our Protestant conviction as to the authority of Christ. We believe that a man or woman is directly confronted by the claim of Christ and is summoned to decision. Faith is a *personal* relationship between us and Christ. We believe also that it is the Church that brings this Gospel to us, and it is within the community of believers that this decision takes place. But for us the Church is simply the instrument of Christ, the body of which He is the Head. Therefore, nothing—not even the most punctilious performance of every obligation of churchmanship—can replace the simple, direct trust of a man or woman in their Saviour. Faith is not assenting to a set of propositions, or following a religious code. It is trusting Christ with our lives as we would trust a friend with our most precious possession. When we so find Christ we know that we are complete in Him. And that is the most invincible conviction that a man or woman can have.

This central conviction has some implications that we believe to be decisive for the strength and purity of the Church.

I

If "we are complete in Him" then we acknowledge that He alone is sufficient for all our needs in this world and the next. Every book of the New Testament tells us this in unmistakable language. "I am the way, the truth, and the life; no man cometh unto the Father, but by me"; "My grace is sufficient for thee"; "All power is given unto me in heaven and in earth"; "Jesus Christ, the same yesterday, and today, and forever." "There is one God and one mediator between God and men, one man Christ Jesus"; "God shall supply all your need according to his riches in glory by Christ Jesus."

He is sufficient. Therefore nothing needs to be added to what He has done. We cannot add to His perfect life by any merits of our own. We cannot supplement His perfect sacrifice by any rites of the Church. When He opens up the way to the Father we have no right to interpose any other mediators or to suggest the need of any indirect approach. When I hear a speaker on television say that when we find Christ's front door to heaven too forbidding we can go round to Mary at the back door, then I know why we had a Reformation, and need one still. There are, of course, a hundred ways in which the Church, as the Body of Christ, can minister to us His grace and power. But surely it must never dare to suggest

129

that He Himself is not sufficient for our salvation, not open to our direct approach. We are complete in Him.

The question we have to ask ourselves this morning is whether we Protestants really believe that today—"not only with our lips, but in our lives." The man who truly believes that Christ is sufficient for his and his neighbor's life, both here and hereafter, will surely not be found giving equal place to some secular society, however good, or making side-bets with psychiatry, however sound. The woman who truly believes she is complete in Him will not be drawn to esoteric cults, or psychic séances, nor will she be likely to feel safer with some saintly medallion on the dashboard of her car. I know how superstitious we all tend to be, and perhaps these ancestral whisperings can never be totally silenced; but if we are "complete in Him" we must surely see all such practices as symbols of our lack of faith. The cure for superstition is the sufficiency of Christ.

II

The next implication of this simple trust that we are complete in Christ concerns the nature of our Christian life and the methods of the Church.

If we are complete in Him then we draw the inspiration for our daily life, the guidance for our decisions, the pattern of our behavior, from our communion with Him as members of His Body. The Bible calls this "walking by the Spirit." It means a glad and spontaneous response to the love of the living Christ. The nearest parallel we can find to this is the influence of a good friend, the kind of influence that works silently in the depths changing our habits and ourselves and making us continually aware of new dimensions of the good life.

Now we are all so made that it is easier for us to try another way, what the Bible calls "living by the Law." That means following a code of religious and moral duties which we accept as binding—and do our best to impose upon others. A set of rules, a discipline of the religious life is a good thing—and we could do with more of it in our Protestant Christianity—*provided* these are freely accepted for ourselves as part of our "walking by the Spirit." But when we *substitute* these for our loving, grateful, direct relationship to Christ we have, as St. Paul says, "fallen from grace." "O foolish Galatians," he wrote to early Christians who had made this mistake, "who hath bewitched you?—Received ye the Spirit by the works of

130

the law, or by the hearing of faith?" "The hearing of faith"—this is what we live by when we know that we are "complete in him." Our concern will be to keep in touch, to respond, to grow in His likeness —and not simply to go through the motions, the minimum notions of a conventional Christian. This is a Reformation that must begin with ourselves.

This conception of the Christian way as Spirit and not Law has a direct bearing on the methods of His Church. The Protestant, believing that we are complete in Him Who is Love, and that the Christian life is love, not law, ought never to consent to the imposition of his standards upon others by legal, still less by military, force. It is this conviction that makes a vital Protestantism a necessity for the safeguarding of our freedoms, including the freedoms of those who do not have our faith. Protestants have not always resisted the temptation to impose the Christian way by force, but today almost universally the Protestant churches are content to be "complete in him" and are therefore the opponents of any kind of civil or ecclesiastical dictatorship.

III

"Ye are complete in him." There is one more implication that stems from this invincible conviction. "In him dwelleth all the fulness of the Godhead bodily, and ye are complete in him which is the head of all principality and power." What else can that mean but that Christ, and Christ alone, is the infallible Head of the Church?

In the New Testament we read that our Lord committed His Gospel to His followers, that He ordained apostles to whom He gave authority and great responsibility in the Church. We read in the epistles of other officers—ministers, presbyters, bishops, deacons are some of the names used—who had a vital part to play in the life of the Church. But nowhere do we read of any Head but Christ. He has not abdicated the control of His Church.

What does that mean for us today? The time has passed when we would claim that the Presbyterian system is the *only* scriptural method of church government. We respect the officers and dignitaries of any church no matter how foreign they may be to us. And we pray for God's blessing upon them. But when we look in longing to that day when Christians can again be one, there is one point at which our conviction is invincible and unshakable: union will never come by submission to the authority of any man, however holy, however powerful, as Head of the Christian Church. We are "complete in him"—and in Him alone.

Here again we must turn the question in upon ourselves. How faithful are we being today as Protestants to this great rediscovery of the Reformers? Would Luther, or Calvin, or Knox, clearly recognize in this vast network of Protestant Christianity the unmistakable leadership of Christ? They would certainly be baffled by the complexity of our commissions and committees, astounded by the techniques that are employed in the service of the kingdom, and utterly confused by the multitude of our organizations. Might they perhaps turn on us and say: "But this is where we came in. We found a church tremendously organized, we found a church cluttered with a thousand things that had little to do with the Gospel, we found a church where power and prestige and success seemed to matter more than the Kingship of Christ. And this was the church reformed by the word and the Spirit at tremendous cost. Are you going the same way?"

What would you answer? No one can say what a fair answer would be. But this we do know: that the Church of today, here and everywhere, stands under the judgment of Christ its King and is in desperate need of His reforming power. And we begin, not with a criticism of other churches, not with a blast against bureaucracy and administration, not even, in the first place, with a re-appraisal of the life of our own congregation. We begin with ourselves. Do I really recognize the Kingship of Christ, that He is the Head of this particular member, and that I am complete in Him?

When we begin there, a wonderful vista of true Reformation begins to unfold. When each member returns to Christ as supreme Lord, then a congregation is reformed in Him. When our congregations are thus reformed, a new and vitalized United Presbyterian Church goes into action across the nation and the world. And as this happens in other communions we find our total Protestant witness immeasurably strengthened and unified. And who can tell that by God's good grace this may not be eventually the way in which all Christians may be brought, in humility and deep conviction, to the one-ness for which He prayed. For it is "in him" that we, by whatever label we are known among men, are finally complete.

Faith Which Can Never Die

Right Reverend Bo Giertz, D.D.

BISHOP OF THE LUTHERAN DIOCESE OF GOTHENBURG, SWEDEN

It is appropriate that there should be included in this volume a sermon by a preacher who represents one of the great historic churches of Europe. The author of this sermon is well known in America after visits to this country in 1953 and 1957.

Bishop Giertz has had a distinguished career as a writer. His religious books and essays—and even two novels—mark him as one of those who has a special gift in communicating the Gospel. He is known as a preacher of depth, sincerity, and prophetic insight. He is the Primate of the diocese of Gothenburg and asserts a significant spiritual leadership among the people of his country. He has taken a strong stand on controversial issues on numerous occasions and has borne the banner of Christianity in the midst of a secularized society.

Bishop Giertz was pastor of Linkopings in 1935, and was Komminster (Copastor) in the parish of Torpa from 1938 to 1949. His preaching and church program won respect and attention and in 1943 he became preacher to the King of Sweden. In 1948 he became a bishop.

The sermon which is included here is a witness of the eternal character of the Christian faith. The sermon has been translated by Dr. Clifford Ansgar Nelson of St. Paul, Minnesota, who has also translated other of the bishop's works (including a novel called THE HAMMER OF THE LORD, *to be published this year), and whose sermon "Look Who's Here" also appears in this volume.*

SERMON NINETEEN

"This is the victory that overcometh the world, even our faith," I John 5:4

ST. JOHN OF EPHESUS knew whereof he was speaking when he wrote these words. With his own eyes he had seen the incredible miracle—that the Christian faith beyond all expectations and all logic had taken shape in a church which was being built up everywhere in the Roman Empire. At its inception, almost any worldly-wise person would have put up odds of one thousand to one that *this* faith would never play an important role in history. It was doomed from the start. Roman justice had condemned its founder to execution, respectable religious piety had condemned Him as a blasphemer and a charlatan, even providence itself seemed to have condemned Him by permitting Him to die a shameful death, though He claimed to be the Son of God. His own followers had played the most despicable role possible. And furthermore He was a Jew! His whole teaching was but a variant of the ridiculous messianic faith in which the Jewish national culture had expressed itself. That and all else that came from Judaism was condemned from the beginning to be met by the derision of the learned and the most intense hatred of the crowd. It is also a fact that there is not found on record in a whole century in the ancient world a single reference to Christianity from without that does not start from an absolutely clear and absolutely sure judgment that it is a question of a coarse form of superstition that only deserves sympathetic rejection or radical persecution.

And yet—St. John has seen it with his own eyes: "This is the victory that overcomes the world, even our faith." The impossible had taken place and it was taking place day by day before his very eyes, in Ephesus and all around the world. This faith was conquering. It won people, it refashioned their lives. It made slaves and drunkards, who all their lives had lived in the ordinary sins of their times, in falsehoods, treachery and thievery, into honest and decent people who worked with their hands, who shared with one another and lived in an entirely new fellowship of love and good will. Opposition crystallized, martyrdom threatened, but the cause still went forward. This was the victory.

But when St. John says that this victory is our faith, he does not put into those words what an irreligious person would read into them. He does not mean that it is the Christians' points of view, or their philosophy, their program or their ideas which possess this mysterious power of victory. When a man who does not believe listens to a Christian speaking of his faith, it is perfectly natural that he should be angry. There is something so terribly pretentious in this faith. It is so sure of itself and so intolerant. How can anyone claim that his faith is more correct and better than that of another? We are all simply human, and we will have to make as plausible a theory about reality as we can. But isn't it narrow-minded and arrogant when someone comes and thinks he has a monopoly on faith?

Well, that is what they said. And yet the venerable, humble, admirable St. John said: "This is the victory—*our faith.*"

When he said this, however, he did not put any special emphasis on the word *our*. It did not occur to him that he came with any of his own ideas, or that he should have reasoned out some marvelous theories which would be able to compare with or even supersede the deep philosophies of others. His faith has nothing to do with theories and speculations, or such interpretations of life as men could produce by the keenness of their intellect. Instead, it is more like the joy and certainty of the comrades of Xenophon when after their dangerous expedition they saw the sea beyond the mountain heights and, knowing they were saved, shouted: "*Thalatta! Thalatta!*" His certainty is the confidence of the traveler who has been lost in the forest and suddenly finds himself on the highway. When he calls: "This is the road," he does not mean that he has discovered a new theory about the right direction so that he too can participate in the discussion that his comrades have had out in the woods. Instead he is sure that he has seen something that makes all theories superfluous. He has great good news to tell that will put an end to the discussions. It is not a matter of his intelligence or his wonderful mental abilities, nor is it a matter of arrogance or cocksureness. He simply states the fact, "This is the road."

This is how John speaks. He does not bother about theories. He has seen a fact. "That . . . which we have seen with our eyes, which we have looked upon and touched with our hands, concerning the word of life—the life was made manifest, and we saw it, and testify to it, and proclaim to you the eternal life which was with the Father and was made manifest to us" (R.S.V.).

That which St. John calls *our faith,* that is therefore certain facts, which he has seen and for which he will risk his own life. This faith *must* overcome the world. That he knew, even before experience had substantiated it. Even before his great gamble had been taken, before he had gone forth as an apostle, he knew that there was something which was above all else and therefore must triumph.

How could he know that?

The answer is: *he had been a witness of the Resurrection.* He had talked with the Risen Lord, he had eaten and supped with Him, he had stood in the presence of something which was absolutely real and yet absolutely different from anything else he had known. When all seemed to be lost, when the enemies had triumphed and the Master was killed, then God had stepped into the scene and the miracle of miracles had taken place and had proven at once that this Jesus truly was the Son of God, and that these historical acts were the most important in the history of the world, and that the destiny of every man rested in the hands of the Son of Man. That which previously was ridiculous, was now a reality. It was the Risen Lord Himself Who had asked them to go out and make disciples of all nations. It was perfectly obvious that they must obey. Who could overpower Him Who had challenged death? It was also obvious to them that it would go with them exactly as it had—they would be met with a storm of bitterness, ridicule, and persecution—and still they conquered. It could not be otherwise. They did not preach either their own faith or their own studied speculations. They preached Christ, and behind them stood One Who had been given all power in heaven and on earth.

And there was still another thing. This faith was not only the certainty of something that had happened. Christ still lived. He was with them. Faith meant the daily fellowship with the Risen Lord. They were not simply bearers of a new theory. They were sharers in a new life. They had an unbroken fellowship with Christ. They were members of His body, branches in the Vine, born anew, grafted into Christ—as they expressed it in their own or their Master's words.

When, therefore, St. John says that it is our faith which overcomes the world, he means by faith this certainty about the tremendous fact that Christ is risen, that He is God's Son. And by faith he means this living relation with that Christ, that mysterious life which comes from God Himself.

All this is made very clear in the context in which the words concerning the victory of faith are found. The (R.S.V.) context reads: "For whatever is born of God overcomes the world; and this is the victory that overcomes the world, our faith. Who is it that overcomes the world but he who believes that Jesus is the Son of God?"

That is why faith can never die. All other theories and philosophical systems, all other speculations and convictions are a product of our own fumbling or keen attempts to come to terms with the reality that surrounds us. They are the heroic attempts of our minds to interpret the great mass of facts that existence offers us.

136

Faith is something different. It is fellowship with Jesus Christ. That is why it can never die—"for we know that Christ being raised from the dead will never die again."

That is the reason why all the arguments of unbelief are impotent against faith. Only a few generations after the death of St. John, Celsus wrote his famous polemic against Christianity, in which he gathers together so many logical, reasonable, moral and ironical arguments against the Gospel, that one of our own most famous radicals in the last decade states with a sigh that reason must be singularly weak in a world where almost everything that can be said about the unreasonableness of Christianity was said already in the first century; and where later it has been repeated over and over again that Celsus certainly missed the boat when he made the satirical remark that it is the most insane thing about these groveling Christians that they imagine that their faith—this foolish superstition—should one day become any kind of a world religion.

No! Faith can never die. If all the arguments of unbelief could destroy faith, they would still have to put a stopper at the very source of faith. That is what the high priests tried, when they brought our Lord to the cross. They did not succeed—God raised Him up. The Risen Christ is still less vulnerable to the attacks of denial. The source of faith, its foundation and its power of triumph are beyond all that any dictator or professor in this world can invent. Those who believe can be put to death or persecuted. The dogmas and confessions and teachings can be criticized and made fun of, but the resurrected Lord still lives. That is why faith cannot die.

But there are some observations that must be made at this point. First, that a faith which can never die must mean a real life of fellowship with Christ. Otherwise, it is just as mortal as everything human. There is faith which is called Christian but which is nothing else than a theory without life. It was very common in the days when it was the popular thing for everyone to be a Christian. Christianity then became for most people just simply an interpretation of life, a theory about the origin of the universe and of a life after this, and a kind of practical ethic. What was lacking was exactly this mysterious something, that makes faith—Christian faith—in other words, a living fellowship with Christ. This loss does not show up at a superficial glance, but becomes real when, for example, you examine what a person thinks and experiences with regard to sin and grace. If he is minus what we call a knowledge of sin, if sin does not cause him any distress, if he does not understand that because of sin he is under condemnation that can only be lifted when Christ becomes his Saviour and Redeemer, then his faith is almost surely one of the theoretical kind, that is, not a real Christian faith. It can also be determined if one knows a man's prayer life, and observes how often and how earnest is the prayer for forgiveness or what Christ means to him with regard to the forgiveness of sin. Christian faith is that assurance which St. John expresses thus—"Your sins are forgiven you for his name's sake." Where there is fellowship with Christ, it is built upon this, that we have a right to be Christians because He has died for us and He is our peace. One can also know how it is with a man by the way in which he treats what the Bible calls "the flesh"; the old Adam, the egotistic self, with all its selfishness, its pride, and its desire for worldly gain. The old Adam, to be sure, still remains with those who believe. But when faith is genuine, and a real life-fellowship with the Risen Lord, then faith means a constant strife with the flesh. The life of faith is revealed in the constant battle between the Christ-life and selfishness. If, on the contrary, faith is only a theory, then the old Adam can do as he pleases if he only stays within the bounds of ordinary decency.

Still another observation. Our faith, and my faith, can die, even though it has been genuine. What there is in me of faith—in other words, of Christ—that may vanish. It is not a question of anything that I have brought to light, or have discovered, or of anything that I have charge over. It is a life that comes from God. That life must be nourished and kept alive. We are branches in Christ Who is the Vine. The branch must be sustained by the Vine. And this divine life comes through the Word and the Sacraments. They are the means through which the Spirit of God creates and sustains the life of faith. Christianity without the Bible, without worship, and the Lord's Supper is nothing more than an intellectual faith. The faith which overcomes the world is deeply rooted in the Word, Baptism and the Holy Communion. Therefore, St. John continues in our lesson: "This is he who came by water and blood . . . There are three witnesses, the Spirit, the water, and the blood." The Word, Baptism and Holy Communion belong together in the same manner that seeds, sunshine and rain belong to the harvest which grows in the field.

Faith can thus very well die in the individual Christian. There are branches in the vine which wither. But the vine does not die. Whole provinces of Christendom may die. Great areas of the Christian church have thus been destroyed in the Orient. But faith is not crushed; it lives on in new lands, among new people. And when a man earnestly remains by the sources of faith in the church, then a faith is renewed within which can overcome the world. "If you continue in my word, you are truly my disciples, and you will know the truth, and the truth will make you free."

Does faith, then, overcome the world by disregarding reason and logic, and refuse the witness of science and intelligence?

Not at all. Faith does not let itself be overwhelmed by the arguments of unbelief, not because it knows less than unbelief, but because it knows more. There are today, as always, believing Christians who stand at the peak of the culture and learning of their age. A man may be an atomic specialist or a lung specialist with a world-wide reputation and at the same time be loyal to the Christian confession with all of life and soul, without either science or faith suffering on that account. There is no contradiction between faith and knowledge. But there is a clear contradiction between him who knows nothing about God and His Son and him who knows something about these realities. If one knows God, then all of life comes into a new sphere, and one cannot stay by the half-truths that the atheist is content with. It is just about the same as when a prominent mathematician is also a gifted musician. As a mathematician he can explain all of music with mathematical calculations. And still a sonata of Beethoven will open a whole world for him which no figures can express. It is entirely natural that he should give both time and energy to exploring this area of beauty. And if some tone-deaf colleague comes to him and tries to prove that the whole sonata is simply a combination of ether waves that no intelligent person should expend any time on, then it is almost certain that the musical professor will get angry and tell his colleague to shut up. He is talking about things which he has no ability to understand.

This parable is incomplete because there is a fundamental difference between the world of beauty and the reality of God. But it can, perhaps, make clear to us how a man who knows the Risen Christ, who talks with Him daily and knows His influence over all his life, must react to the critics who try to explain away things which they have never seen or experienced or understood. In that situation a Christian will feel as Columbus would have felt if someone after his visit to America had told him that he had simply imagined all that nonsense about the New World, since there obviously were no birds, or animals, or flowers such as he was decribing. Such arguments are hopelessly futile. One does not even

139

listen to them seriously. For, "That which we have seen with our eyes . . . proclaim we to you." And he that has seen will not be instructed by him who has not seen.

The faith which overcomes the world, and which never can die, is faith in Christ. The power of faith comes from the Risen Lord. As soon as human pretensions begin to overshadow even a little of the fact that Jesus is the Son of God, then it loses its power. Then it is our faith, Professor Harnack's faith, or Browning's conception, or Mr. Smith's private idea—and that will not overcome the world. That faith which a man himself commands even a little bit is nothing more than a human idea among many others, and it will deserve the same fate, to be superseded and destroyed like other human ideas. There was a time when in foolish, good intention, it was considered the proper thing to correct Christian faith according to the world view which was then in vogue. Since that world view was dominated by unchangeable laws, and since the laws of nature were considered to be known, then faith was supposed to be fitted into the great, revolving machinery of the world. The Saviour thus could not possibly have been born of a virgin, and the grave could not have been empty, plus many other things. Such faith looked a bit reasonable to the people of that day. But strangely enough, it was entirely powerless. It won no converts. People who had inherited their Christianity and wanted to keep it, retired within this new bastion of the faith. But they took no doubters with them. The faith which was on the offensive and converted people, was the ancient faith with the ancient language of sin and grace, the cross and the Resurrection.

There are many criticisms that can be leveled at the Christian Church today, within all denominations and all areas. She has often been unfaithful to the message that has been entrusted to her. Sometimes she has been faithful, but has imprisoned the pure Gospel in forms of expression that once were fresh and vital, but have become obscure and difficult to understand. It is entirely correct, if one demands to have the Gospel sound and pure, warm and evangelical, that formalism and smug complacency shall be challenged. But one must not demand that the Christian faith shall become anything else than a fellowship with the Living and Risen Christ in Word and Sacrament. That faith is what it is, since the resurrected Lord remains the same to all eternity.

Even this can be ascertained through experience. It is a fact that there are a great number of people who believe in God, but who are not really active members in the Christian Church. All kinds of polls and statistics have shown that the overwhelming majority in my country believe in God in our time. But not even half of these believers are living members of the church. That might be interpreted to mean that there was some other religious confession than Christianity that would meet the needs of modern man. That thought has even been expressed. But the strange fact remains that though there are many who speculate about religion and are out to find some faith for these times, the results to date have been absolutely negligible. Of course people can try to speculate about the kind of God that can find acceptance with the modern mind. But no one believes such things when they are presented. They seem to have no power to overcome the world. They do not help men out of their doubts and difficulties. They have no decisive challenge to their action, and they have no gift of forgiveness of sins and peace of soul.

For him who seriously reckons with the Living God, it remains obvious that if it really were the will of God that faith in our time should be clothed in a new garb, by having new revelations of God given to us, then God would long ago have sent us new reformers with a new, great, releasing truth. Instead God still continues to guide earnest, seeking people back to the ancient verities. Those who are not satisfied with a little religious atmosphere and their own speculations, but really through prayer have come in touch with the Living God and without reservation commit themselves to Him, become Christians. To begin with they perhaps do not understand the ancient doctrines, but in the measure that they make trial and experience the truth of God, in that measure does their understanding find clarity. Here it is true as our Lord said: "If any man's will is to do his will, he shall know whether the teaching is from God or whether I am speaking on my own authority." Those who in real seriousness are led by God will not be led to all manner of new truths. They will be led to Him, Who is the Truth.

This is a fact which anyone can corroborate in his own environment. Out of the great mass of seeking, uncertain, and fumbling contemporary people, who somehow believe in God but still are not Christians, there comes no new religious pattern, no joyous confident assurance in believing, no new strong characters who live by some other faith than the Christian. Instead one of two things occurs. Either they move farther and farther away from all belief, until the last residue has vanished and they land in the darkness where nothing is certain any longer, nothing right, nothing holy, and where almost anything can take place—concentration camps, child murder, conscious falsifying, euthanasia, etc. etc. This is the type of man that has created the despair of Europe. Or there is also the possibility that these religious types come closer to the reality of faith and begin to see more of that which the people of faith have always lived by, that which has carried and sustained our Western cultural ideal and its humanitarianism. They begin to realize that it is not a question of happenstance, or fluctuating theories, but they have stumbled on the most vital of all, that which is the solid and eternal basis of all existence. Then there remains only the question of whether the Lord Whom they have met shall be permitted to direct their whole life. That is the most important question in their existence. On their answer to that question depends their destiny, whether life shall be meaningful or in vain, if the world shall conquer them, or they shall overcome the world.

For who else can overcome the world except those who believe that Jesus is the Son of God?

FAITH

Faith of Our Fathers

The Honorable John Foster Dulles, LL.D.

In this lay sermon Mr. Dulles presents a discussion of the Church and the faith which the men and women of yesterday built and have left for us. The editor is happy to include this sermon by a man who was an important officer in our national government and in world affairs. When he died on Sunday, May 24, 1959, men and women all over the world felt that a great man had passed. Washington honored him with a state funeral in the National Cathedral and a tomb in Arlington National Cemetery. People of many nations mourned him, while Chancellor Adenauer and many West Germans wept. Russia allowed her May 27 Berlin deadline to pass unnoticed. Perhaps he accomplished in his death what he had devoted his life and faith to achieve.

John Foster Dulles, the son of a Presbyterian minister, was born in Washington, D.C., on February 25, 1888. He attended Princeton University; after his graduation in 1908, he spent a year at the Sorbonne in Paris and later took his LL.B. at George Washington University. He began the practice of law in New York City in 1911. He has been a leader in the Rockefeller Foundation and the Carnegie Endowment for International Peace; he was a trustee of Union Theological Seminary, was secretary of The Hague Peace Conference in 1907 and was a member of the Second Pan-American Scientific Congress. In 1917 he was sent as a special agent of the Department of State to Central America; then he was an officer in the United States Army during 1917 and 1918. After the war he was a counsel to the American Commission to Negotiate Peace in 1918 and 1919, and was a member of the Reparations Commission in 1919; he was American representative at the Berlin Debt Conference in 1933. He was a member of the United States Delegation at the San Francisco Conference on World Organization in 1945, a representative to the United Nations General Assembly in 1946, 1947 and 1950, and acting chairman of the United States Delegation of the U.N. General Assembly in Paris in 1948. He was Special Representative of the President, with the rank of Ambassador, to negotiate the Japanese Peace Treaty in 1951. When President Eisenhower was elected, Mr. Dulles was appointed Secretary of State, taking office on January 21, 1953. He represented the United States at every major international meeting from 1953 to 1959 and worked unceasingly to bring understanding among the nations.

He was the author of WAR, PEACE AND CHANGE *and* WAR OR PEACE, *and wrote and delivered many important papers and addresses, including "Our Experiment in Human Liberty," "The Peace We Seek" and "The Moral Foundation of the United Nations." Mr. Dulles was well qualified to occupy a pulpit and did so on many occasions by invitation. His work was recognized with the honorary LL.D. from Princeton, Tufts, Wagner, Northwestern, Union College, Pennsylvania, Lafayette, Arizona, St. Lawrence, Johns Hopkins, Fordham and Harvard.*

SERMON TWENTY

A NOBLE HERITAGE

THIS IS THE 150TH ANNIVERSARY of the founding of our church. To me this church is richer in memories than any other earthly spot. My father preached here for sixteen years and radiated a spiritual influence that is still felt here, and elsewhere, as I have learned in my travels about the world. Our family life revolved around this church. Before me is the pew in which we sat three times on Sunday and frequently during weekday evenings.

At times the church services seemed overlong and overfrequent. But through them I was taught of the two great commandments, love of God and love of fellow man. Ordained ministers are uniquely qualified to deal with the relations of man to God. But laymen, who have to deal with national and international problems, are perhaps qualified to make some observations on the relations of man to fellow man.

* * * * *

Our American political institutions are what they are because our founders were deeply religious people. As soon as a community was founded, a church was built. Also, wherever a community was founded, its members developed practices and ways of life which reflected their belief that there is a God; that He is the Author of a moral law which all can know and should obey; that He imparts to each human being a spiritual dignity and worth which all should respect. Our founders sought to reflect these truths in their political institutions, seeking thus that God's will should be done on earth.

The Bill of Rights puts into our supreme law the concept of the Declaration of Independence that all men are endowed by their Creator with "certain unalienable Rights." Our Constitution says, in unmistakable terms, that men, even in the guise of government, cannot lawfully deny other men their fundamental rights and freedoms.

From the beginning of our nation, those who made its laws and system of justice looked upon them as means to assure what seemed just and right. Thus we became heirs to a noble heritage.

NEED TO REVITALIZE THE WORDS

We must, however, remember that that heritage is not inexhaustible. Our institutions of freedom will not survive unless they are constantly replenished by the faith that gave them birth.

General Washington, in his Farewell Address, pointed out that morality and religion are the two pillars of our society. He went on to say that morality cannot be maintained without religion. "Whatever may be conceded to the influence of refined education on minds of peculiar structure, reason and experience both forbid us to expect that national morality can prevail in exclusion of religious principle."

Arnold Toynbee, the great student of civilizations, has recently

144

pointed out that the political and social practices of our civilization derive from their Christian content, and, he says, they will not long survive unless they are replenished by that faith. His profound study convinces him that "practice unsupported by belief is a wasting asset."

Many other nations have modeled their constitutions after ours. But they have not obtained the same results unless there was a faith to vitalize the words.

The terrible things that are happening in some parts of the world are due to the fact that political and social practices have been separated from spiritual content.

That separation is almost total in the Soviet Communist world. There the rulers hold a materialistic creed which denies the existence of moral law. It denies that men are spiritual beings. It denies that there are any such things as eternal verities.

As a result the Soviet institutions treat human beings as primarily important from the standpoint of how much they can be made to produce for the glorification of the state. Labor is essentially slave labor, working to build up the military and material might of the state, so that those who rule can assert ever greater and more frightening power.

Such conditions repel us. But it is important to understand what causes those conditions. It is irreligion. If ever the political forces in this country became irreligious, our institutions would change. The change might come about slowly, but it would come surely. Institutions born of faith will inevitably change unless they are constantly nurtured by faith.

THE POWER OF MORAL FORCES

It may be asked, may not aggressive material forces prevail unless met by materialism? It sometimes seems that material power is so potent that it should be sought at any price, even at the sacrifice of spiritual values. Always, however, in the past those who took that path have met disaster. Material aggression often is formidable. It is dynamic, and we must admit that the dynamic usually prevails over the static.

But it is gross error to assume that material forces have a monopoly of dynamism. Moral forces too are mighty. Christians, to be sure, do not believe in invoking brute power to secure their ends. But that does not mean that they have no ends or that they have no means of getting there. Christians are not negative, supine people. Jesus told the disciples to go out into all the world and to preach the Gospel to all the nations. Any nation which bases its institutions on Christian principles cannot but be a dynamic nation.

Our forebears felt keenly that this nation had a mission to perform. In the opening paragraph of the *Federalist Papers* it is said that "it seems to have been reserved to the people of this country, by their conduct and example," to show the way to political freedom.

Our Declaration of Independence meant, as Lincoln said, "liberty, not alone to the people of this country but hope for the world for all future time. It was that which gave promise that in due time the weight should be lifted from the shoulders of all men and that all should have an equal chance."

THE GREAT AMERICAN EXPERIMENT

What our forebears did became known as "the Great American Experiment." They created here a society of material, intellectual, and spiritual richness the like of which the world had never known. It was not selfishly designed, but for ourselves and others. We sought through conduct, example and influence to promote everywhere the cause of human freedom.

Through missionaries, physicians, educators and merchants, the American people carried their ideas and ideals to others. They availed themselves of every opportunity to spread their gospel of freedom, their good news, throughout the world.

That performance so caught the imagination of the peoples of the world that everywhere men wanted for themselves a political freedom which could bear such fruits.

The despotisms of the last century faded away largely under the influence of that conduct and example. There is no despotism in the world which can stand up against the impact of such a Gospel. That needs to be remembered today. Our best reliance is not more and bigger bombs but a way of life which reflects religious faith.

FAITH AND THE ATOMIC AGE

Do our people still have that faith which in the past made our nation truly great and which we need today? That is the ultimate testing of our time. Admittedly some have come to think primarily in material terms. They calculate the atomic stockpiles, the bombers, the tanks, the standing armies of the various nations and seem to assume that the victory will go to whichever is shown by these scales to have the greater weight of armament.

146

Unfortunately under present conditions we do need to have a strong military establishment. We are opposed by those who respect only visible strength and who are tempted to encroach where there seems to be material weakness. Therefore, without military strength, we could not expect to deter aggression which, even though it would ultimately fail, would in the process cause immense misery and loss. But your government does not put its faith primarily in material things.

The greatest weakness of our opponents is that they are professed materialists. They have forcibly extended their rule over some eight hundred million people, a third of the people of the world. They are seeking to make these people into a pliant, physical mass which completely conforms to the will of the rulers.

But these people are religious people and they are patriotic people. They have shown that over the centuries. We believe that the Soviet rulers are attempting the impossible when they attempt to subject such people to their materialistic and repressive rule. We believe that the subject peoples have faith and hopes which cannot indefinitely be suppressed.

PUTTING FIRST THINGS FIRST

The President, the Cabinet, and the Congress all recognize the priority of spiritual forces. We do not intend to turn this nation into a purely material fortress and to suppress the freedom of thought and expression of the inmates, so that our people would more and more assume the likeness of that which threatens and which we hate.

There are a few within this nation who do not share that viewpoint. They honestly feel that the danger is so great and of such a kind that we must give an absolute priority to material efforts. There are others who honestly feel that the danger is so imminent that we should impose uniformity of thought, or at least of expression, abolishing diversity and tolerance within our nation and within our alliances.

Such points of view, while often heard, represent a small minority. Certainly there is some confusion of thinking, which needs to be dispelled. But I believe that the great majority of the American people and of their representatives in government still accept the words of the prophet: "Not by might nor by power, but by My Spirit, saith the Lord of Hosts."

How shall we surely become infused with that spirit? That is my concluding concern.

There is no mystery about that. The way to get faith is to expose oneself to the faith of others. It is not only diseases that are contagious. Faith is contagious. A strong faith, rooted in fact and in reason, inevitably spreads if contacts are provided. If, therefore, we want spiritual strength, we must maintain contact with those who have it and with those who have had it.

That is above all the task of our churches. The Bible is the greatest book because, as Paul pointed out to the Hebrews, it is a story of faith. It recounts lapses from faith and their consequences and revival and restoration of faith. Most of all, it is a story of men who lived by faith and died in faith, bequeathing it to successors who molded it into something finer, truer, and more worthy.

Our American history, like Hebrew history, is also rich in the story of men who through faith wrought mightily.

In earlier days our homes, schools, and colleges were largely consecrated to the development of faith. They were places of prayer and of Bible reading. Parents and teachers told daily the story of those who had gone before and who had lived by faith.

THE BURDEN OF THE CHURCHES

Today our schools and colleges and, I am afraid, our homes largely omit this study in faith. That throws a heavier burden on our churches. They today provide the principal means of drawing together the men, women and children of our land and of bringing to them knowledge of the faith of those who have gone before, so that today's faith is a contagious and vital force.

As our churches, synagogues and other places of worship thus carry an ever greater share of vital responsibility, they should be strongly supported by all our citizens, for they all profit from the institutions which faith inspires.

Sometimes we feel that we are indeed compassed about by a great cloud of witnesses. Each of us knows that, in terms of loved ones who have gone before. We know it as we have heard read the great Book of Faith and as we are taught the lessons drawn from the story of the great prophets and disciples of the past.

Let us maintain spiritual communion with them. Let us draw faith and inspiration from their lives. Let us act as we know they

would want us to act. Then we, in our turn, will run with stead-
fastness the course that is set before us. Then we, in our turn, will
play worthily our part in keeping alight the flame of freedom.

FAITH OF OUR FATHERS

Our fathers have left us a rich spiritual legacy. Surely it is our
duty not to squander it but to leave it replenished so that we, in
our generation, may bequeath to those who come after us a tradition
as noble as was left to us.

A church spire is symbolic. It points upward to the Power above
us, from which we derive our spiritual strength. It marks a building
as a place where we can gather for a communion that renews our
faith.

Let us be ever thankful for the church of our forebears, remembering those who founded it. Let us remember also those who during the succeeding decades maintained it, enlarged it, beautified it
and enriched it with their Christian labors. Let us dedicate ourselves
to follow in their way.

What Makes Men Good?

Elton Trueblood, Ph.D., LL.D., Litt.D.
SOCIETY OF FRIENDS (QUAKERS), PROFESSOR OF PHILOSOPHY, EARL-
HAM COLLEGE, RICHMOND, INDIANA

*This sermon raises questions many people avoid all of their lives.
Dr. Trueblood discusses the fundamental greatness of life and shows
its importance in developing character and making us the kind of
people we really are. "What Makes Men Good" was given at Stanford University.*

*Dr. Trueblood is a man of many interests, professor, preacher,
author. Born in Iowa of Quaker parents, he attended Penn College
and Harvard University, studied for his Ph.D. at Johns Hopkins
and has taken an active part in the American Philosophical Association. From 1947 to 1952 he was chairman of the Friends World
Committee for Consultation and is a member of the board of the
Church Peace Union.*

He has been professor of philosophy and Dean of Men at Guilford College. At Haverford College he taught philosophy; at Harvard he was acting chaplain. At Garrett Biblical Institute he was a visiting professor, and at Stanford University he was chaplain and professor of philosophy of religion; he was Swarthmore lecturer in England in 1939, was editor of "The Friend" from 1935 to 1946, and since 1946 has been professor of philosophy at Earlham College.

Dr. Trueblood's preaching and writing have won him a unique place among the religious leaders of our country. He has a clear, penetrating style which stimulates thought; he bases his religious beliefs on sound philosophical reasoning. He is known as the author of ALTERNATIVE TO FUTILITY, YOUR OTHER VOCATION, THE LOGIC OF BELIEF, THE PREDICAMENT OF MODERN MAN, THE LIFE WE PRIZE, THE RECOVERY OF FAMILY LIFE *(with Pauline Trueblood),* FOUNDATIONS FOR RECONSTRUCTION *and* PHILOSOPHY OF RELIGION. *For several years he was chief of religious information in the United States Information Agency in Washington.*

SERMON TWENTY-ONE

"Hold fast what is good," I Thessalonians 5:21, R.S.V.

ONE OF THE MOST STRIKING FACTS of the world is the fact of moral difference. Men differ from one another in a thousand ways, but all other differences fade into relative insignificance in comparison with differences in goodness. Though goodness is difficult to define, it is wonderfully easy to recognize. Often the difference is observable on first contact with another person, so radically do selfishness and greed, as well as their opposites, influence the whole man, even affecting his external appearance in many ways. This does not mean that the understanding of ethical problems is easy or simple, but it does mean that we know goodness when we see it, and to see it is a thrilling experience.

The paramount importance of goodness in human life becomes evident when we ask ourselves what kind of people we are willing to have as companions for long periods. For steady companionship it is sheer goodness that we prize most, providing we mean by goodness genuine excellence of character and not some trivial standard of conduct. The one whose companionship we prize is not the person who puts on a show of virtue for the sake of private gain, the self-centered man, or the man who would seek to use us for his own ends. Mere cleverness would finally become tiresome, dominating personalities are ridiculous after a time, humor we want in small doses, but goodness is permanently satisfying. Sometimes, indeed, we hear of people who are accused of being too good, but that merely indicates that these persons are superficially pious or are marked by an affectation of gentleness or generosity. When we think of the best people we know, we realize that they have something which cannot be overdone. The heart of goodness is *trustworthiness*, and there cannot be too much trustworthiness in the world.

In view of the fact that goodness is of paramount importance in the life of human beings, it is obvious that we should do all we can to learn how it is achieved or produced. There could be no more worthy task than that of discovering the conditions under which moral excellence arises, since the deliberate cultivation of these conditions might facilitate the development of the goodness we so greatly prize. We are tempted to conclude that goodness is born and that effort is therefore futile, but it is a fact that character can be changed. It is not surprising, therefore, that some of the best thought of great and good men has been devoted to this problem since the rise of civilization.

Before attempting a positive answer it is worthwhile to note some of the conditions which are not sufficient, either separately or together, to produce moral excellence. Perhaps the most obvious one of these is *wealth*. Money does not make men good and neither does poverty, inasmuch as we find all degrees of goodness combined with all degrees of economic standing. Rare beauty of character sometimes flourishes in city slums, but it is also found in homes of millionaires.

Socrates was a poor man of Athens, and Marcus Aurelius was the emperor of Rome with vast resources at his command, but both lived beautiful lives. In some sections of New York City the slum and the avenue are separated by only a few feet, but they are no closer geographically than they are morally. This is not to say that economic conditions have no bearing on the problem, but it does mean that they are not sufficient conditions. Certainly some conditions make goodness unusually difficult and these are chiefly the extreme conditions. The economic condition which presents the fewest hindrances to the development of goodness is one removed as far as possible from great wealth on the one hand and from dire poverty on the other.

Another condition which cannot account for goodness is *educa-*

tion. As in the case of wealth, it can be truly said that all degrees of goodness are actually combined with all degrees of training. Some moral giants have been rude, unlettered persons. The conspicuous example is that of the first apostles, Galilean fishermen. Almost everyone is acquainted with some genuine saint, usually of restricted circumstances, who may have read only a few books in his life. The best person I have ever known never went to college. On the other hand, there sometimes develops in educated circles a spirit of jealousy and struggle for personal power that makes us profoundly discouraged. Goodness is clearly much deeper than mere learning.

This holds in moral education as well as in strictly secular education. It is possible to study the moral standards of different peoples and argue endlessly about competing ethical theories without being made one whit better. Ethical scholarship and personal goodness are two different things.

In the same way we can say that a man's *profession* is not a sufficient condition of moral excellence. There seem to be good men in every kind of work and disgusting men in every kind of work. It is possible that some tasks make goodness easier, especially those which involve contact with the soil or which provide some physical work without the labor which exhausts. For example, gardeners often seem to have a high degree of what we most prize in men. At the same time there are tasks which are not consistent with moral dignity at all, particularly those by means of which some men are parasites. How nearly independent goodness is of profession is especially clear when we realize that participation in the ministry is no guarantee of goodness. In spite of pious words, and an unctuous manner, there are clergymen who, by a realistic test, are evil men. Churches are often scenes of bickering and bitterness. We can say, then, that occupation bears on the question, but is a minor consideration.

Another possible condition is that of beautiful *physical surroundings.* Some men live their entire lives in the presence of physical ugliness and filth, whereas others are in the presence of mountain lakes or carefully tended parks and lawns. It is very hard to see how goodness can ever come to flower in the sordidness of the average mining village, where flimsy houses are crowded together on a narrow street and where the only view is obstructed by a pile of slag. But the miracle does happen. At the same time persons surrounded by great beauty may be far from good men.

152

When I began my teaching career I lived in North Carolina in a section which commanded a fine view of some mountains which were the first outposts of the Appalachian Range. It became my habit to look at these mountains daily, and I often thought how fine it would be to live among them. The people on those slopes, I said to myself, could hardly fail to be grand people, considering their surroundings. Later I visited the people who lived there and found that, for the most part, they were quite unaffected by the beauty about them. Indeed, most of them seemed unaware of the beauty, and there were evidences on every hand of moral decay. I went home knowing that physical beauty of surroundings, while it may help, is certainly not enough.

What, then, is enough? There is no perfect recipe in the sense that we can be completely sure of our results, but there is a great deal of accumulated wisdom on the subject, and, according to this wisdom, the prime conditions are two: *contagion* and *discipline*.

The *contagion* of goodness is well demonstrated in the experience of the apostles who, in spite of conspicuous limitations in other ways, became good men chiefly as a result of their acquaintance with Christ. We often use the word contagion only for what is evil, but the truth is that goodness is like a disease which must be caught from another who has it. Fortunately, however, the contact need not be direct in order to be efficacious. Thus goodness can be contagious at long range, and the life of Christ may have an effect on men today much like the effect it had on Peter and John. Goodness has about it an inherent attractiveness that is far more effective than all the arguments in the world. One example may be worth a thousand commands. This is another way of saying that goodness is really unique and that goodness is the only thing which will produce goodness.

If this is true we should act accordingly and try to provide for ourselves the constant opportunity of contagion. You cannot make yourself catch a germ, but you can at least place yourself where the germs are. Professor Whitehead has put this point in a memorable sentence by saying, "Moral education is impossible apart from the habitual vision of greatness." So act that you bring yourself in steady contact with the highest excellence you know, for the soul grows by what it touches.

The *discipline* of goodness is only a special application of the principles of contagion and suggests the steady control which is necessary. When men do not respond to goodness it is because they are not sufficiently sensitive themselves to be helped by it. We need discipline to break down the barriers which hinder contagion. Back of anything that is really well done there is usually a long period of self-mastery which has so refined the powers that they seem to act spontaneously. It is well known that good "extempore" speakers are men who have made the most painstaking preparation. Perhaps they have not prepared the individual speech, but they have prepared the long background of the speech. Is it reasonable to suppose that excellence in character needs no discipline, when excellence in speaking needs so much?

The discipline for each task must be one appropriate to it. The appropriate discipline for the opening of our lives to the contagion of goodness is that which comes from times of personal quietness when we refuse to let our minds run hither and yon in a lazy fashion and hold them steadily to high things. The habitual practice of public as well as private prayer, not when we feel like it but with complete regularity, is comparable to the discipline of the musician who forces himself to practice in season and out.

Logan Pearsall Smith has put us in his debt by telling how Whistler learned to paint. The final painting in each case took an incredibly brief time, but before the final painting, literally hundreds of others, of the same subject, were made and discarded. He painted with speed, but it was long discipline that made the speed possible. We see the successful last effort and tend to forget what preceded it. It doesn't take much effort or time to do anything if you know how, but it usually takes a long time to learn. It doesn't take long to throw a javelin, but days of training are what make the throw good.

By the same token, goodness is difficult, and there is no royal road to character. But there is a road, and a road which men are at liberty to choose. That road is one in which we place our lives in contact with contagious goodness and so discipline our spirits that we are able to profit by the experience.

Where Your Hopes Come True

Reverend Norman Vincent Peale, D.D., L.H.D., LL.D.
MINISTER, MARBLE COLLEGIATE CHURCH (DUTCH REFORMED), NEW
YORK, NEW YORK

*Dr. Peale's preaching touches thousands of people all over
America. Visitors to New York consider it an event to hear him, and
his church is filled to overflowing every time he preaches.*

*What is it that he says which attracts such a serious and steady
following? Why do people listen to his sermons so raptly and read
his books in such great numbers? The sermon included here partly
answers these questions, for it is an excellent example of Dr. Peale's
preaching. He shows the excitement that is possible in worship and
in seeking the inherent splendor of the Christian faith.*

*Born in Bowersville, Ohio, on May 31, 1898, Dr. Peale studied
at Ohio Wesleyan University and Boston University School of Theology, and began his ministry in the Methodist Church at Berkeley,
Rhode Island, serving from 1922 to 1924. He then went to Kings
Highway Methodist Episcopal Church in Brooklyn, where from 1924
to 1927 he attracted much attention by his preaching and made this
church grow rapidly. He moved to Syracuse, New York in 1927,
remaining there until he was called in 1932 to Marble Collegiate
Church, where he has been ever since. Year by year his preaching
becomes more popular with people who have problems in business
or personal life. His sermons are designed to help people to become
their better selves through faith.*

*He has recorded much of his philosophy in his books, which
include A GUIDE TO CONFIDENT LIVING, THE POWER OF POSITIVE THINK-
ING, STAY ALIVE ALL YOUR LIFE and THE ART OF LIVING. He has been
honored with the doctorate by Syracuse, Ohio Wesleyan, and Duke
Universities, and by Lafayette and William Jewell Colleges.*

*With all his great following, Dr. Peale keeps his sermons simple,
his delivery direct. He stands at his pulpit without notes and talks
with his congregation as though all were his personal friends in the
privacy of his home. His preaching is always easy to follow, yet it
grips men and women with its feeling and its homeyness. He steps
beyond technique to reach the human heart.*

155

(Psalm 73:17)

WHEN WE COME TO CHURCH we ought to come with a feeling of excitement. Christian worship should never be merely formal or perfunctory. We ought to have a consciousness of the fact that the church is a place literally filled to overflowing with actual power. It is the House of God and, as such, it partakes of God's spirit, so that if you come to it in an attitude of expectancy and humility, and in willingness to give yourself to God, God will give Himself to you.

You never know when the greatest experiences of life may take place. Suddenly, there it is—the biggest thing that has ever happened to you. It might happen right now. And nowhere more often than in church does it happen that people suddenly get the answers to their big problems, that lives suddenly are changed.

Years ago, I was preaching one night at Marble Collegiate Church. It was a cold, rainy night. That night there was a certain man walking restlessly back and forth along Fifth Avenue because he was inwardly ill at ease and dissatisfied with his life. He was a man who occupied an important position as comptroller for a big New York City chain of hotels. But life had no rich, full meaning for him. He was not a bad man; he just wasn't a very good one, and he was strangely dissatisfied with himself and his life.

In the course of his walk this man happened to come by the Marble Collegiate Church. It was shortly after eight o'clock. He saw the lights inside. Though he had not for a long time been in the habit of going to church, he paused. He heard the great, soaring sound of that wonderful old hymn, "What a Friend We Have in Jesus." It drew him. He entered the church and took a seat in the balcony.

The sermon preached that night was not extraordinary. Few of my sermons are. It was just a regular sermon. But it was preached, however imperfectly, by one who meant it. And on that occasion we were talking, as we often do, about the wonderful transformation that occurs in a human life when an individual surrenders himself to Jesus Christ. At the conclusion of the service we suggested—according to a custom we still follow—that any person present who wished to signify that he wanted to accept Christ and become active in the Church should fill out and sign the card provided in the pews for that purpose. This man took a card, looked at it, took out his pencil and started to sign. But then he hesitated. He was one of those modern men who are terribly afraid of emotions. He said to himself, "This I don't like. This is evangelism." To him evangelism was something emotional, and therefore, for some reason, wrong. He was moved and stirred, and he wanted to sign that card, but at the same time he resisted it. So he took the card home with him.

He went to the hotel where he lived, went to bed, slept fitfully until three or four o'clock in the morning. Then he awoke. There came back to him the scene in the church and the challenge. He was in conflict, but he knew somehow or other that this was it, that here was the answer he was seeking. He got out of bed, got down on his knees by the bed and prayed. And finally he signed the card. Then he put on a bathrobe and walked down the hall to the mail chute. He told me afterward that as he dropped the card down the chute and saw it flash for a second as it passed on its way to the mailbox below, all of a sudden something happened to him. It seemed as if burdens left him, as if weights on his mind were lifted. He became wonderously happy and, as he phrased it, "organized on the inside."

The next morning he telephoned me and asked if I would come and see him. Something in his voice told me his need was serious, and I went. I found him in a huge office, surrounded by a barricade of secretaries. When we were alone he told me about the card. When he had finished he asked, "What happened to me last night?" Then, to my utter surprise, he put his head forward on his arms and started to sob. Now it always bothers me to hear a man weep. I am used to women weeping, but with a man it's something different and to me always a little embarrassing. However, the mechanism of tears is a releasing agent and I let him cry.

Finally he said, "I'm ashamed of myself, but I'm just all stirred up inside. Actually, I'm crying for joy." He went on to relate to me how he had been away from the church for many years, and how he had lost sight of his early hopes and dreams and high attitudes toward life. Now, he said, they had all come back again, and he struck off this phrase which I have remembered through the years: "The church is a place where all your hopes come true."

That man entered into the life of the Marble Collegiate Church and became one of its most active members. And seldom have I known anyone to give as generously as he gave. First he tithed ten percent. Then it went up to fifteen, twenty, twenty-five, thirty percent. In fact, he wanted to give so many things that actually, to my own consternation, I found myself telling him not to give so much. And that, I assure you, is something I seldom do.

At the same time he interested himself increasingly in social welfare work. He gave to every Christian agency he knew of that was working to bring about better conditions among men. When finally he died and I took his body to Philadelphia for burial, there were three or four railroad cars filled solidly with men who were making that journey in his honor. One after another they came to me on the way to Philadelphia and back, asking, "What in the world did you do to Bill?"

And I said, "I didn't do anything to Bill." What could I do to Bill? I continued, "I'll tell you Who it was that did wonderful things to Bill."

They answered, "You needn't tell us, we know."

Now the unfortunate fact is that when you learn of something like that happening to someone, you are likely merely to marvel and think, isn't that wonderful? But what I, as a minister, would like for you to say to yourself is, "I want that to happen to me." You are as acceptable to Christ as was this man whose story I have been telling. For you, too, the church can be the Gateway of Heaven where life comes alive and rises to its best. But you must want it, you must stop resisting, you must yield yourself.

What a tragedy it is that many men appear to live and die with all their possibilities still within them. There is in each of us, if you please, an imprisoned splendor. Years ago I used to give a lecture on the subject, "Imprisoned Splendor." Of this I was reminded the other day when I came across a little folder put out by a lecture bureau upstate some thirty years ago when I was living and preaching in Syracuse, New York. It was a folder describing me and my lecture, "Imprisoned Splendor." I must confess I was impressed with my own picture on the front page, if I say so myself. It was the picture of a young man, with head up, shoulders thrown back, very young face, and there was a light in the eye.

Now I remember what caused that light in the eye. I was a young preacher, and I believed that I was commissioned by Almighty God to try to change men and human society in the name of Christ. And I believed that I could persuade men that their lives could be better. So I went around giving this lecture, "Imprisoned Splendor." The theme of the address was that Almighty God has built a splendor into each of us, and that by the power of God it can be

158

released so that ordinary people can lead extraordinary lives and can become great souls.

In the days when I used to travel about giving that lecture, a certain businessman in Syracuse asked if he could go with me and hear me give it. I was highly complimented, for if I were to mention the man's name today it would be recognized by practically everybody who was more than a child at that time. He was president of a company that manufactured one of the most famous American products. This man had had only about three or four years of school education; yet he was a well-educated man. Whenever he came across anybody who struck him as having, as he put it, anything "on the ball," from which he could learn, he would "fasten himself like a leech" to that individual until he got the knowledge he was after.

Well, after sitting one night as I gave my speech in a little high school at Tully, New York, he said to me, "Norman, that is it, imprisoned splendor. That is what has always carried me on. I've had a longing to be somebody, and to do something in the world for people. It's the imprisoned splendor. That's what it is. And I know it was given to me by God. You pray to the Lord that I'll really use it, won't you?" He did use it, too. I was present on the day when Syracuse University conferred upon him the degree of Doctor of Laws. And when the Chancellor of the University put on the hood and gave the citation, stating that this was one of the great scholars of our time, what did that fellow do but give me a great big wink —as if to say, "*You* know I'm no scholar, but you know that I *am* one of the fellowship of the imprisoned splendor, following my hopes and following my dreams."

Dreams are among our most precious possessions. When you were born, God put dreams in your heart. I don't know exactly what the Lord will say when you come up in front of the great White Throne at the Judgment, but I wouldn't be at all surprised if He were to say, "What did you do with those bright and shining dreams and ideals I gave you as a boy or as a girl? Have you let them grow dull and tawdry? Have you lost them altogether?"

The great French author Flaubert says, "The principal thing in this world is to keep one's soul aloft." I think that sentence is worthy of immortality. When you are in church under the preaching of the Word and the singing of the great old hymns and the reading of the Scriptures, what it does to you is to send your soul aloft. Then you are able to live with power and to be faithful again to the dreams and hopes you had as a boy or as a girl. That is why people love the church, because it helps them keep the soul aloft.

This is a beautiful world, filled with glory and loveliness, but it is also a cruel world, filled with pain and suffering and confusion and war and death. It is not an easy world, and only strong men and women live in it successfully. God never meant that this world should be easy, for He wants His children to be strong. And the only way to do that is to keep your soul aloft.

A friend in Houston, Texas, sent me a newspaper clipping about a boy in Baylor University School of Medicine, who was a shining illustration of keeping the soul aloft in the midst of the pain of this world. This boy came from Colorado. He had been top student in his high school, and at college top man both in scholarship and in athletics. Then he came to Baylor University School of Medicine, because all his life he had wanted to be a doctor. In his first year there, again he was top man. He had an enthusiasm for medicine that inspired the professors as well as the students. He loved it. He used to say to his fellow students, "Isn't it wonderful? We're going to be doctors."

Well, in his second year at medical school this boy, Rick Fox by name, developed a pain in his stomach. It grew worse. He went to the hospital and one day the doctor sat down by his bed and said to him, "Rick, I've got to give it to you straight. You have terminal cancer, son, and you can't live."

Rick said, "Doctor, let me have thirty minutes alone with God." The doctor and nurses went out and left him. When he called them back his face was shining, and this is what he said, "Now, what I want to do is to stay in the hospital and have you use me as a laboratory specimen. I will keep a memo of my reactions so that my illness will help you fight this disease and cure others of it in the future." A doctor, you see, to the last; thinking not of himself.

The students would come in day by day to see Rick, and he would say, "Be a good doctor." When, finally, Rick was told he had only two or three more days to live, he said he wanted to go home to Colorado to see his loved ones and the mountains again. So they took him in an ambulance to the airport and sixty students of the medical school lined up to say good-bye to him. They wheeled him in a wheelchair down the line, and he shook hands with each one and called each one by name. Then, before he was wheeled onto the plane, he turned around and gave them a wonderful smile and said, "Remember, be good doctors."

160

They watched as the little silver plane passed into a cloud and was gone. Two days later the body of this boy was dead, but only the body. And as long as they practice medicine through the years, sixty men will remember the indomitable spirit of one whose imprisoned splendor triumphed in the face of death.

One great message of the church is that there is no adversity that, by the help of Jesus Christ, you cannot triumph over. So, into a church that can tell people this, should we not pour our hearts, our lives, our money and our love? In the course of human life we get confused, we mess things up, we destroy the purity and goodness of our lives, we suffer failure, we meet moral and spiritual defeat. But for every kind of failure or defeat, the church has a great message. I wouldn't argue about what is message number one, but I suppose the chief message of the New Testament is love. As you read the Gospels, you feel the impact of One Who is telling us to love: to love the poor, the needy, the suffering, the dispossessed, the people who are victims of prejudice; to love people generally; to love one's neighbor as oneself, not more than oneself, but as oneself, for if you don't love yourself you can't love your neighbor. If you don't esteem yourself, you won't esteem your neighbor. So, the full normality of life comes through love of God, love of self, love of others, love of life.

Also, the New Testament tells us about a wonderful transformation called the new birth. You can be born again. You can be reborn in such a way that you leave behind you all your sins, all your weaknesses, all your faults and failures. You get a fresh, new start. How would you like to live your life all over again? Wouldn't it be wonderful to go back and correct the foolish, stupid, bad things you have done? Well, you cannot do that physically, but you can do it spiritually. You can separate yourself from those things as far as the East is from the West and begin again with new power and new strength. You have to pay for past mistakes, all right—you can't get away from that—but by rebirth in Christ you can gain victory over them and go forward. This, too, is the message of the church to every man.

Not long ago a rather young minister of my acquaintance told me what a marvelous thing he thought it was to be in the ministry. You could see that he was really on fire with it. I asked him what had happened to get him so stirred up, and he told me an experience he had had.

A seventeen-year-old girl who lived in his community had asked for an interview and came in to see him. First she asked whether what she wanted to talk about would be kept confidential. He assured her, of course, that all pastoral counseling is confidential. She said, "I'm so miserable, I'm so unhappy."

The minister asked her to go ahead and tell him all about it.

"Well," she said, nervously clasping and unclasping her hands, "you know the magazines seem to tell us that what the church says about personal purity isn't so. They make light of it and you read these stories in the magazines where parents are doing the same things that the young people are doing. I wonder, is there any goodness anywhere? I was brought up," she went on, "with the idea of being a pure, clean girl. But plenty of my classmates tell me that's all out of date and old-fashioned, and the boys come along and give you a big line about how they love you and then they make demands and tell you they're not going to love you any more or date you any more unless you do what they want. I didn't want to give in, but finally I did. And now I'm in pretty deep. I don't get any fun out of it. I'm just miserable. I feel so dirty, soiled. And I'll be this way the rest of my life. I'll end up an old hag."

The minister said to her, "Honey, don't despair. Against all that stands Jesus Christ. These things have left scars on you, and those you will have to bear, but Jesus Christ can make you clean again. He can change your life."

She looked at him, he told me, just like a little child. Then he took her into the church to the altar in front of the pulpit. She knelt down and they prayed together, and the girl asked the Lord to change her, to give her rebirth. The minister was then moved to do something he had never done before; he put his hand on the girl's head and said, "Let the healing grace of Jesus Christ take away your sins and make you clean again."

"When I saw the look on that girl's face when she stood up," he said to me, "I knew why I was in the ministry. I knew why I loved it so. That girl will go straight now. I know it. How good God is."

It is my great privilege to stand in the pulpit and say to one and all that no matter what you have done, you can be different. The church can make your hopes come true. That is what it does for people. That is why people are willing to devote their prayers, their gifts, their service for the church. All of us get lost in the world, and our hopes and dreams grow dull. But in the church they are restored to us again through Jesus Chirst our Lord. The church is where your hopes come true.

162

Prayer: Our Heavenly Father, we ask Thee to bless us all and grant that all of us, through Thy wondrous church, may experience rebirth of our high ideals and dreams and hopes and so come alive again and live in Jesus Christ our Lord, for now and eternity. Amen.

How to Get Rid of Jesus

Reverend D. Martin Niemöller, D.D.

MINISTER, THE EVANGELICAL CHURCH IN GERMANY (LUTHERAN), WIESBADEN, GERMANY

In this distinguished sermon, Dr. Niemöller emphasizes the "comeback" of Christian faith today, and shows how the church and individual Christians must meet the challenge of Christ if they are to face the world courageously and successfully.

In World War I Martin Niemöller was a U-boat commander. With the rise of Hitler and Nazism he opposed totalitarianism in its restriction of personal and religious liberty. The Lutheran Church in Germany has come down from the time of Luther as a state church, and has consistently maintained the purity of its doctrine; therefore, when the Nazis attempted to silence the church, Dr. Niemöller and a number of loyal clergy of the Lutheran Church went to prison rather than compromise what they believed.

Pastor Niemöller, who had been pastor of the wealthy church of Dalhem-Berlin, was imprisoned in Dachau, and for eight years was a special prisoner of Adolf Hitler. From 1937 until he was released by the American forces in May, 1954, he endured loneliness and privation rather than submit to the Nazi system and repudiate his religious beliefs.

As soon as the war had ended, he worked ceaselessly to help rehabilitate Germany, and tried to create renewed understanding between his country and the people of England, France, Switzerland and the United States. Today he is president of the German Lutheran Church.

He received the honorary D.D. from Eden Theological Seminary in 1934, from Pine Hill Divinity School in 1946 and from the University of Göttingen in 1946. He visited the United States from December, 1946, to April, 1947, and spoke in a number of the leading cities

across the country. At that time he discussed the "guilt" of the Church in Germany and of the German state in World War II.

SERMON TWENTY-THREE

John 11:45–53

THE CHRISTIAN RELIGION is having a "comeback" these days. At least this is the general assumption in what we call the Western world, acknowledged even by those who for their part do not believe in Christ but accept religion only as the last resort in warding off materialism and the Communist ideology and in buttressing our spiritual foundations. This revival recalls the fact—for a fact it is —that our whole culture and civilization was built on Christian ideas and represents a definitely Christian tradition. Thus it is with a note of pride that we identify our Western world with the Christian world, and our Western way of life with the Christian way of life. In this "comeback" we are merely recovering what we have lost, we are preserving what we have kept and striving to bring the whole back to life.

In the Gospel story, which we have just heard as our text, the situation is different so far as Christ is concerned. Here people honestly want to get rid of Him at any cost; they are fervent about it. What the high priest Caiaphas proposes is a genuine conviction, and it becomes the conviction and the objective of all who take council with him. Surprising as it may be, this was not a conspiracy of atheists, this plan to get rid of Jesus. These planners were the religious people of their day: Pharisees and priests, the high priest himself, people who hoped for the Messiah, and who longed for the Christ. But they did not want Jesus. And the reason why they sought to get rid of Jesus is just as surprising: Jesus had raised Lazarus from the dead. That was one miracle more, and they feared that "all men will believe on him," and that the result might be that the Romans, the occupying power, would put an end to their already restricted autonomy. Jesus was becoming politically suspect, becoming a danger for the nation itself. These conspirators were not afraid of Jesus as a person. There was no reason for them to fear either His miracles or His teaching. His teaching, in its religious aspect, was not contradictory to their established religion, and His miracles were not directed against anybody. What troubled

164

their minds was consequences which might follow. If people followed Him, acknowledging Him as their master, the position of the nation over against the Roman invaders would be weakened. It was the main interest of all Jewish authorities, and of the Pharisean group in particular, to keep alive the spirit of national resistance at any cost, and it was as a threat to this interest that they had to fear the influence of the new prophet from Nazareth. He was teaching quite a different attitude and behavior toward one's enemy. He taught to resist not evil but to overcome evil by doing good. His precept was, Love your enemies; bless them that curse you, do good to them that hate you; and pray for them which despitefully use you and persecute you! This was the basis of their enmity against Jesus. Political authorities did not, and they do not, believe in the efficacy of the methods which He enjoined and demanded. On the contrary, this tactic, as they see it, will only weaken and endanger their own position.

From this point of view the miracles were extremely dangerous and threatening indeed. As long as Jesus did nothing else than teach a new way of life, a new attitude toward the enemy, He might be regarded and treated as just one among the many queer idealists who are to be found in every generation. These visionaries arise, they talk, they disappear, they vanish and are forgotten. But in Jesus Somebody was speaking with authority. This authority was being confirmed and exemplified by His deeds and it was stimulating and strengthening the confidence and trust of the multitudes. Thus it came about that the leaders of the nation and all true patriots wanted to get rid of Him! They wanted the Messiah, they wanted the Christ, but Jesus they rejected.

Now again we have to face the question of whether or not this rejection has any meaning in our own situation and to our attitude. Our Christian world is not as Christian as we think, and even our Christian Church by no means is. Do we really want Jesus? Do we actually agree and confess that He is the Christ, that He is right, right in the sense that we are bound to follow His advice and command? His words certainly have not changed. He has not revoked a single one of them. He has confirmed them by the testimony of His death. He obeyed these Himself when He ordered Peter not to use his sword for His defense and when He renounced the assistance of His Father's angels. Yet His Church has acted differently. Certainly, His Church has not adhered to His words, but has tried again and again—and is trying again and again—to be rid of them and to get rid of Him, justifying herself and her disobedience the same way as Caiaphas did, by pointing to the consequences: how can we defend ourselves and survive, if we love our enemy and venture to overcome evil by doing good?

So the Church finds herself caught in an insolvable dilemma. She is willing to confess Christ as her Master and Saviour, as the only hope she may rely upon and which she has to offer to a world in despair. But she is determined at the same time to reject Jesus and to get rid of Him. She is afraid—we are afraid—of the consequences which will follow: the Romans will come and take away both our place and nation. This then is the awkward dilemma in which we find ourselves; how can we keep Christ and yet get rid of Jesus? The entire history of the Christian Church is marked by the unceasingly repeated and continued effort to escape from this choice. This moreover is by no means the problem only of the Church; it is —is it not?—a personal problem with which each of us is struggling day by day. To be Christians and still to keep our own way, to confess Christ and yet to get rid of Jesus and of the necessity to follow Him: that is for you and me to decide. He is an obstacle each of us must encounter.

Caiaphas and his collaborators were convinced that they could solve the problem by putting Jesus to death. They thought it expedient that one man—this one man specifically—should die in order to save the nation. Our idea is practically the same: get Him out of the way and forget about Him! We have found an even better and more effective method of accomplishing the deed. Jesus stated and stressed the one great commandment, that we shall love God only and our neighbor as ourselves. But we have found a better commandment to put first: Thou shalt love thyself! This leaves us free to serve ourselves as we are inclined and to make our contribution to God and to our fellow man according to our own discretion and judgment. We are rid of Him, for His authority is no longer absolute. His authority is restricted by what we regard as the highest authority: the law of nature itself, the law of self-preservation. But how safe are we? Have we really silenced the voice of Jesus?

The act of Caiaphas, as we know, proved to be mere self-deception. The death of Jesus did not work. Or perhaps we must say: it worked too well. Are we ourselves not in the same plight that befell Caiaphas? Let me tell the story of the gallows, or more accurately the story of the sermon of the gallows. There was in front of my cell window in Dachau Concentration Camp a gallows. I often had occasion to pray for those who were hanged on it, poor souls. This gallows put a question to me: what will happen when one day they bring me to this test and wrap the rope around my neck? Will I then, with my last breath, cry out: "You criminals, you think you are justified in executing me as a criminal; but there is a Living God in heaven and he will show you!"? And then the second question followed: "What would have happened, if Jesus had died, cursing His enemies and murderers?" We know the answer: the world would be rid of Him, there then would be no Gospel, no good tidings of great joy, no salvation, no hope! Not for anyone, not for you! But —thank God—Jesus died otherwise! He did not curse His murderers, but prayed on their behalf: Father, forgive them; they know not what they do! They could not get rid of Him, for He held on and kept them in His forgiving love. His Father heard His prayer and was well pleased with His Son. So, there was no escape; this death worked too well. And there is no escape; this death marks His final victory: I have overcome the world! How overcame He the world? By overcoming hatred with love, by overcoming our evil with His good!

We strive to save our life by fighting our enemies. But Jesus says, Whosoever shall save his life shall lose it! In desperation we strive to get rid of Him. But this we cannot accomplish. He prayed for us, He died for us who are His enemies. So He has overcome our enmity, thereby setting an example for us in an undeniable way. Our way does not work, we know it, everybody knows it. Instead of scheming to get rid of Jesus and His way, we must get rid of our ways. We must yield ourselves, if we really want to live. This is what the Gospel story tells us. The words of the high priest are and were God's own word, if we have the insight to understand: Jesus should die for that nation, and not for that nation only. He should gather together in one nation the children of God that were scattered abroad.

How to get rid of Jesus? In our unregenerate state we all want to get rid of Him. He does not allow us to live as we want to live; we all sentence Him to die, to get Him out of our way. We are willing to worship Him, but we are not willing to obey Him. We consent to pay Him our reverence, but never the obedience due Him as our Master and Lord. He summons us to be His servants, His followers and friends. His is the last decisive appeal, for in dying He speaks His final word: Even My death is meant for you, you may accept Me, you may reject Me; but one thing you cannot do, you cannot get rid of Me; I remain either your Saviour or your Judge. This is the alternative left us. Jesus is the Christ! Jesus is He that was dead and liveth, and is alive forevermore!

Blessed are they who put their trust in Him; and blessed are we, if we put our trust in Him!

LOVE

Still the Greatest Thing in the World

Reverend Thomas S. Kepler, Ph.D., D.D., S.T.D.

A MINISTER OF THE METHODIST CHURCH, AND PROFESSOR OF NEW TESTAMENT LANGUAGE AND LITERATURE, OBERLIN COLLEGE GRADUATE SCHOOL OF THEOLOGY, OBERLIN, OHIO

This sermon represents Dr. Kepler's mature thinking on the doctrine and equality of love. Using the Greek words, philia, eros, and agape, he discusses the meaning of love in the New Testament as an essential part of Christian living.

Thomas Kepler was born in Mount Vernon, Iowa, in 1897, attended Cornell College, took his D.D. and his Ph.D. at Boston University, then did graduate study at Marburg University in Germany and at Cambridge University. Cornell College in Iowa conferred the D.D. upon him in 1940 and Baldwin-Wallace (Ohio) the S.T.D. in 1950. He began his professional life as a director of athletics in Rock Springs, Wyoming, was coach of athletics and teacher of mathematics in Greater Boston, then became pastor of Pawtucket Congregational Church in Lowell, Massachusetts. In 1930 he became Professor of Bible and Philosophy at Mount Union College (Ohio), then from 1934 to 1946 he was Professor of Religion and Bible at Lawrence College in Wisconsin. Since 1946 he has been Professor of New Testament Language and Literature at Oberlin College Graduate School of Theology.

He has published a great number of books and has been the editor of many others. Among those of his own writing are JESUS' DESIGN FOR LIVING, CONTEMPORARY RELIGIOUS THOUGHT, A JOURNEY INTO FAITH, THE FELLOWSHIP OF THE SAINTS, CONTEMPORARY THINKING ABOUT PAUL, PATHWAYS TO SPIRITUAL POWER, JESUS' SPIRITUAL JOURNEY—AND OURS, RELIGION FOR VITAL LIVING *and* THE BOOK OF REVELATION: A COMMENTARY FOR LAYMEN.

Dr. Kepler is one of four associate editors of THE INTERPRETER'S
DICTIONARY OF THE BIBLE, *for which he is supervising the writing of
many articles dealing with personalities or background of the New
Testament and is giving special attention to maps, photographs, and
illustrations dealing with the Holy Land, Greece, and the Mediter-
ranean area where Jesus and Paul lived and journeyed. He has edited
Francis de Sales,* THE DEVOUT LIFE; THEOLOGIA GERMANICA; *Martin
Luther,* TABLE TALK; THE JOURNAL OF JOHN WOOLMAN; *François
Fenelon,* LETTERS AND REFLECTIONS; *John Wesley,* CHRISTIAN PERFEC-
TION; *Pascal,* THOUGHTS; *Jeremy Taylor,* HOLY LIVING *and* HOLY DYING;
Lancelot Andrews, PRIVATE DEVOTIONS *and* THE SPIRITUAL RICHES OF
JOHN BUNYAN; *and* THE IMITATION OF CHRIST.

SERMON TWENTY-FOUR

"Love never ends," I Corinthians 13:8

ONE OF MY MOST DRAMATIC EXPERIENCES occurred on the evening
of December 7, 1941, when my wife and I with a group of friends
in our living room listened to Handel's *Messiah,* broadcast from the
Lawrence College chapel. We heard the beautiful music from that
oratorio—the Hallelujah Chorus, the arias, the great choruses—all
telling about the way by which the world ought to live, that of a
Messiah and His way of love. Then with a slight turn of the radio
dial we heard of the bombings at Pearl Harbor, the way of force
as the means to obtain a nation's ends. Since that evening I have
often reflected: the religious philosophies behind the events of Pearl
Harbor and Handel's *Messiah* represent the two choices we today
must face: one is the way of cultural suicide, the other is God's
plan for humanity. Every person must decide on which side he will
throw his allegiance; there is no alternative.

In 1890 Henry Drummond, in his famous essay on I Corinthians
13, called love "The Greatest Thing in the World." He developed
the theme that love is where religion is, where God is, Who Christ
is, where Christ is, where the kingdom exists. This theme was true
in 1890, it is equally valid today; *love is still the greatest thing in
the world.* Robert Southwell has vividly expressed it: "Not where
I breathe, but where I love, I live." The apostle Paul voiced the
theme even more penetratingly when he said, "If I have all faith,
so as to remove mountains, but have not love, I am nothing. If I

give away all I have, and if I deliver my body to be burned, but have not love, I gain nothing." In this age of atomic energy we are no longer speaking about love from an "armchair" in a theoretic way as "the greatest thing in the world." It is the only way of living that can save the world! Unless we solidly tie love in its various ways into the complexities of everyday living, world annihilation is our only other choice!

I

Christian love is a complex quality, with three kinds of love woven into our living. The first kind of love is *philia*. In this type of love there is a loyalty to a common ideal which binds us together. When Jesus asked Peter, "Simon, son of John, do you love me?" Peter answered three times, "Yes, Lord; you know that I love you (i.e., have *philia* for you)." Peter possessed a loyalty for his Risen Lord, and with others felt an undying allegiance to everything for which Jesus had lived and died. Through the Christian centuries Christians have had *philia* for the kingdom of God and for the Church; this *philia* has bound Christian believers into their fellowship, at the center of which has been their Lord. But *philia* is seen elsewhere in everyday living. A man who has membership in Rotary or Kiwanis, a woman who belongs to a literary club, and a student in a college fraternity or sorority are examples of individuals who have *philia*. An alumnus of a college is loyal to his alma mater; he gives of his finances to her support; he comes back with eagerness to her campus at home-coming or commencement; he sends his children to this college for their education; the spirit which binds him and the other alumni to alma mater is *philia*.

Many of us have been reared in communities which several generations ago were nonexistent. As our forefathers wended their way westward into the prairies of the United States, they built homes, a school, a church, places of business—all because within their midst there existed *philia* which solidified them around a common ideal. *Giants in the Earth,* by Raalvag, illustrates how the Scandinavians, cemented together by philia, left Minnesota to build their new homes in the Dakotas.

Today two ideologies are vying for supremacy in the world: one is Communism, the other is democracy. Communism is based on atheism with its concept of slaves as obedient to masters; democracy is based on a belief in God, where men have freedom, and in their common relationship to God as Father share brother-

170

hood with one another. This feeling of free men bound together by *philia* in a democracy is poignantly expressed in the words of Lincoln:

> Abe Lincoln was a quiet and a melancholy man.
> But when he spoke of democracy
> This is what he said: he said,
> "As I would not be a slave, so I would not be a Master.
> This expresses my idea of democracy.
> Whatever differs from this, to the extent of difference
>   is no democracy."

It is the Christian's faith that if God and freedom can be deeply ingrained within our ideology of democracy, the democratic ideal cannot be defeated—because *God* working in history cannot be defeated! Christians should share in their deep faith the words of Woodrow Wilson to one of his friends, after they had been talking, during Wilson's last illness, about the League of Nations: "Nothing can stop God!" But what God can and will do depends greatly upon the *philia* we have to the ideal of the Kingdom of God as taught and lived by Jesus Christ. With this *philia* we need to beckon again to Gamaliel's words to the early antagonizers of the Christian movement: "If this plan or undertaking is of men, it will fail; but if it is of God, you will not be able to overthrow them. You might even be found opposing God!"

II

The second kind of love is *eros*, a selfish desire of a person for value from an object which will add worth to his experience. *Eros* is sometimes associated with eroticism and a stress on sexual desire. But it can be on a high cultural plane where a person desires value for himself from friendships, music, literature, worship. William L. Stidger deeply expresses the higher meaning of *eros* in a person in these words:

> Man does not live by bread alone,
> He lives by truth and right,
> By beauty, brotherhood, and hope,
> By laughter, dreams, and light.
>
> Man lives by music and art,
> By dawns, and noons, and nights,
> By starlit skies and milky ways;
> These are the soul's delights.

171

Man lives by symphonies and psalms,
By sunsets, roses, trees;
By essays, poems, romance, love;
These are the victories.[1]

Eros is found in one's desire for learning and education. A friend of mine, one of America's leading university presidents, reread Shakespeare's plays with a new set of commentaries in one year as he traveled about this country. Why did he do this? Because within him was this *eros* by which he wished to obtain a deeper understanding of the meaning of life through the great English writer. Emily Dickinson expresses the way by which *eros* in man is satisfied through books:

There is no frigate like a book
To take us lands away,
Nor any courser like a page
Of prancing poetry.

Music, perhaps more than any other aesthetic medium, satisfies the *eros* which man has for beauty and purpose. I have been made aware of this the many times I have heard the Cleveland Symphony Orchestra play under the skilled baton of George Szell. Edna St. Vincent Millay describes this *eros* for value from music in her poem "Concert," where a girl leaves her lover to attend the symphony concert alone. Before she leaves she says to her lover,

Come now, be content.
I will come back again to you, I swear I will,
And you will know me still.
I shall be only a little taller
Than when I went.[2]

All experiences of value, which satisfy *eros* within us, make us "a little taller than when we went." As books and music make one "taller," so does one's worship of God. Every sensitive person has a deep hungering *eros* for God in his private and corporate worship, if his total selfhood is to be realized. Augustine in the first paragraph of his *Confessions* expresses this *eros* for God: "Thou madest us for Thyself, and our heart is restless, until it repose in Thee." Gamaliel Bradford put this desire for God in similar words:

[1] From "Man Does Not Live by Bread Alone" in *I Saw God Wash the World*, The Rodeheaver Hall–Mock Co., Winona Lake, Indiana.
[2] From *Collected Poems*, Harper & Brothers, by permission of Norma Millay Ellis, copyright 1923, 1950 by Edna St. Vincent Millay.

172

My one unchanged obsession
Wherever my feet have trod
Is a keen, enormous, haunting,
Never-sated thirst for God.

Jesus knew this gnawing *eros* in the heart of man when he said, "You, therefore, must be perfect, as your heavenly Father is perfect." Paul likewise felt it: "I press on toward the goal for the prize of the upward call of God in Christ Jesus." While the word *eros* never appears in the Greek in the New Testament, it is deeply woven into its pages as a part of a Christian's yearning for the divine and Christlike values of life.

III

A third and distinctive kind of Christian love is *agape*, an unselfish and redemptive love which gives value to one's environment and the persons who live there. Wherein *eros* is a selfish love to obtain value for oneself, *agape* is an unselfish love to contribute value to the objects outside of oneself: namely, to other people.

Especially in three of His parables Jesus illustrates what *agape* is like: the Prodigal Son, the lost coin, the lost sheep. The Prodigal Son was lost, "out of circulation," but after his repentance "while he was yet at a distance, his father saw him and had compassion, and ran and embraced him and kissed him." The coin in the home was "out of circulation," having neither intrinsic nor instrumental value until the woman sought and found the coin, again putting value into it. Likewise the lost sheep had no value until the shepherd found it and put value into it by rescuing it. From these parables Jesus is illustrating that at the heart of the universe God has *agape* by which He is trying to seek and to find and to put value into any of us who are willing to receive His love. Likewise, as we obey His will and become channels of His *agape,* we too in an unselfish way must seek, find, and redeem the unfortunate and lost persons in the world; in such fashion *agape* works in Christians. Paul described the features of *agape* in a Christian: "Love (*agape*) is patient and kind . . . not jealous or boastful . . . not arrogant or rude . . . not irritable or resentful . . . bears all things, believes all things, endures all things."

In Northern Italy in the Waldensian Valleys, Pastor Tullio Vinay in 1947 started a community called Agape. About this community he said: "Agape wants to be in the midst of troubled Europe as a large cross whose arms are extended toward everybody for reconciliation in the love of Christ." Should not these words depict the motive of every Christian community? In a neighborhood ought not each cross street as a symbol of the cross remind us of the arms of the cross reaching out in redeeming love through us as we live with one another?

In my study of the Christian saints I find *agape* the ethical quality of each saint, incarnate in his redemptive acts toward his fellow men: I observe it in William Law buying four milk cows to give milk to the poor children in his neighborhood; I see it in John Woolman when on August 28, 1758, he vows to eradicate the holding of slaves by Quakers; it is portrayed in the experiences of Jane Addams in founding Hull House in Chicago, and Muriel Lester in starting Kingsley Hall in London; it is dramatized in the labors of Albert Schweitzer in the Lambaréné area in Africa and of Toyohiko Kagawa in the slums of Kobe. It is clearly observed in the unselfish redemptive acts of numberless Christians in their daily living with their fellow men. *Agape* is the test of the worth of *eros* and *philia* in a Christian's life.

Agape in a Christian's life is nowhere more beautifully shown than in the life of the great New Testament scholar, Caspar Rene Gregory. Born in Philadelphia, he finished his biblical studies in Leipzig, Germany, where he remained the rest of his life as a great manuscript scholar. But he felt that intellectual labor was not enough for a Christian; he was also obligated to do something redemptive through *agape* for the unfortunate—so he chose the German laboring people as his laboratory for *agape*. When World War I began in 1914, Professor Gregory, at sixty-eight years of age, enlisted in noncombatant service to continue his ministry to the laboring man of Germany. In this labor of love he was killed by a bomb. In reviewing the life of Gregory, Martin Dibelius said that he knew of no Christian who better illustrated the words of Jesus: "Greater love (*agape*) has no man than this, that a man lay down his life for his friends."

"Love" seems to be the one "word" which today can be given in answer to the destructive forces of our era. In 1949, Elizabeth Hunter, disturbed by the fears of our atomic age, dedicated a poem to Albert Einstein, in which she wrote:

> Quick, dreamer, bring some word
> Authentic, that shall gird
> Our hearts with strength against this self-willed fate!
> We know, past time and space,

174

God moves in love and grace.

His mercy is most stern and most compassionate.

Yes, love is the one "word authentic," and it is still the greatest thing in the world! And for the Christian there are three kinds of love—*philia, eros* and *agape;* but the greatest of these is *agape!*

Man Against Himself

Reverend David B. Watermulder, D.D.

MINISTER, FIRST PRESBYTERIAN CHURCH, OAK PARK, ILLINOIS

This sermon discusses man's war within himself—the battle of the self against God, of man's drive for material success against the danger of losing his life spiritually—and the power of faith even in a power-crazy world.

David Watermulder first attracted wide attention by the strength of his preaching at the First Presbyterian Church in Watertown, New York, from 1950 to 1955. Previously he had been minister of the First Presbyterian Church in Hightstown, New Jersey, from 1945 to 1950, where he also ministered to boys at the Peddie School.

During the summer of 1953 he was exchange preacher to Great Britain, under the auspices of the National Council of Churches of America and the British Council of Churches. He has been visiting instructor in homiletics at McCormick Theological Seminary in Chicago since 1956. He is a member of the General Board, National Council of the Churches of Christ in America; of the Board of Directors, The University of Dubuque and Dubuque Theological Seminary, Dubuque, Iowa; and of the Board of Trustees, Princeton Theological Seminary, Princeton, New Jersey.

Dr. Watermulder studied at the University of Kansas and Princeton Theological Seminary; Parsons College in Fairfield, Iowa, conferred the honorary D.D. upon him. He has done further study at Union Theological Seminary in New York.

In 1953 he returned to Drew, where he is now Associate Professor of Old Testament. In addition, he has found time to head Bible study groups in various centers in New Jersey and New York, has had articles published in religious and scholarly journals, and has been in demand as a preacher in many churches of the area.

*His most important recognition to date came in December, 1955,
when the American Schools of Oriental Research in Jerusalem
awarded him a fellowship to engage in archaeological study in the
Holy Land during 1956 and 1957. In the summer of 1957 he was a
member of the archaeological team which conducted excavations at
ancient Shechem under the joint sponsorship of Drew Theological
Seminary and McCormick Theological Seminary.*

SERMON TWENTY-FIVE

> "Not many days later, the younger son gathered all he
> had and took his journey into a far country, and there he
> squandered his property in loose living. And when he
> had spent everything, a great famine arose in that coun-
> try, and he began to be in want." Luke 15:13, 14, R.S.V.

DR. KARL MENNINGER is one of the foremost psychiatrists in the
United States of America. He is also a Christian, active in the church.
In 1938 he wrote a book, *Man Against Himself*. It was a popular
interpretation of psychiatry, and still remains a much-quoted book.
It is from this book that we take the title of our sermon today.
The thesis of Dr. Menninger's book, stated by many themes and
variations, is that man is continually against himself, seeking to
destroy himself.

Says Dr. Menninger: "In the end each man kills himself in his
own selected way, fast or slow, soon or late. We all feel this, vaguely;
there are so many occasions to witness it before our eyes." He goes
on to say that our world is full of hatred, that men destroy one another, and that there is a spiritual malignancy within us. All of us
seem to have these tendencies towards self-destruction, expressed
in various ways.

It is a long distance indeed from Dr. Karl Menninger in the
twentieth century to Jesus and the Parable of the Prodigal Son. But
the message is the same in both cases. Whether it be in the pic-
turesque language of the parable or in the scientific jargon of the
psychiatrist, man can become his worst enemy. Man is against himself.

The Parable of the Prodigal Son has been called "the greatest
short story in the world." Here is a story—a very brief story—packed
with feeling, movement. It has been called the Gospel in miniature,

176

for here in a picture is the whole story of the Gospel of the grace of God. Here we see ourselves and here many of us begin to find ourselves.

You remember how it begins: "There was a man who had two sons; and the younger of them said to his father, 'Father, give me the share of property that falls to me.' And he divided his living between them. Not many days later, the younger son gathered all he had and took the journey into a far country, and there he squandered his property in loose living." There we have a picture of ourselves, for Jesus meant for the son to represent us, and the father to represent God.

I

This is the story of man against himself. It is our story. Like the younger son, we take the many blessings which God has heaped upon us and separate ourselves from God. We live in the far country of our own willfulness and self-centered desire.

And like the Prodigal Son, we probably mean well. There is no reason to think that he was a bad man when he left home. It wasn't unusual for a father to distribute his properties to his children, and to see those children use their initiative and find their ambitions fulfilled. But, much like ourselves, the young son gives all the evidences of being rather headstrong. "Give me the share of property that falls to me," he demands as he thinks of himself, quite certain of his own wisdom. Like us, he was after both success and freedom, but he had never really stopped to understand the meaning of success or freedom. And, like us, he squandered his property in loose living. The very things that were meant to build him up, tore him down. All that could have become a blessing became a curse. He was his own worst enemy; he was a man against himself.

It is a timeless picture of each of us as our blessings become our curse. The Bible begins with this picture in the matchless story of Adam and Eve—the Hebrew words for *man* and *woman*. The story of Adam and Eve is the story of everyone: made to be children of God we rebel against God and try to live without Him. God gives us freedom, and we use that freedom to have nothing to do with God! This is what the Christian really means by the word *sin*. Sin exists whenever we separate ourselves from God. *Sin* means trying to substitute ourselves for God, however subtly we do it. *Sin* means fooling ourselves into believing that we can be free if we are responsible only to ourselves. All of the little sins of life stem from this one big sin: rebelling against God's authority.

This throws a new light on sin, doesn't it? We are accustomed to think of sin solely in terms of physical and sensual abuses. But sin is basically a spiritual matter. It stems from pride, or thinking we are more important than God. Sin is not nearly so much the animal within us as it is the higher spiritual nature within us rebelling against God and asserting independence.

This helps us understand "original sin." *Original sin* means that this desire to assert ourselves above God and have our own way is common to all of us. Adam, the representative man, tried to make himself more important than God, and we try to do the same. Here is where we begin to understand our true selves. "All have sinned and come short of the glory of God." All of us are like the Prodigal Son in finding that the very gifts of life which were meant to be a blessing become a curse. All of us, like the Prodigal Son, take our journey to a far country to escape from God, only to find that we become enslaved by those very desires that drive us on.

II

Where is the far country? We don't need to be told; we've worn a smooth path into its regions. Each can chart another road which takes us there.

Let it be noted in passing that *the far country is that place where we can't stand success.* Do we recognize the fact that a good many people simply cannot stand success? They are couples and families who have more than they ever dreamed they would have; who have advanced further than they ever supposed possible; who are experiencing a higher standard of living and have more things at their command than they ever imagined. They are part of a more complicated world than they ever dreamed possible. They have everything they wanted, and they can't stand it.

Shakespeare's whole story of Macbeth is the story of a man who could not stand success. He tells his wife that the witches which tempted him to a great crime "met me in the day of success." The witches would not have bothered him if he weren't going places and weren't greedy for greater success. But his ambitions were stronger than his principles and he was ready to pay any price to fulfill them. After he commits his crime he declares, "Had I but died an hour before this chance, I had lived a blessed time."

That is a terrible thing to say, but we all say it when we get

178

into the far country and separate ourselves from God. What tragedy that such a good world can become such a terrible curse, that the blessings of ambition, prosperity and achievement can become the demons which destroy us! This is sin. This is the far country. This is man against himself.

Says Dr. Menninger, "A large number of people demonstrate that they cannot endure success. They seem to be able to succeed in everything but succeeding." This is the story of the Prodigal Son, isn't it? The man demanded his share of the blessing. Apparently it was a big share because we read that the father lived on a big estate with many hired servants. When the son's wish was granted, he had everything and he went away with everything, but it turned out to be nothing. Life was too much for him.

A letter appeared in one of our news magazines recently, commenting on the death of one of our most successful business tycoons. This man of success, head of one of our nation's largest industries, friend of the influential business interests throughout the country, took his life a few weeks ago. The letter remarked that this had to be the inevitable consequence of a man whose life became so totally absorbed in his success that he became its slave. Success relentlessly drove him to his own destruction.

In this particular case, the man ended his life rather dramatically with a shotgun. But what shall we say about the rest of us to whom Dr. Menninger referred? Those who are so set on success that they are too busy to live, only to come to the day of old age and look back on glorious years which have slipped through their fingers and disappeared forever? Or those who are so immersed in getting ahead that they become too irritable to be loved or to love? Or those who are so consumed in getting and acquiring that they have lost one of the greatest gifts God has given to anybody—the capacity to care, to show concern and compassion toward someone else? Or those who are so involved in this mad pace of life that they need sleeping pills to sleep and stimulants to awaken? Or those who are so afraid to face the stark realities of their situation that they drown themselves in drink and try to live in a dream world rather than face what must be faced?

A recent book, entitled *The Lawless Decade*, presents a pictorial history of our country after the First World War. What prosperity, what gaiety, what crime—everywhere! While we went wild, the rest of the world seethed. We can look back on it now. We're far enough away from it to know that there were ten, fifteen or twenty precious years when the good Lord had given us the blessings of creation which we directed toward ourselves and our own self-destruction.

Looking back on the roaring twenties we can see how we didn't know how to stand success, nor did we know what to do with peace and plenty. We're too close to the decade following the second war which grew out of that era, but who is to say that we have known how to use the blessings which have been given to us? When we separate the blessings of life from the God who gives them, we find ourselves in the far country.

> If, drunk with sight of power, we loose
> Wild tongues that have not Thee in awe . . .
> Lord God of hosts, be with us yet,
> Lest we forget—lest we forget.

III

Not only in our inability to stand success do we take our journey into the far country. We also journey into that waste land away from God *when we become mixed up about what really matters, and our standards disappear.* Winston Churchill wrote a novel called *A Far Country* which represented a land where there was the loss of standards and ideals. It happened to the Prodigal Son. At home, life stood for certain responsibilities and attitudes. While life had its obligations, it also had its dignity. He threw that away when he left; he thought he was liberating his soul. He found that he became the slave of the worst kind of tyranny.

It's not easy to hold to standards and ideals in any generation, but it becomes doubly hard in a generation like ours when one age is dying and another is coming to birth. Since the last war we have come to think in terms of nuclear weapons and total destruction, to say nothing of adventure into outer space. Since the war, "the organization man" has emerged full-blown. No longer is the salient characteristic of the American one of individuality, courage and restlessness. Now it is group belongingness, crowd culture, and security —what David Riesman in his book *The Lonely Crowd* calls an "other-directed" culture, where we make sure that we are not different and that we agree with the corporation and the crowd. Suddenly we have become terribly sensitive to group approval, and are likely to be branded as traitors if we do not think and dress and act exactly as everyone else does. The words of Peter, "We must obey God rather than men," have real meaning for us in this day when business and social pressures try to make us conform until all individuality is gone.

But how can we obey God if we don't know Him? How can we know Him if we don't take the time to let our childish notions of Him become mature? H. G. Wells tells of an Indian prince who wanted to erect a lovely memorial for his dead wife. He had the best artist in the land carve a beautiful alabaster tomb so exquisite that many people came to visit it. Still it wasn't enough, so the prince had a lovely pavilion built over the tomb, and it became the most famous monument in all India. For a time this satisfied the prince, but he felt that something even finer had to be built. Finally, he planned the most beautiful mausoleum the world had ever seen. It was built over the tomb, with high vaulted ceilings and beautiful landscaping surrounding it. At last, the memorial seemed adequate to express his feelings, but still he felt an unrest. Pacing the high galleries of the mausoleum, it suddenly dawned on him what else was needed. Calling in his architect he pointed down to the original tomb of his wife still standing in the middle of the marble floor, and said to the architect, "Remove that thing, for it is a blemish on the beauty of this place."

We become so absorbed in the structures we create, whether they be for business interests or family life or social pleasure, that before long we have forgotten the purpose for which these things exist. We simply go on creating more massive structures, forgetting what life, with its business, family, and society, is for. We are indeed in the far country when we forget who we are, or why we are, or what life is for.

IV

In so many ways, which we could sit down and catalogue out of our personal experiences, we have wandered into the far country. At the base of all these wanderings is the fact that many of us have lost the power of the Christian faith. Nowhere is man more against himself, nowhere is he his own worst enemy more than *when he relies on hate instead of love.* As he heaps out his hate, revenge, unforgiveness and bitterness toward other people, he denies himself the blessings which God has given His children.

Medical men are quick to tell us of the effect of hate upon the physical system. Hatred, unforgiveness, revenge, soon take their toll upon our emotional systems. Soon our nervous systems are affected until our physical resistance is weakened. When illness strikes we are incapable of throwing it off; we have not allowed the healing powers to do their work in our bodies. Hate kills. Hate destroys. Yet we employ it as though it were our friend and weapon.

Hate is the far country because God is love. If God ever had full reason to retaliate with hate, it was at the cross. But He responded in love. We see the same love in the father of the Prodigal. If any man had a right to denounce his son and never see him again, he did. But the father ran to meet him, threw his arms around him and kissed him.

What is love except the way we express our faith? What is love except faith in action, faith at work? We begin to find the miracle of faith and feel its power when we express ourselves with Christian love, which means we identify ourselves with the other fellow, understand his situation, look at life through his eyes, and respond to him with a loving concern. Then something happens to that other person, something happens to that bad situation, and something happens to us. A redeeming power, as real as the power that makes grass green, comes into life and begins to work. Then we know we are a part of God's redeeming process within the world.

It was this kind of love that the Prodigal Son threw away when he went to the far country. At last he found himself living among the swine. Thus do we find ourselves in our pigpens of pampered prejudice, self-martyrdom, self-assertion. With hatred and an unforgiving spirit we build our pigpens in the far country.

v

Not only as we rely on hate instead of love, but *when we refuse to accept the love of God for ourselves,* do we end up in the far country. God surrounds us with spiritual resources, but we refuse them or ridicule them. When we become incapable of accepting God's gifts we have wandered into the far country without knowing it.

Do you know what I mean? We may become so pleased with what *we can achieve* and what *we can do* that we are deceived into thinking that even our faith is of our own manipulation. God becomes a little toy which we push around for our pleasure or satisfaction. Even good Christians who ought to know better become victims of a "faith" like this.

We are proud of our achievements, and we want to be self-sufficient. But we are not the creators of life, we are the created! There is no way we can feel the arms of faith enfolding us and giving us the poise and power we need, except the way of humility in the presence of God. *"To have faith"* doesn't mean feverishly to work at a project of doing in the church or the community. *"To have faith"* does not mean to grin and bear it under terrible circum-

182

stances. *"To have faith"* does not mean to devise some stoic philosophy of life so that we can take it.

To have faith means to put ourselves in the hands of God because we are His children and He is our Father, and to let Him hold us up where we are unable to stand by ourselves. To have faith means to accept the promises of God as a child accepts the love of a parent.

Moreover, to have faith means to express toward other people the same feeling that God has expressed toward us. It means to try to understand why they are the way they are, and to see life through their eyes. This is love, Christian love. The Bible tells us that God is love. This kind of love is nothing but faith in action.

To have faith means to return to God as the Prodigal returned to the father and say, "I am not worthy of thy blessings, but here I am. Do with me what you want to, where you want to, how you want to. I make no claims, save that I look to you for what I need. Do what you will." To have faith means to surrender self and situation to God.

And then, to have faith is to find Him greeting us as He greeted the Prodigal Son! He greets us, as we are and where we are: not after we have succeeded in overcoming our difficulties, nor after we have done some valiant good work in our community, but as we come back to Him with the stench of the pigpen still on our bodies, clothed in all our false pride and failure.

To have faith is to feel Him throw His arms around us and dress us in His mercy and lead us back home. We have been homeless, homesick, and now we are home! We may have been "man against himself." We may have been our own worst enemy. Through the love of God in Christ all of this has passed away and we have become new people, living in a new world. Now we are sons of God and if God be for us, who can be against us?

To have faith is to hear Him say to us, "This my son was dead and is alive again. He was lost and is found." God give us the grace to leave our far country and find the Father longing to welcome us back home!

> Just as I am! Thou wilt receive,
> Wilt welcome, pardon, cleanse, relieve;
> Because Thy promise I believe,
> O Lamb of God, I come!

The Case Against Parental Delinquency

Reverend R. J. Robinson, Th.D., D.D.

PASTOR, FIRST BAPTIST CHURCH, AUGUSTA, GEORGIA

This sermon combines timeliness, spiritual insight, knowledge of city conditions, and an interest in parents, children, education, and community welfare. It is a powerful treatment of a difficult theme—delinquency, adult and juvenile—a problem which plagues nearly every city and town in our country today.

Robert Jackson Robinson is minister of historic First Baptist Church of Augusta, Georgia, a church of 3,200 members, where the Southern Baptist Convention was organized in 1845. He studied at Baylor University, Waco, Texas; Southwestern Seminary, Fort Worth, Texas; and Temple University, Philadelphia, Pennsylvania; then he did additional graduate study at the University of Edinburgh, Scotland. He obtained his Th.D. from Southwestern Seminary and a D.D. from Howard Payne College, Brownwood, Texas.

He has preached in a thousand churches in the United States in the last fifteen years, averaging 100,000 miles of traveling a year, has studied and preached three times in Europe and the Holy Land, conducted a Crusade in the Hawaiian Islands, preached and visited mission points in South America, and spoke at the Baptist World Alliance Youth Congress in Rio de Janeiro.

While at Baylor University, he was all-American basketball player from 1946 to 1948, winner of the Outstanding Athlete award in 1947 and a member of the 1948 Olympic basketball team.

More than eighteen hundred new members have been received into First Baptist Church during his six-year ministry. More converts were baptized this past year than in any previous year in the church's illustrious 139-year history. Such crowds attend on Sundays that two morning services are imperative and there are three Sunday worship hours.

SERMON TWENTY-SIX

"And, behold, Cushi came; and Cushi said, Tidings, my lord and king [David]; for the Lord hath avenged thee this day of all them that rose up against thee. And the king said unto Cushi, Is the young man Absalom safe? And Cushi answered, The enemies of my lord the king, and all that rise against thee to do thee hurt, be as that young man is. And the king was much moved, and went up to the chamber over the gate and wept: and as he went, thus he said, O my son Absalom, my son, my son Absalom! would God I had died for thee, O Absalom, my son, my son!" II Samuel 18:31-33

ORDINARILY I enjoy preaching, but frankly, I wish that I did not feel compelled to deliver this message.

For some time juvenile delinquency has been an acute national problem. Now it presses upon us in harsher fashion, constituting a real and powerful menace to the welfare of our country.

The current upsurge in juvenile delinquency that we are witnessing began in 1948. From then until the present the increase in population of the nation's children in the age group between ten and seventeen years has been 8.1%. In the same period the number of children in serious trouble increased seven and one-half times as rapidly as the population growth of that age-span.

By 1960 this country will have a greatly increased population of young people between the ages of ten and seventeen. If the rate of juvenile delinquency also continues its upward trend, it is estimated that no less than 1,500,000 children will be in grave trouble with the police in 1960.

The offenses which children commit range from truancy to murder. The Uniform Crime Reports for the United States published by the Federal Bureau of Investigation show that last year a total of 53.6% of the persons arrested for auto theft were juveniles. Nearly half, 49.3%, of all persons arrested for burglary were not yet eighteen years old. Juveniles comprised 50.6% of those arrested for crimes against property. (Such crimes include: robbery, burglary, larceny, auto theft, embezzlement and fraud, buying and receiving stolen property, forgery, and counterfeiting.)

In 1955 arrest of persons under eighteen years of age increased 2.3% to include 269,831 youths, while arrests of adults decreased 1.9%.

Most of us knew these facts as mere cold statistics, unimportant and highly impersonal.

Then the scene of action moved closer to home. Rumblings began to come from the capital city of Georgia. Atlanta was having her troubles! Broken windows, chain whippings, and deadly speeding became fashionable as more and more teen-agers were getting into trouble. Authorities threw up their hands in desperation, admitting their inability to cope with the matter.

Several meetings were held in schools and churches with civic, educational and church leaders having their say.

Out of it all Atlanta invoked a midnight curfew as a weapon in the war they are waging against juvenile delinquency. Atlantans under eighteen have been ordered off the streets by midnight. The police are "To question, report, and if necessary, lock up any juvenile disobeying the order." This police curfew followed a recommendation by Fulton County Grand Jury which recently investigated Atlanta's alarming and much publicized outbreak of crime among juveniles.

Still, I hoped that this sermon would not be necessary, but this problem moved still closer.

I have a letter in my file from the managing editor of the *Augusta Chronicle,* Mr. Chris Brady, who says, "A preliminary study in the problem of juvenile delinquency in the Augusta area indicates the problem is critical and no solution is in sight. I would greatly appreciate your views on the subject in general, and specifically on what you think should be done to combat the growing problem."

So we are faced with it! The problem of juvenile delinquency confronts every thinking Augustan.

This morning, without any fear or favor, I am going to place the blame exactly where it belongs. We are not faced with a problem of juvenile delinquency, rather parental delinquency. Our problem is not the teen-agers and youth, but adults and parents!

Face the facts! No less a person than John Edgar Hoover declares: "In twenty-five years as director of the Federal Bureau of Investigation I have found that juvenile criminals are generally the product of neglect and improper training. The actions of the majority of them were and are directly related to the conduct of their parents. The harvest of juvenile delinquency is reaped from seeds planted by adult delinquents."

Augusta school authorities and community leaders are doing and will do their utmost with this situation. This is not a time for church people to be silent! Juvenile delinquency, yea parental delinquency, is a Christian problem. Who can remain mute in such an hour?

Listen again to J. Edgar Hoover from an April 25, 1955, Crime Report from Washington: "The continuing flood of immorality and crime on the part of the youth of America accompanies an all too evident substitution of a secular, materialistic philosophy for our historic reliance upon Divine guidance which has been the cornerstone of our democracy. The teachings of God, if followed, will prevent criminality. The stabilizing force of religion is needed today more than ever before. A child who has been taught to respect the laws of God will have little difficulty respecting the laws of man."

To me, the entire difficulty is reminiscent of a great drama from the Bible.

The story of Absalom's rebellion is one of the most exciting yet saddest tragedies in human history. Absalom with his stately form, his flowing hair, his pride and cruel tiger heart is not the central figure of the drama; rather, King David.

When Absalom rebelled against his father, David's forces were far inferior in number to Absalom's army. So David divided his soldiers in three groups and met Absalom at three different points. The battle is reported to have taken place in the Wood of Ephraim. It probably occurred in a wood in Gilead. King David had the advantage of choosing his ground and was a great military leader with able generals.

The aged king was prepared to take part in the battle, believing that his presence would be helpful to his men. His people would not allow the risk.

There was a great slaughter that day as twenty thousand men died. David remained behind the lines eagerly awaiting news about the tide of affairs and concerning the well-being of his son.

Absalom's troops began to fall back; next they broke and ran. Absalom does not appear to have made any attempt to rally his followers. Riding on a mule in haste to escape, he probably plunged into some part of the wood where his hair came in contact with the mass of prickly oak. Struggling to make a way through it, Absalom only entangled his hair more hopelessly in the thicket. Then as he raised himself in the saddle to free himself, his mule went from under him and left Absalom caught, maddened by pain and raging at the absurdity of his plight.

Absalom's sad hour had come. General Joab came upon the scene and thrust three darts through Absalom's heart. Then ten armor-bearers slashed and mutilated his handsome figure. Finally the body was cast into an unmarked grave.

Now the son of Zodak the priest offered to carry the news to David. He came into the presence of the king but was afraid to reveal the facts of the death of Absalom. Up rushed the Cushite who broke the tidings. Whereupon this broken-hearted father cried, "O my son Absalom, my son, my son Absalom! would God I had died for thee, O Absalom, my son, my son!"

David's grief was for the dead, but more. It was the grief of a conscience-stricken man. He grieved to lose a son; he grieved to lose a son in rebellion; he grieved because he knew that the rebellion was a direct result of his living.

Events which had happened years before in David's life testified against the king in this sad hour. David had violated domestic sanctity, had taken another man's wife and sent that man to his death. With the coming of Bathsheba there came to his home strife, hatred and division. It is a terrible picture of perpetual quarrels and bloodshed in a family.

The worst tragedy of all was that as his entire household rotted in sin, David had no power to stop it. His hand was paralyzed! For had not he himself been the first and chief transgressor? He had sowed to the wind of lust, and now the whirlwind of Absalom's rebellion was upon him. David's heart cry, "O Absalom, my son, would God I had died for thee," was too late. So it may be with parents and children today.

Our young are chips off the old block. They are the result of what we make them. Of course, there are exceptions to this rule. There have been cases where, in spite of the influence of Christian homes and Christian training, a child develops a defiant attitude and deliberately chooses to go wrong, sometimes even experiencing a fiendish thrill out of hurting loving parents. This, I am glad to say, is unusual; and I repeat, it is the exception to the rule. Juvenile delinquency exists as a result of parental delinquency. Parental delinquency takes two forms:

First, the form of neglect. Modern psychologists are practically unanimous in speaking about the importance of tender love and care to the well-being of a child. "T L & C," as they put it, is imperative in the development of proper personality traits.

I had the unhappy chore recently of trying to help a family where a thirteen-year-old boy had gotten into serious trouble. He had robbed a man and stolen a car. Prying into the reason for this, I found that both father and mother worked and were seldom at home. They neglected their son. Whenever they said anything to him it was in a harsh tone, punctuated by cursing. Repeatedly the parents slapped the child's face.

Last week a nurse showed me a patient in the University Hospital. I felt sick at heart as I viewed a thirteen-month-old child that weighed less than twelve pounds. The reason for this discrepancy in weight was nothing but unadulterated neglect! The father and mother simply failed to feed the child.

Neglectful treatment like this horrifies most of us, but what about more subtle neglect of which we must plead guilty? We fail to feed their need for security, and might as well slap the faces of our offspring as ignore them.

I am told that a recent poll reveals that the average professional man in America gives his children only three to five minutes of undivided attention per day. What an accusation!

Second, the form of overindulgence. This week popular Bishop Fulton J. Sheen was interviewed at the Atlanta airport, and he puts his finger on this when he maintained that juvenile delinquency is the result of the current freedom from restraint. He stated that to have a tame horse, the colt must be restrained. Americans have forgotten how to say "no" to their children, he declared.

This past week a fine schoolteacher described to me the hostile parents who had practically attacked her in censuring her for giving the pupils not too much homework, but any homework at all. Their accusation was that the children did not have enough time for all their social functions if they had to study. I tell you that it is time for some Augusta parents to stop and take stock. If your children are in that fix, they have too much social life and you need to cultivate the fine art of saying "no." Begin with the church and school affairs, doing right by them. If other time exists, well and good. Otherwise, stop worrying about your child participating in every affair in town. Use the bridle! Learn to answer in the negative.

Our children did not ask to be born, and if they are unwanted, overindulged or neglected, it is not their fault, it is our fault. Then what are we to do? The problem of parental delinquency needs much prayer and thought, but to begin with:

We need to trust in God and teach our children this faith. The place where discipline begins is at home. The schools and churches can help, but the parents must take the lead. To do this many homes must make drastic changes. Actually, the home situation will never be what it ought to be unless we have God at the core.

The 1955 Congressional Record, page 1991, contains this statement by President Eisenhower; says he: "Only Christianity perpetually renewed is equal to the challenge of today's youthful tyrants."

We need to nurture our children in discerning right from wrong.

189

This presupposes the fact that we ourselves are capable of making such choices and have high ideals. Can there be a better place for this to be done than in the churches of our community?

Again I quote from the Director of the F.B.I., who asks and answers this question: "Shall I make my child go to Sunday School and church?" with a resounding affirmative. "What do we do when Junior announces that he is not going to take a bath? He bathes, does he not? Then why all this timidity in the realm of spiritual guidance? What shall we say to Junior when he announces that he does not like to go to Sunday School and church?" Hoover says that is easy to answer. "Tell him in our house, we all go to Sunday School and church, and Junior, that includes you."

Then we need to set the right example. Recently, one of the boys here at First Baptist, and if I were to call his name almost everyone present would know him, exclaimed to me in despair, "I don't care about my father's position. I don't care about his money. I don't care about a beautiful home. I only wish that Daddy could be decent. I just wish he would stay sober and live right so I could hold my head up among my friends at school." To you in this sanctuary this morning such a testimony is terrible, but more and more children are saying it, or ought to.

You need not only to see that your child gets to Sunday School and church, but you need to bring the child yourself. My heart aches when I see cars pull up in front of our church after Sunday School, and parents come by to pick up their children. How will a child ever come under conviction and be converted unless he comes to the worship service, and how will he come to the worship service unless parents dress, come and bring him?

I know of a father that learned his lesson about the example that he was setting for his child the hard way. He was living haphazardly, taking his child to Sunday School and church occasionally. One day this father was puttering around in the yard and had taken off his shoes, which were loafer-style, and put on some old work shoes. As he was working in the back yard and striding along, he thought he heard a noise and looked over his shoulder and found his young son walking in his loafers, trying to stretch his little legs out far enough to step in the tracks his father was making in the damp soil. The truth flashed home to that parent, and needless to say, that father's example was completely transformed.

Young people, live right! Parents, wake up! Let us stop this

190

problem before it becomes worse. Wake up! Wake up! before your broken-hearted cry becomes, "O my son Absalom, my son, my son Absalom! would God I had died for thee, O Absalom, my son, my son!"

Christianity and Racial Tensions

Reverend Edward Hughes Pruden, Ph.D., D.D.

MINISTER, FIRST BAPTIST CHURCH, WASHINGTON, D.C.

This sermon on the race problem is clear, fair and well-done. It tackles the whole matter from the standpoint of Christ, makes a dynamic presentation of a subject needing study, prayer and all the religion, wisdom, patience, love and good judgment men of our time of all races possess. We are proud to present Dr. Pruden's courageous discourse.

Born in Chase City, Virginia, he was educated at the University of Richmond, Southern Baptist Theological Seminary, and Yale University, and at the University of Edinburgh, Scotland, where he received his Ph.D.

He has had pastorates at First Baptist Church, Petersburg, Virginia, and has been at First Baptist Church, Washington, D.C., since 1936.

He was guest professor of English for one year in the University of Shanghai, China, has been president of the American Baptist Convention, the Washington Federation of Churches, the District of Columbia Baptist Convention and the American Baptist Foreign Mission Society. He is a member of Executive Committees of the Baptist World Alliance and the Southern Baptist Convention; the Board of Managers of the American Baptist Foreign Mission Society; and the Boards of Trustees of the University of Richmond and the University of Shanghai, China.

He has been awarded the honorary D.D. by the University of Richmond, and is a member of Phi Beta Kappa, University of Richmond.

He is author of INTERPRETERS NEEDED *(1951) and has made numerous contributions to religious books and magazines. He was the President's pastor during Harry S. Truman's administration.*

191

THE SUBJECT with which we are dealing this morning is one which usually arouses deep emotional responses. We should therefore approach it in that spirit of love and humility to which Paul refers when he wrote: "For I say, through the grace given unto me, to every man that is among you, not to think of himself more highly than he ought to think; but to think soberly, according as God hath dealt to every man the measure of faith" (Romans 12:3); and "Do nothing from selfishness or conceit, but in humility count others better than yourselves" (Philippians 2:3, R.S.V.).

I have no desire to be controversial. As is the case with most people, I much prefer to be affable and agreeable; to say the thing that will be acceptable to the largest possible number of people. That is human nature! The minister of Jesus Christ at his best, however, must be the prophet of God, and therefore is not at liberty to follow his own inclinations. He must study the current scene carefully and prayerfully, and then attempt by all possible means to bring the will of God to bear upon all contemporary problems.

The Church of Christ cannot afford to be silent amidst turmoil and discord. The question we ask this morning is the question Zedekiah, the king, asked of Jeremiah, in the long ago: "Is there any word from the Lord?" and Jeremiah answered: "There is." We, too, believe that God has a word for us in the midst of our national crisis. I have prayed very earnestly that He would speak that word through me today.

What I shall have to say is addressed to Christians—those who have acknowledged their need of a Saviour, and are seeking that spiritual rebirth by which we become new creatures. To those who are not Christians, any plea for humility, patience and genuine brotherhood is to no avail. Paul said that *before* he became a Christian he loved certain things and hated other things; but *after* he became a Christian and received Christ into his heart, the things he once hated he now loved, and the things he once loved, he now hated.

Not only do I address myself to Christians, but I trust that I am speaking to Christians who recognize the incompleteness of their religious experience. Not one of us has attained to the fullness of the life in Christ. At a midweek service a number of years ago, we departed from our usual procedure and asked members of the congregation to share with us the problems they were facing, in the hope that we could help them through prayer and encouragement to find solutions to those problems. Finally, one of our older deacons got up and said: "I think some of you know how difficult I can be at times; and how hard it is to get along with me under certain circumstances. But," he said, "you should have seen me thirty years ago." And then he went on to say, in true humility, that while he had not reached the ultimate goal he was seeking, nevertheless, in the intervening years God had led him step by step into a more Christian spirit. All of us are incomplete, unfinished Christians. Let us keep this in mind regarding race relations and all other difficult problems with which the human spirit is confronted.

I am also speaking this morning as a Southerner whose grandfather was a slave-owner, and whose boyhood hero was Robert E. Lee. I am speaking, too, as a Southerner whose three children attend integrated schools. Two of them have had Negro teachers for whom they have great admiration and respect. And as a Southerner, I speak against the background of two specific declarations made by our Southern Baptist Convention, both of which accepted the Supreme Court decision as the law of the land and called upon all our people to conduct themselves in the spirit of Christ. I am also speaking against the background of the fact that all six of our Southern Baptist Theological Seminaries are integrated. Negro students are received in all of them.

As a Southerner, and as a Christian, I recognize that extremists on both sides of the question have created a great deal of trouble which might have been avoided. Politicians on both sides of the question have sought to make political capital out of it. And some individuals have seen in such a controversy a chance to put themselves in the limelight, and advance their own personal fortunes. Such things, however, should not deter men of good will from trying to discover spiritually constructive means by which such a problem can be solved.

Let me suggest that we keep several things in mind. Consider first, that *as Christians, all of us are committed to the spiritual principle of human dignity and the sacredness of personality.* I don't believe there is a Christian in the world who would deny these vital concepts. Even the Psalmist, before the time of Christ, asked the question, "What is man?" and answered his own question: "Thou hast made him a little lower than the angels, and hast crowned him with glory and honor." Not *some* men, but *all* men, are born into this exalted estate. Wherever Christianity has gone, the dignity

193

of man has been recognized and practiced. Women have been given opportunities and privileges they have never known before. Children have been recognized and protected as never before. Lepers and outcasts, who were looked upon as the scum of the earth, have been taken into the fellowship of the concerned and ministered to in love and mercy. *All* men have received a higher status because of the concept of man which comes to us out of our Christian faith. And this concept of man must influence our relationship with all sorts and conditions of men, regardless of race, color or nationality.

Our Lord told the story of the good Samaritan for the purpose of illustrating that our mercy and good will should be extended not only to an inner circle of congenial persons, but to those also who occupy areas far removed from our own. And when He spoke of children, He said: "Rather than offend one of these little ones, it were better for a man that a millstone were hanged about his neck, and that he were cast into the midst of the sea." Christ was not speaking only of *white* children!

In the second place, let us never forget that our religion requires of us more than one finds in others. Jesus said to the Hebrews: "What do you more than others?" the inference being that they were committed to certain spiritual ideals and principles, and therefore more was expected of them. The Christian can never sink to the level of the average, popular opinion of men. He must espouse and defend certain exalted ideals which come to him out of his faith, and which he cannot in honesty deny. The Christian faith carries with it certain inescapable imperatives. It requires of us a certain quality of thought and spirit which is not to be found in others who do not share such a faith.

In the third place, let us remember that it isn't easy to be a Christian. Following Christ goes counter to many natural tendencies with which we were born. Following Christ sets us apart from the man in the street, who is untouched and uninfluenced by the Christian Gospel. Paul, speaking to the early Christians, said to some of them: "Are you not behaving like ordinary men?" the inference being that they had no right to behave like ordinary men, for they possessed an extraordinary faith and experience. It is *hard* to be a Christian!

And let us keep in mind, too, that our immediate reactions are hardly ever *entirely* Christian. Though we are professing Christians, we're still in the thick of the spiritual struggle between the spiritual man and the natural man. Paul bears testimony to this in a bit of spiritual autobiography, when he tells us: "What I *would* do, I do not, and what I would *not* do, I do." "Every day," he said, "I struggle to keep my body under." These words were not written before he became a Christian, but after he had received Christ into his heart. Never assume that your immediate reactions are wholly Christian, but test them and try them against the norm of the spirit and life of Jesus Christ.

Remember also that it is practically impossible to put ourselves in another's place. How easy it is to say, "If I were a Negro I would do this, and that, and the other; I would be patient, I would wait, I would not insist on anything"; but how do you *know* what you would do, since you are *not* a Negro? It is simple enough for us to say, "Why did this matter have to be hastened? We were making progress; one of these days it would all have been worked out calmly and peacefully." That reaction is fine for *us*, but suppose *your* child were being adversely affected; his self-respect being violated by the impact of a social order which treats him as a second-class citizen? Could you then be as patient as you are now? The Golden Rule is admired and quoted by all of us, but frequently we forget its practical application: "Do unto others as you would have them do unto you."

Still again, let us be assured that if we do what is right we can leave the consequences in the hands of God. We are reminded of the old story of the ship coming into the harbor in the midst of a great storm, when the waves cast it upon the rocks, and it was in danger of being beaten to pieces. The captain of the Coast Guard called his men together and said: "You must go out and bring the people in before they are drowned." One of the sailors said: "Captain, we may *reach* the ship, but I doubt if we'll ever get back." To which the captain replied: "That isn't your business. As a member of the Coast Guard, when people are in danger, it is your duty to go to them. Whether or not you get back is an entirely different matter altogether." Our duty as the children of God is plain. Any consequences which may follow in the wake of doing His will as we see it will be cared for in His own way by an infinite, merciful, wise God. We can afford to leave the consequences with Him.

Then, finally, while most of us believe that kindness and brother-hood cannot be legislated, nevertheless we must recognize that there are times when laws serve a most useful purpose in the area of guaranteeing human rights. When Paul was arrested in a Roman city, his captors were on the point of thrusting him into prison, subjecting him to severe persecution, and perhaps even death, when suddenly they were reminded that he was a Roman citizen, and that under Roman law he had certain rights which could not be violated. Instantly the Roman soldiers changed their attitude. They had no disposition to show Paul mercy; they were not inclined to be kind and thoughtful; but they were under law, and because they were under law, Paul got a fair trial and decent treatment.

We have labor laws in the United States to protect the working man. They would never have been necessary if Christian people had exerted their influence. But almost every advantage the laboring man has won has been under legal pressure; not because people were kind-hearted or generous. Now, of course, almost everybody agrees that these laws are just and right. In the beginning, however, they were vigorously opposed by almost everyone who occupied a place of leadership in the realm of industry. It would be better if we were governed by conscience and humanitarian impulses, but until the consciences of men have been touched by the Holy Spirit of God, and the humanitarian impulses of men are sufficient to guarantee to every man that which is due him, we shall need certain legal decrees by which all men are protected.

May God give us grace to live calmly in the midst of confusion; graciously in the midst of cruelty; and constructively in the midst of chaos. Peter, on the housetop at Joppa, saw the vision of God, and heard the words of the Almighty: "That which I have cleansed, call not thou unclean." What every man needs is the ability to hear the voice of God, and to acquire the spirit of humility by which we may follow His will wherever it may lead. "Love suffereth long, and is kind."

God-Fearing Leaders

Irwin Jacob Lubbers, Ph.D., Litt.D., LL.D.

PRESIDENT, HOPE COLLEGE, HOLLAND, MICHIGAN, AND MEMBER OF
THE REFORMED CHURCH IN AMERICA

This sermon highlights the quest for firm ground in political and national life and emphasizes the need for authority—proper author-

*ity that does not abuse its power or the people under its rule. The
Christian way, Dr. Lubbers shows, is the way to victorious living.*

*Irwin Jacob Lubbers is a layman of the Dutch Reformed Church
and a college president. He was born in Cedar Grove, Wisconsin;
attended Wisconsin Memorial Academy, Hope College, Western
Theological Seminary, and Columbia University; and took his Ph.D.
at Northwestern University. He received three doctorates in 1945:
the LL.D. from Central College and the Litt.D. from both Hope
College and Rutgers.*

*He was in the U.S. Army Air Force in 1918; lecturer in English
at Voorhees College, Vellore, India, from 1919 to 1922; instructor
in English at Hope College from 1923 to 1929; instructor in Education at Northwestern University in 1929 and 1930; assistant to the
president and instructor in Psychology and Education at Carroll
College, Helena, Montana, from 1930 to 1934; and president of
Central College, Pella, Iowa, from 1934 to 1945. He became president
of Hope College in 1945.*

Three of his writings have attracted attention: COLLEGE ORGANIZA-
TION AND ADMINISTRATION, ARE COLLEGE ENDOWMENTS SAFE? *and*
WHO CONTROLS THE LIBERAL ARTS COLLEGES?

*This layman's clear-cut faith and emphasis upon religion in daily
life and affairs are good to meet in our time.*

SERMON TWENTY-EIGHT

"If the trumpet give an uncertain sound, who shall prepare himself for the battle," I Corinthians 24:8

I

CONFUSION is characteristic of our time. Under similar circumstances Paul wrote to the people of Corinth about the need of
disciplined authority. He posed a rhetorical question: "If the trumpet
give an uncertain sound, who shall prepare himself for the battle?"
The figure of speech is taken from primitive warfare when com-
manders were on the field with their soldiers. It is reminiscent of
Napoleon in his Italian campaign. The battle was going against him.
In one of his rare moments of caution he ordered the bugler to
sound retreat. The lad, new in his task, said, "Sir, I have not learned
the retreat but I know how to sound the charge." The charge was

sounded and the battle was won. By such intangible things of the
spirit are great issues decided. Is the present battle going against
us? If so, we need the trumpet which gives a certain sound.

II

The quest for authority is an age-old quest which is innate to the
human spirit. *Authority* has always asserted its control over human
actions. Our language reveals its nature and influence. *Author* and
authority are the same root word. That which is creative and un-
folding is the object of man's quest.

We submit readily to authority when it expresses our inner convictions and opens doors of opportunity. When it is alien to our
spirit and restrains us we protest and challenge it. When we succeed
in deposing unwelcome authority we proceed immediately to replace it with another. We are constantly seeking to find a horizon
for our living. We want to have established rules for playing the
game. Man must be under authority to live and move and have his
being.

III

The simplest form of expression through which authority asserts itself is the pressure of the group. There are still extant
primitive villages where under bright oriental stars the elders gather
in council to deliberate, to punish and to praise without the benefit
of law or judge. In the assembly of the United Nations representatives of great powers strive to have their grievances listed on the
agenda for discussion. Man seeks constantly to plead his case before
the bar of public opinion.

Slowly but surely, primitive man sensed the shining through
of another order, an order not human. Conscience spoke to him of
obligation beyond that which is expedient. From the most primitive
superstitions and taboos to the most elaborate rituals, profound
theological tenets and organizational patterns, religion has been
mankind's most feared, most honored and most respected authority.
The great religions have exercised ultimate power over large masses
of humanity.

Kings and dynasties appropriated to themselves the prerogative
of authority. The theory of the divine right of kings was promulgated
to give their usurpation religious sanction. Emperors were deified for
the same purpose. State Churches were established and the state
attempted to make itself God and claim men's complete allegiance

and subservience. Even democracy proclaims that "the voice of the people is the voice of God." By such varied and devious methods do men seek to establish authority in response to men's inborn quest for certainty.

IV

The pages of history are replete with illustrations of effective authoritarian power. For a thousand years after Augustine, *The Church* exercised absolute control over the Western world. The manifestation of the authority reached its climax in the courtyard of the Vatican in Cannes. The emperor of the Holy Roman Empire had refused to obey the orders of the head of the church. For this defiance he was excommunicated. In humble contrition he stood for three days and nights barefooted and bareheaded in the snows of winter outside the papal palace to be finally forgiven and to receive the Church's benediction upon the promise of appropriate penance and future good behavior.

The Protestant Reformation sought not to overthrow the Church but to proclaim a new source of authority. For Protestants the Bible is this source. The great era of Protestantism evidenced in the building of churches, the world-wide program of missions, the establishment of schools and colleges, the permeating of society with its spirit and ideals are evidences of its vigor. The power of the "Word of God" over the minds and hearts of men and of nations is one of the most remarkable chapters in the history of man's quest for certainty.

Men have turned also to secular agencies for authority. With the growth of nationalism, love of country was exalted. Patriotism was preached as the noblest virtue. Dying on the field of battle was openly announced as the certain road to Elysium. In Washington, in Whitehall and elsewhere the Tomb of the Unknown Soldier became a national shrine.

The industrial age brought tyranny in a new form. Mass production lines reduced free men to a new serfdom. And so the labor movement was born. It was led by great prophets and built on lofty principles. Through the years the unions have grown powerful and rich and they speak with an authority more vital than that of church or state in the lives of millions.

But authority is constantly undermining itself. The Church at the height of its power was weakened by corruption in high places. The very strength of Protestantism became its weakness, and its freedom led to friction and confusion. Nationalism capitalized on patriotism to make the twentieth century a century of fratricidal wars. The closed shop and the arrogance of union leaders drove labor to defy its own authority in the secrecy of the polling booth.

Thus are men victimized by their own quest after a voice that shall speak to them with authority.

V

But man is not an animal driven by instinct to a certain goal of survival or destruction. At war in his spirit with the quest for authority is the quest for freedom.

Spirit-led men seeking constantly a fuller revelation of God strike off the shackles of superstition. Brave men rise up against tyranny and lead their fellow men to liberty and self-government. Inquiring minds usher in the age of science that men may be masters, not victims, of the forces of nature.

In education, in religion, in politics, in all realms of action, men seek truth in the sure knowledge that the truth will make them free.

VI

This quest too has had its high moments recorded in the pages of history. When King John signed the Magna Carta he surrendered for all time the pretense that kings were appointed to rule by divine sanction. At Runnymede the quest for freedom embarked upon the road of high adventure. In the French Revolution the damned-up resentments of the oppressed burst open with violence the flood gates and released in turbulence the human aspirations to be free. The American Revolution nailed the Bill of Rights to the door of freedom's temple for all the world to read. Free men served notice on those who would be masters over them that "all men are created equal" and that their endowments are from the Creator and not by permission of men.

The quest is not limited in time or space. In the words of Russell Davenport "Freedom here means freedom everywhere." In the dark days of World War II, Roosevelt and Churchill met to draw up the Atlantic Charter and proclaimed the Four Freedoms as the goal of our common endeavor. The United Nations is a monument to man's desire to organize the forces that will secure freedom.

Does freedom seem an elusive ideal? Such it must always be, for its life lies in the quest itself—a process that is never consummated.

VII

The quest for freedom is a continuing quest accompanied always by the never-ending quest for authority.

"Every nation, every epoch, every thoughtful human being, has again and again to establish the landmark between freedom and authority; for, in the absence of authority, liberty degenerates into license and chaos ensues; and authority becomes tyranny unless it is tempered by freedom." (Stefan Zweig, *The Right to Heresy*)

In no age has this recurring task assumed the proportions that it has in the present. Nearly half the world is held in thrall by Godless authorities while the other half struggles to remain free. The tragedy of our time is revealed in the contrast between the trumpet calls that summon the contending forces to the contest. From beyond the iron curtain comes a sure and certain sound. In the free world we hear a feeble and wavering note.

"The Communist world has very clear ideas about what it conceives to be the rottenness, the decline, the decadence, the evil, of the rest of the world. It is therefore moved by a Messianic view of its own destiny vis-à-vis the outside world. Furthermore, the Communist world is armed to the teeth and disciplined to the hilt, but what do we see on the other side? Politically, we see bickering and squabbling and disunity; psychologically, we see softness and a weakening of moral resolve; economically, we see material greed vitiating and obscuring the larger issues!" (From an address by Charles Malik of Lebanon).

"If the trumpet give an uncertain sound who shall prepare himself for the battle?"

Can the landmark be established if authority refuses to acknowledge the rights of man or recognize the rule of God? Can authority be overthrown without the sacrifice of freedom? Is there no reconciliation of the twin quests except through Armageddon? We are faced with a fearsome question. Can the iron curtain be dissolved only through the terrifying heat of atomic destruction?

VIII

There is a way out of the dilemma. Men must be ruled by God or they will be ruled by godless men. *God-fearing leadership* is the bridge that will span the chasm between untempered authority and unbridled freedom. Leaders who love and fear God will love and serve their fellow men.

The scribes and Pharisees were in the seat of authority in ancient Israel. Yet it was said of Jesus that the people heard Him gladly because He spoke as one having authority and not as the scribes and Pharisees. The secret of His authority was in the premise which underlay His life and teaching: "Love the Lord thy God with all thy heart . . . and thy neighbor as thyself."

Leadership is a spiritual quality. The new cleric, calling on his most famous parishioner, said, "What does this parish need most?" Answered the great Thomas Carlyle, "What this parish needs most is a man who knows God other than by hearsay."

When Joseph Stalin died, a sigh of relief was heard around the tense, uneasy world. When Robert A. Taft died, men mourned the passing of a great leader—a servant of the people—a man who feared God.

The landmark between authority and freedom will not be established in our time by might nor by power. If God-fearing men will lead, Americans will follow and the peoples of the world will follow. Only such leaders can preserve liberty under law. *Only God-fearing leaders can exercise authority without endangering freedom.* Only those who put their trust in God can meet violence unafraid.

The road may be long, the obstacles seemingly insurmountable, the cause well-nigh hopeless. If in such a plight the trumpet sound is uncertain nobody will prepare himself for the battle. If the trumpet sounds a clarion call, what then? Free men will rise and conquer evil.

> Make me a captive, Lord
> And then I shall be free
> Teach me to render up my sword
> And I shall conqueror be!

God Is Revealed in Nature

Reverend Vere Vander Hyden Loper, D.D.

MINISTER, FIRST CONGREGATIONAL CHURCH, BERKELEY, CALIFORNIA

Dr. Loper combines philosophy, religion, and a knowledge of people in his outlook on life and in his preaching. In this distinguished sermon he discusses the revelation of God to man through nature and through Christ, and shows God as a God of justice, as Creator.

Vere Loper was born in Des Moines, Iowa. He studied at Grinnell College, took his divinity work at Yale and was ordained a Congregational minister in 1919. That same year he began his ministry in Great Barrington, Massachusetts, where he served until 1921; his next pastorates were at Great Falls, Montana; Minneapolis, Minnesota; and Wilmette, Illinois. From 1930 to 1939 he was at the First Plymouth Congregational Church in Denver; then he was called to the important First Congregational Church of Berkeley, California, where he has been for twenty years in his ministry just off the campus of the University of California.

In World War I he was a second lieutenant with the 338th Field Artillery. He has been president of the Berkeley Community Chest and Rotary Club; in 1948 he was awarded the Benjamin Ide Wheeler Medal as Berkeley's Most Useful Citizen. From 1950 to 1952 he was National Moderator of the Congregational Christian Churches. He is at present President of the American Board of Foreign Missions and Lecturer in church administration at the Pacific School of Religion.

Dr. Loper's preaching has a freshness and vitality greatly needed in our time.

SERMON TWENTY-NINE

GOETHE ONCE SAID that nature is the only book upon whose every page a significant message is written. We are concerned to turn a few pages of the book on nature to read what God has written about Himself in the physical universe. We would find Him where He seeks to reveal Himself to us. In most instances our guides in many fields would be the scientists who have given us a clearer idea of God by giving us a more accurate concept of the universe. Each new discovery of science is fresh insight into God's relationship to nature.

This is not to say that nature gives us our most important insights into God. These are revealed by Jesus Christ, Who brings us our truest conception of the saving love of God, enabling us to find our permanent place as members of His family. Moreover, it must be admitted that faith is necessary if God is to be discovered in nature. If we turn to nature absolutely devoid of any previous knowledge of the Bible or faith that God is seeking His children everywhere in His creation, we might miss Him where we will endeavor to find Him. Many do not see God in the natural world, and nature does not bludgeon them into that belief. In fact, some factors in nature tend to make difficult our belief in God. But nature, taken as a whole, presents many aspects which reveal God at work in His universe to all who are sensitive to His Eternal Presence.

I

Let us turn to the book of nature where on the first page is written—God is orderly, dependable process. Nature plays no favorites. It does not give the righteous the inside track on its benefits. It does not protect them from the evil which comes to other men. It is possible to believe in a personal God, but we would need something more than nature to make us certain at this point. Nature seems to be a Dr. Jekyll and Mr. Hyde, who goes forth in the morning in in the guise of Dr. Jekyll with healing and kindly ministries visiting the earth with beauty and blessings. Evening comes, and Mr. Hyde is abroad to scatter death and destruction by volcanoes, earthquakes, living creatures red in tooth and claw. Actually, nature is neither Dr. Jekyll nor Mr. Hyde. Nature pours its riches upon all men alike and brings pain to all according to the same dependable process.

Jesus made this clear. He said to us, "God makes his sun to rise on the evil and the good, and sends rain on the just and on the unjust." We need to accept this fact and be grateful that God does act in such a way through His universe that we can depend on Him. This enables us so to relate ourselves to God as dependable process that we will be in tune with the universe. Its power will then lift us and its devastating floods can be escaped. If we could not rely upon God as dependable process, life would be chaos, and we would not know how we could become co-workers with Him. We are too prone to think of God primarily in terms of what we please to call miracles.

The parable is told of a king who once demanded of his counselor a sign of the wondrous works of God. The counselor replied, "Here are four acorns. Will your majesty stoop and plant them—then stoop and look into this pool of water?" The king looked and saw four oak trees where he had planted the acorns. "Wonderful," said the king, "this is indeed the work of God." "How long were you standing by the pool of water?" asked the counselor. The king looked at his garments and found they were threadbare. He saw his reflection in the water and realized that he had become a very old man. "There is no miracle here," said the king. "Yes," replied the counselor, "it is God's work whether He did it in one second or eighty years."

They also asked Jesus to perform a miracle or to give them a sign. He replied that it was an evil generation which sought signs, and no sign would be given except the sign of Jonah, which was the preaching of righteousness to a corrupt city. In short, Jesus told the people that this universe is an orderly, dependable universe—morally as it is physically. They must act accordingly or suffer. God comes to us in an aspect of true greatness through the dependability of His universe. Ancients often thought He was capricious. We look at nature and know that it is dependable process. This is not religion at its highest, but it is at least the religion of the naturalist, based upon the firm foundation of the universe where it cannot be shaken. It is an irreducible minimum and on it impressive superstructures of faith can be built.

II

We turn to the second page of the book of nature—God is known in nature as Creator. Augustine went to nature with a number of preconceived ideas which proved to be false. But when he stood with an open mind before nature, hoping to hear the inanimate speak, the creatures of nature said of God in united voice, "He made us." Coleridge stood at the foot of Mont Blanc in awe. He asked the mountain a question and received an answer—

> Who made you glorious as the gates of heaven
>   Beneath the keen full moon? Who bade the sun
> Clothe you with rainbows? Who with loving
>   Flowers of loveliest blue, spread garlands at your feet?
> God! Let the torrents, like the shout of nations answer
>   And the icy planes echo, God!
> And they too have a voice, yon piles of snow.
> And in their perilous fall shall thunder, God!

Nature is a rich field of God's creative activity. He has been at work since the beginning of time drawing the raw materials of the universe together into creations which meet every fundamental need of man. This is the process which we carry back to the beginning of time, believing God is at work creating order out of primitive chaos. This is a process which we believe to be at work in the contemporary scene. We see spiral nebulae in the heavens and are told they may well be a universe in process of being born. The astronomer adds, "Our galaxy is a spiral nebula consisting of about 100,000 million stars, of which the sun is a representative sample, in no way conspicuous except to us, and then only because our little planet revolves around this particular star." With the telescope on Mt.

Palomar we can photograph a billion other galaxies similar to our own. It appears that this fraction of the universe which we can study is a tiny fraction of a universe probably infinite in both space and time. From the heavens we go into the forest with Lew Sarett and hear him say to us—

> Oh, I can hear you, God, above the cry
> Of the tossing trees—
> Rolling your windy tides across the sky
> And splashing your silver seas
> Over the pine,
> To the water line
> Of the moon.
> Oh, I can hear you, God,
> Above the wail of the lonely loon—
> When the pine trees pitch and nod—
> Chanting your melodies
> Of ghostly waterfalls and avalanches,
> Washing your wind among the branches
> To make them pure and white.

It is a part of the divine creation as Jesus taught us that God shall supply our need for bread as well as beauty. When He saw fields clothed with flowers, it suggested God's concern for the practical needs of man as well as God the Creator of beauty. "Behold the lilies of the field. They toil not, neither do they spin. Yet I say unto you that Solomon in all his glory was not arrayed like one of these. If God doth so clothe the grass of the field which today is and tomorrow is cast into the oven, shall He not much more clothe you?"

At the very beginning of the Bible we are taught that God has created the values in the universe for the benefit of man. When we look at nature through the eyes of our faith, we see it as a storehouse of infinite riches which God continues to create through all time for the enrichment of the life of man. Nature reveals to us God, as creative energy, inspiring the spirit of man with a creative urge that he may share the divine work of a Creator God.

III

We turn to a third page to read—God is discovered in nature as Eternal Presence. He links all time into one mighty drama. We can scarcely grasp what the author of the Book of Revelation means when he speaks for God to say, "I am the Alpha and the Omega, who is and who was and who is to come." Science makes us at home in the great stretches of time. It speaks of the history of this globe in terms of billions of years. It sets a vast stage for the drama of God in His universe.

We need a God of whom we can truly say—He is the Eternal Presence. He was present at the beginning of time. He is present now. He will continue to be present in the future. Man seems to be such a fleeting shadow so far as this earth is concerned. He comes forth in the morning and is cut down in the evening. We can only find ourselves in vast stretches of time by linking ourselves with a God to whom a thousand years are but a watch in the night when it is gone. We need Him to gain a setting for the ultimate solution of the problems of humanity. We need the Eternal Presence as a comrade for life eternal which we live within the wide horizons our faith opens for us. History will help us here, but nature, through science, sets vaster scenes. Go into the great Sequoias of California. The Eternal God waits for you there. Among those trees you are living for the moment with those who lived when Washington led our country to liberty. They were undisturbed when Napoleon shook a continent. They were in their places when Caesar consolidated the Roman Empire. They were old when the happy songs announced the birth of a Babe Who was wrapped in swaddling clothes and laid in a manger. They were part of the world which Alexander longed to conquer. He could have seen them if he had marched this way. At the heart of each tree is a small sack-like structure which discharges a secretion making these giants practically immune to everything except the ruthlessness and carelessness of man. How they bridge the centuries and make us at home with the God of the ages!

We do not need to go to the Sequoias to visualize God's hand at work over the stretches of time. We can look out from the hills upon San Francisco Bay. How modern it seems, but how ancient it is! Thirty thousand years ago the great glaciers were melting. The ocean rose four hundred feet and more, and finally broke through the Golden Gate, and the Bay was born, twenty thousand years ago. God was at work there. Go to the top of Mt. Diablo or Mt. Tamalpais and look out at the Sierras in the distance. Now the Sequoias become infants in the family of God, and the Bay a thing of yesterday. For fifty million years ago the Sierras were born. We plunge further into time as we find on the top of the highest peak a remnant of life which existed when that mountain top was a part of the sea floor. We pick up a bit of limestone, and we must at least double the age of the Sierras to know when God made it. And when we hold a piece of granite in our hands we count time in several hundred million years since it came out of chaos. The astronomer looks at the heavens and goes back five billion years—the estimated current age of the universe. Surely here is the commentary that can be made—that of the ancient Hebrew: "Lord, thou hast been our dwelling place in all the generations, before the mountains were brought forth or ever thou hadst formed the earth and the world, even from everlasting to everlasting, thou art God."

IV

We turn a fourth page in the book of nature and upon it we read—God is discovered in nature as inexhaustible power. Theologians have always told us that God is omnipotent. But how are we to envisage the power of God? Nature reveals powers beyond our comprehension. Aid has been given by the scientists' insights into nature, revealing the power God has made available for us. What the scientists reveal in nature brings the power of God closer to us. In the disintegration process of radium, alpha particles are hurled out with velocities of the order of 4,000 miles per second. In its radioactive disintegration uranium emits beta rays. These high-speed electrons emerge with velocities varying from about 37,000 to 175,000 miles per second. In the fission of the nucleus of a uranium 235 atom, gamma rays and also neutrons are emitted, both capable of penetrating several feet of concrete or approximately a foot of iron.

The energy released in the fission of a gram of uranium 235 is equal to that released in the burning of about 3,000,000 grams of coal. If you could possibly assemble one gram of electrons and release their power, you could pull a train of loaded freight cars six thousand miles long at 30 miles per hour on the level for slightly more than a half hour or a distance of about fifteen miles. Have you noticed with what difficulty a double-header sometimes pulls the train of average length, especially on a mountain grade? These are the most powerful engines man can make, but the power of nature's God dwarfs them into insignificance.

The *Nautilus* has been in the news frequently. How thrilling it is to realize that this great submarine can go at the rate of twenty-five knots night and day for a whole year and all the power necessary for that year will have been released from 26.15 pounds of uranium 235, and we could hold it in the palm of our hand.

Everywhere nature speaks of the power of God—power which you and I can use not only to discover the God of nature but also to increase our adequacy for daily living.

208

V

We turn one more page; on it is written—God can be discovered in nature as unseen essence of the seen. To visualize God as spirit is difficult. How can God, Who has no physical body located in space, express Himself through physical mediums? We would not expect help from nature at this point, but we do receive it.

The scientist has been subdividing this physical universe with the zeal of a real estate agent who has just gained control of a valuable tract. The scientist does not stop with fifty-foot lots. He wants the smallest possible unit. He goes back through atoms, those fascinating minature universes, to protons, electrons, and neutrons. At the moment, he suggests that these are the smallest physical units—the building blocks out of which the physical universe is made. "What are they?" asks the layman. The scientist answers, "Protons and electrons are positive and negative charges of electricity; neutrons are electrically neutral particles." "But what is electricity?" The answer will probably be given in terms of "energy." An unseen nucleus bombarded by an unseen power produces effects which can be photographed. Such scientific phenomena increase our capacity to see God also as an unseen power producing visible results. If nature in one aspect be power or energy, then God is also. The ultimate in nature becomes close to the ultimate in religion, and God is discovered where we least expected to find Him.

But we do not stop here. The most beautiful sights which nature offers have no physical reality in the ordinary sense of bodies. Here is the glory of the western horizon—a sky which is a blaze of color. Upon it the many hues of gold and red and purple blend in a masterpiece which can be depicted only weakly by the artist. And yet the western horizon has no reality in the ordinary sense. It is only an apparent meeting of the earth and the sky. It is partially an optical illusion but like the life of God of which it is a part, it is a daily witness of the God of nature Who is in part an actual meeting of the divine and the human. It makes all who have eyes to see a little nobler, a little broader, a little deeper. The man who gazes upon it can discover, if he will, the other source of beauty which also can have no body.

Here is the rainbow. From ancient time men have associated it with God. It was the promise that God would not visit them with devastating floods. The rainbow can be a path to God. But never think that you can stand at the foot of a rainbow. It cannot be done, for it flees from you. It has no physical reality in the ordinary sense. The rainbow appears in the sky only as you witness certain phenomena of nature from exactly the right angle. When you stand so that the light of the sun catches the remaining mists in the sky, reflecting and refracting the light, you then see what appears to be a great bow of dazzling beauty in the heavens. It has physical causes but no physical reality in the usual sense. A man who does not look from your angle might say, "Rainbow, nonsense. I see no rainbow. Bring it to the laboratory and we will examine it." But you say, "I see it, and it can never be brought into any laboratory." "O," says the skeptic, "something like God." "Yes," says the man of faith, "something like God." You can discover Him if you view the phenomena of nature from the right angles.

I wish we might wander leisurely through the book of nature instead of taking hasty glances at a few pages. We could read of the intelligence of God in the flight of birds and the labor of ants. The nesting birds could show us that something loving and tender in man is shared by many of God's most humble creatures. It was this quality which caused St. Francis to find birds such delightful companions. And trees—of them Bryant said, "the groves were God's first temples." The sanctity of ancient worship still lingers in them. May we so sense it that we will walk in them with the consciousness that we tread holy ground.

We have turned only a few of the pages in nature's book. We leave it in your hands and hearts as the tool of the richest discovery of the human soul—the discovery of God. God gave it to you in the hope that it would bring you into His presence. May the book fulfill the purpose of the Author in your life.

Nonconformity

Reverend Ernest Gordon, T.D., S.T.M., LL.D.
DEAN OF THE CHAPEL, PRINCETON UNIVERSITY, AND A MINISTER OF
THE PRESBYTERIAN CHURCH, PRINCETON, NEW JERSEY

Dr. Ernest Gordon, Dean of the Chapel at Princeton University, speaks out of wide experience with life and faith and suffering. During World War II he was a Captain in the Argyll and Sutherland

Highlanders. After being wounded in Malaya, he escaped on the downfall of Singapore to Sumatra, where he organized an escape system which took care of fifteen hundred men, and women, including nursing sisters, wounded soldiers, and children. After the conquest of Sumatra by the Japanese, he escaped again in a sailboat with eight others, but after twenty-four days on the Indian Ocean was recaptured by the Japanese Navy.

For three and a half years he worked on the infamous "Railway of Death" between Thailand and Burma. During that time he helped organize and teach in the "Jungle University," which helped keep morale up, and in addition, served as a lay minister to his fellow prisoners of war. He was ordained in 1950 at Paisley Abbey, where he served three years as deputy minister. For a year he was Chaplain to Presbyterian students at Princeton University prior to his appointment as Dean of the Chapel in July, 1955.

He did his undergraduate work at St. Andrews University in Scotland prior to the outbreak of World War II in 1939. He later completed his studies in theology at Edinburgh University, Hartford Theological Seminary in Connecticut, and at Glasgow University. He is the author of A LIVING FAITH FOR TODAY *(1956) and has conducted Religious Emphasis Week on various university campuses. He is the founder and first President of the Church Service Society.*

His preaching has become an event at Princeton Chapel where his sermons are eagerly listened to week by week by students and faculty. This sermon shows his understanding of life and people and the need to be one's own self and to have a personal faith.

SERMON THIRTY

"And he [Jesus] said unto them, The Sabbath was made for man, and not man for the Sabbath: Therefore the Son of man is Lord also of the Sabbath," Mark 2:27, 28

THERE IS A GREAT DEAL of physical comfort to be had from being in the fore ranks of those who conform to the customs, mores and folkways of contemporary culture. We feel quite satisfied with ourselves when we know that the suit we are wearing conforms to the sartorial laws of the high-priced tailors; that our tie is striped the right way instead of the wrong way; that our shirt collar buttons down instead of up; that our shirt is pink but our politics blue; that our bank account is balanced; that the family we come from is neither too small nor too large; that our grade is passing; that our ideas are the same as everyone else's; that we are not too bad nor yet too good; and that we are not likely to suffer from anything worse than that of having a high-powered wife, the seven-year itch, the commuter's blues and athlete's spread!

There was once a man who learned to brush his teeth at an early age. He got up in the morning, brushed his teeth and at the end of the day brushed his teeth and went to bed. In due course he went to a good preparatory school where he got up in the morning, cleaned his teeth, and at night cleaned his teeth and went to bed. Without questioning the ordering of his life he went to a University, from which he duly graduated after having got up in the morning, cleaned his teeth, and at the end of the day cleaned his teeth and went to bed. Eventually, after a great deal of teeth-cleaning, he became an exceedingly successful man in the eyes of the world, and still he got up in the morning, cleaned his teeth, finished his work and came home at the end of the day to clean his teeth and go to bed. Fortunately, there is an end to this story; one day he went for a walk in the country and came to a field where an old-fashioned cow was placidly chewing the cud. After looking into the big brown eyes of the cow for a while he suddenly remarked, "Look here, cow, the only difference between us is that you chew the cud, and I clean my teeth!"

Unreasoned conformity is about the dullest thing there is. The highest it can ever offer us is a place with the cows and the vegetables —although, mind you, they at least are useful! When you have conformed to all the right conventions; known only the right people; done all the right things at the right times in the right places; and have been so unrighteously right in all your dealings with your fellow mortals; then you are still only a body in a gray flannel suit!

Contrary to a great deal of misguided opinion there is no place for such conformity within the bounds of Christianity! *Nonconformity* is not necessarily the sign of a neurotic disturbance, but may well be the evidence of a condition of grace. I am exceedingly glad that my youth was spent in a small community where every individual in it was a distinct and recognizable character. Just as no two bonnets were the same, so no two personalities were alike. Each one had his own particular point of view and everyone disagreed with the theological position of the minister. In that, at least, they were all unanimous! These were not people who were disgruntled with life, but people who accepted gladly the reality of the supreme Sovereignty of God and who feared no one but Him.

Reared on porridge-oats, Shakespeare and the Bible, and the Shorter Catechism, they knew beyond the shadow of a doubt that, "The chief end of man is to glorify God and to enjoy Him forever." In other words, they recognized the will of God as being supreme in their lives, and were ready to disobey the conventions of society whenever those conventions seemed to be in conflict with the will of God. They were always ready to be counted as rebels for God's sake.

When we consider the life of Jesus Christ and His influence upon the world we are sometimes apt to forget that He is probably the greatest revolutionary figure this world has ever known. He can be counted as the top ranking nonconformist! There is very little of the "gentle Jesus meek and mild" about Him when we find Him telling the Pharisees and the Sadducees the truth about themselves. He accused them of allowing their conformity to their interpretation of the Law to be a stumbling block in the way of those who were trying to do what was right. His condemnation of them was so severe that it is no wonder they plotted and schemed to have Him crucified. By His teaching and His deeds He completely undermined the complicated legal edifice that they had built up with such rationalistic thoroughness. His lack of interest in the obviously religious, in the sham ceremonial of the unctuously pious, and in the hard-heartedness of the self-righteous, was a cause for hatred on the part of His enemies. Because of it His family despaired of Him and thought of Him as a renegade. He was so thoroughly nonconformist that none but the down-and-outs and the sincerely religious would have anything to do with Him! To the disgust of His detractors His concern seemed to be with the commonplace things of life, and with the daily happenings of common people. His parables were simple and straightforward, containing no high-sounding phrases nor "highfalutin" ideologies. They were about farmers, shepherds, merchants, housewives, debtors, fishermen, servants, travelers, brides and bridegrooms, poor folk and rich fools, unjust managers and unjust judges, penitent prodigals and heartless elder brothers. To the Pharisees it seemed paradoxical that, professing to come from God, He should plunge Himself into the lot of humanity and make its problems and burdens His own. Righteousness, He taught, was not a matter of conforming rightly to inhumanly objective standards but of thinking righteously, living righteously, loving righteously and worshiping righteously. Righteousness must be before God and man; it cannot be contained but must express itself in action in the daily life. It is not only divine but human: for our conduct and attitude toward our fellow men is directly related to our conduct toward God. The Samaritan who went to the rescue of the robbed traveler was commended for his compassion to his neighbor in need. The publican who knew only too well that he was a sinner was commended for his honest humility and for his recognition of his need for mercy. The harlot who anointed Him with her precious ointment was commended for her sincere love and fellow-feeling for Him. The money-changers and sellers of sacrificial animals were whipped out of the temple because they cheated simple people of their hard-earned money as they came to worship. The thief on the cross next to Him was forgiven and granted a place in paradise because of his distress at the unfairness of Jesus' crucifixion. It was at the point of their human concern, in other words, that they found favor or disfavor in the eyes of God.

Jesus was consistently teaching that God is intricately involved in the human situation, and that He regards the people of His creation as children. The revelation that Jesus bore to God was not that of God as omnipotent and omniscient, but of God as Father. It was this belief and His readiness to accept it as a fact in His personal relationships that marked Him out as a dangerous nonconformist to be crucified.

Our Gospel lesson makes this emphasis of His dramatically clear. Here we have Jesus taking His disciples for a Sabbath afternoon's walk, much as they do in other lands today. They have been talking with one another about the kingdom of God and of its importance in their lives, or of suchlike subject. As they walk along beside a wheat field His disciples pull some ears of grain and mill them between their hands, blowing away the chaff and eating the kernels. To us this seems the most material of actions, for we have probably done the same sort of thing countless times without giving it a thought. But not so the Pharisees. They had gone to the trouble of trying to make the general law regarding conduct on the Sabbath fit as many particular circumstances as they could think of. They delighted in treating men like little children and had formalized Sabbatical observances in such a way that they forced a condition of bondage upon the people, and gave them burdens that were too heavy to be borne. Not only was it unlawful for a man to carry his straw paillasse on the Sabbath, or to heal, or to walk more than the prescribed distance, but eventually it became unlawful to catch a troublesome flea. Now, all this was an obvious perversion of the law. It was a denial of the purpose for which it was brought into being. The law of the Sabbath was given in order that men might

214

have the advantage of one day in which to rest, to think, and to worship—a day which they could regard as their own. It was for the benefit of mankind, to ensure that labor was not exploited or that a man's responsibility to God and his neighbors was forgotten.

I daresay the Pharisees were delighted to see Jesus and His disciples break the Sabbath in this fashion, for to them it was but further proof that Jesus was a nonconformist and a rebel who voluntarily placed himself beyond the pale by His actions. But Jesus was an expert in handling such situations. And so when He was condemned for allowing His disciples to descend to such desperate levels of wickedness, He simply reminded them that they were mistaking their prejudices for principles. "Are you quite certain," says He, "that there is no precedent in our tradition which justifies the conduct of my disciples? How about the time King David, our national hero, disregarded this law and not only that but because of his hunger ate the holy bread which was reserved for priests, and shared it with his companions? Don't you see," He went on to say, "man was never created to be the slave of the law, but its master: for, 'The Sabbath was made for man, and not man for the Sabbath.'"

*   *   *   *   *

The relationship with God, for which man was created, is not a legalistic one but a personal one. God doesn't compel men to be good nor hate them for their failure to meet the law's demands. The history of mankind is the history of His patient dealing with it. To the Old Testament prophets it was incredible that God should withhold His wrath and bear with the obvious transgressions of His sinful children. Jeremiah, for instance, was impatient to view God giving the sinners hell. He says, "But, O Lord of hosts, that judgest righteously, that triest the veins and the heart, let me see Thy vengeance on them." Jeremiah, however, was to learn that this was not God's way; that His way was greater than the law or a nation's obedience to the law, and so he wrote, "After those days, saith the Lord, I will put my law in their inward parts, and write it in their hearts; and will be their God, and they shall be my people." What was so difficult for the prophets, priests, Pharisees and scribes to understand—just as it is for us—is that God's humanity is greater by far than the power of a dead, cold legalism. His relationship with us is that kind which says, "Come now, and let us reason together." Our knowledge of what is righteousness is something which is per-

215

sonally revealed to us by God. Through fellowship with Him we become conscious of His divine initiative for our lives and destiny. The autonomy of our wills is not violated but won over by His Love. When we lose sight of this gracious relationship, then man becomes nothing but an animated dancing doll dangling at the end of a string.

We are redeemed by God's gracious dealings with us. Unworthy as we are, He sends His Son—not to force men to return to Him but to demonstrate His love for them. It is our independence from God, our unwillingness to obey His word addressed to us that makes Christ's sacrifice on the cross essential for our salvation. By our conformity to the laws and conventions of the natural world we forge fetters for ourselves from which the law cannot free us. Only the acceptance of God's rule in our hearts, by faith, can bring us freedom. It is only in that Father-son relationship, in which faith permits us to participate, that true moral and spiritual freedom can be enjoyed. This liberating experience is ours without the necessity of any moral attainment on our part. It is not won by us but given to us, in love. Once salvation and moral attainment are equated we find ourselves standing in the shoes of the Pharisees and claiming that man was made for the Sabbath and not the Sabbath for man. Love, you see, ignores the past in the joy of the present and points us toward the perfection of Jesus Chirst. When the waiting father welcomed the penitent prodigal returned from the far country, he didn't ask the lad if he thought himself worthy of a reconciliation, or ask for proof that he intended to lead a new life according to the normally accepted laws of the family. No, he loved his son and commanded that he be given the very best of everything he possessed. This is how God deals with us, and how He expects us to deal with others!

Sounds obvious and simple, doesn't it? But we don't do it! We prefer to live by the law of the Sabbath! Life that is lived in truly personal terms is only possible to the redeemed man; to the man who has staked his claim in the kingdom of God; to the man who is obedient to the will of his Heavenly Father. To the natural man, all life is centered upon his legalistic conformity to those rules and regulations which are set in space and time. Occasionally I find it necessary to intercede with some authority or other on behalf of a fellow mortal. The answer I usually receive is that there is nothing in the regulations to deal with such a case. And when I complain that I am not dealing with regulations but with a human being in anguish, I am told that there is nothing that can be done. We must live by the law and not by love! Must we? Man was made for the Sabbath and not the Sabbath for man.

Was he?

The temptation for the Church as well as for ourselves is to think that man was made for the Sabbath. Whenever she becomes conscious of the respectable place she has achieved in society or of the glory of her outward trappings, then she draws the fires of the spirit and embeds herself in concrete. The truly Catholic Church, by the nature of the life given unto her by Jesus Christ, is always nonconforming to the standards of the Sabbath and always *protestant* in the confession of her faith. She can never be satisfied with herself, or feel that she has taken over the controls from God, or that she dare deal with the world in anything but a divinely-human relationship. Her task in every age and in every land is that of loving men and women and children into the kingdom, and showing by her life and example that, "The Sabbath was made for man, and not man for the Sabbath."

REDEMPTION

Love in a Slave Market

Reverend Lawrence E. Toombs, Ph.D.

A METHODIST MINISTER AND ASSISTANT PROFESSOR OF OLD TESTA-MENT AT DREW THEOLOGICAL SEMINARY, MADISON, NEW JERSEY

Lawrence Toombs, one of the most vital young theologians, tells the story of Hosea the prophet and his message, focusing on Hosea's repurchase of Gomer, his errant wife, in the slave market. Dr. Toombs illustrates the excellent use of Old Testament insight to preach a sermon on a theme as modern as today.

Born in Charlottetown, Prince Edward Island, Canada, Lawrence Edmund Toombs' early interest in science led him to take both the Bachelor of Science and Bachelor of Arts degree, with honors in chemistry, from Acadia University, Wolfville, Nova Scotia, in 1941, and to do postgraduate work in explosives research in the University of Toronto. During the war he served as meteorologist with the Royal Canadian Air Force. At the war's end he entered training for the ministry and in 1948 took his divinity degree from Pine Hill Divinity Hall, Halifax, Nova Scotia. From there he pro-

ceeded to Drew where in 1951 he received the Doctor of Philosophy degree in the field of Old Testament study.

From 1950 to 1953 he was professor of Old Testament Language and Literature at St. Stephen's College in Edmonton, Alberta. While in Alberta he did a great deal of preaching. Out of his association with the National Young People of Canada he developed a course of Bible study, "A Year with the Bible," which is being used across the Dominion.

SERMON THIRTY-ONE

"When Israel was a child, then I loved him," Hosea 11:1

THE SLAVE TRADE is an ugly and degrading business. Sleek black ships out of Africa with a pitiful cargo of human flesh cowering below decks, the lash, the chains and the filth and squalor of the slave compound are symbols of the bestiality and cruelty of which human beings are capable. But worst of all is the slave market where one man bids against another for the body and personality of a fellow creature. Depravity and greed can reach no lower. Yet once—only once in human history—the slave market was bright with the revelation of the love of God. Its horror was transformed, and it became the arena, not of man's inhumanity to man, but of God's unconquerable love for the human beings He has made.

It happened some 750 years before Christ in an unknown town in the northern kingdom of Israel. A man walked through the streets toward the slave market, and the eyes of the villagers followed him as, with head erect and a look of determination on his face, he strode forward. He was known to them all. His name, Hosea; his occupation, prophet of the Lord. He was the last man on earth who should be going to the slave market on that day, for up ahead on the auction block his own wife was being sold as a slave. Why was he going?

The townsfolk could have been in no doubt as to the answer. They had heard Hosea preach and they knew him for a fiery prophet of the judgment of God—a grim man with a grim message. Anyone, he had taught, was at liberty to sin, but he had better be ready to take the consequences, for they would inevitably follow. Israel, the people of God, had repeatedly disobeyed God's law. They had been rebellious and unfaithful. Now God's patience had run out, and

218

destruction hung over the nation like an avalanche over a mountain valley. Hosea had even gone so far as to give his children names symbolic of his message: Jezreel, to remind the people of the national crime which had been committed in that city when the whole family of King Ahab had been murdered; *Lo-ammi*, "not my people," since God had cast aside His people and abandoned them to their fate; *Lo-ruhamah*, "no mercy," because the healing springs of God's mercy were dried up and would no more nourish the life of Israel.

The rugged man who preached this message had suffered a tragedy in his own home. His wife had deserted him and his family, and gone out to make her own way in the world. It had been no easy road. She had become a public prostitute, and now that her charms had faded she was being sold at public auction. Her body and her future would become the property of anyone willing to pay the price.

The fate of Gomer, the prophet's wife, was a perfect illustration of Hosea's message. She had rejected his love—as Israel had rejected the love of God. She had turned from his home to the arms of other lovers—as Israel had turned from the Lord to idols. The judgment had now fallen upon her and she would be sold into slavery —as the judgment was about to fall on Israel—and the nation would become the slave of a foreign conqueror. It was pat, complete and perfect, an exact verification of everything Hosea had preached. Who among the villagers could doubt that Hosea was walking to the slave market to see his words come true, and to indulge in a rather sadistic "I told you so"?

The whispering voices fell silent and looks of astonishment appeared on the faces of the crowd. An unbelievable thing was happening before their eyes. Hosea, a Hebrew, a member of that race to whom the sanctity of the family is of paramount importance, was standing in the public slave market, in the presence of his neighbors and fellow townsmen, bidding for the purchase of the harlot who had dishonored him. He paid down the price, half in money and half in grain, and walked back through the wondering crowd, leading his faithless wife—his once more at a heavy cost in money and humiliation. Why had the prophet of judgment stepped in to save his betrayer from the consequences of her sin? The answer is both simple and profound. Hosea did what he did because of God.

During the long days after Gomer had deserted him, Hosea had re-examined his prophetic message. He came to a conclusion possible only for a great-hearted man. He had been wrong in representing God as a Being of anger and judgment only. He passed the history of his people in review before his mind, and read a new lesson there. They had been slaves in Egypt, driven, beaten and broken, and God had heard their cry of distress and come down to deliver them. In the wilderness they had built golden idols and worshiped them. They had grumbled and complained against their God. They had followed every selfish whim of the moment. But God's hand had never left them. As He had been their deliverer from slavery, so He had guided them every step of the way into their own land. That was the kind of God He really was—a God of infinite patience, tenderness, and kindness, "teaching His children to walk."

Once Hosea had come to this understanding of what God is like, it became startlingly clear to him what he must do about his wife, Gomer. He must act as God would act. If God is really One Who loves and delivers, then His servants must do the same. His new vision of the love of God compelled the prophet to save Gomer from the horror which lay before her.

The new vision demanded a new language. Hosea took a word from the common speech of his people, and made it the key to the understanding of God's nature. This word appears in English translations of the Bible in a variety of ways—as "loving-kindness," as "mercy" and as "love." In the Revised Standard Version it is "steadfast love." But in the end the word defies translation; we can only recognize it when we see it in life.

First of all, loving-kindness is a deed, not an emotion. The verbs used with it in the Bible make this clear. You *show* loving-kindness, or *do* loving-kindness. You never feel it. Emotion is cheap. You can sit in an armchair before the fire, and love the whole wide world. And it does not mean a thing. It may give a comfortable glow of self-righteousness, but it is in the end only self-deception and does no one any good. Loving-kindness must be expressed in action, and the doing of it may take us into the filth of the slave market.

But what is the quality of the deed called loving-kindness? It is an act of helpfulness—and more—of deliverance. It is offered to those who are unable to help themselves, and in no position to return the kindness done for them. It is easy to do a good turn for the respectable or the well-to-do. They are worthy of our efforts to help them, and may be able to help us out some day when we need their aid. To be helpful under these conditions is a "nice gesture"; but it is a long country mile from loving-kindness. Most of our good deeds are drab, and stained with what we are pleased to call "enlightened self-interest." Loving-kindness soars above this earthbound, calculating, self-centered action, and offers help to the helpless, guidance to the lost and deliverance to the captive, without hope of repayment and without concern for risk or loss. Hosea saw that this unlimited self-giving is the central fact of the nature of God Himself.

There is a direct line from Hosea to Jesus Christ in their teaching about loving-kindness. When the young lawyer, all smiles and false friendliness, stood up to tempt Jesus—the trained legal expert against the unlettered carpenter—he put the difficult question of eternal life. Jesus promptly forced him to answer his own question, "What is written in the law? How readest thou?" The lawyer gave the stock answer. "Thou shalt love the Lord, thy God . . . . and thy neighbor as thyself." With an offhand "That's right," Jesus turned away, as if the matter were closed. But the skilled debater could not let himself be dismissed so easily by a mere peasant. *Wishing to justify himself*, he said, "And who is my neighbor?" Slowly, one imagines, Jesus turned back to him and began to tell the most beautiful of His many parables, the story of the Good Samaritan.

A traveler on the Jericho road was attacked and cruelly beaten by robbers. He lay in the roadside ditch, unable to help himself, unable even to call out for aid. The leaders of religion came by— a priest and a Levite—looked, and winced and went away. But a certain Samaritan as he journeyed came where he was. Forgotten were the thieves who might be lurking nearby, on the lookout for a rich merchant to plunder. Immediately he was on his knees in the dust beside the injured man. He dressed the wounds, walked the long hill to the inn while the wounded man rode, bought him lodging and (the most splendid gesture of all) went away without waiting to be thanked. The young lawyer, educated in the Scriptures, knew what Jesus was talking about. He had just heard the perfect description of an act of loving-kindness. So, when Jesus asked, "Who was neighbor to him who fell among the thieves?" the lawyer replied without hesitation, "He who *showed mercy* to him." After this Jesus' command is simple and inevitable: "Go, and do the same."

* * * * *

The Christian should know from personal experience that Hosea is right. Loving-kindness is the most complete and satisfying description of God. We know this by the cross which stands upon the altar, a perpetual reminder of the agony through which the loving-kindness of God reached down to meet the deepest needs of men. St. Paul grasped the sweep and grandeur of God's action in Jesus Christ, and put it into incomparable words. "For a righteous man no one would be willing to die. For a good man, perhaps, someone might even dare to die. But God commended his love towards us in that *while we were still sinners* Christ died for us." In the cross we have the true measure of the loving-kindness of God.

Now, if we Christians know the love of God, what must we do? The answer is the same for us as it was for Hosea. We must imitate the love of God, reflecting it out of our own lives into the communities in which we live. Wherever there is helplessness or hopelessness there the Christian must be found doing acts of helpfulness and deliverance without hope of reward or repayment, making his deeds reflections, however pale and blurred, of the immeasurable love of God. If Christians are faithful to this calling, it may be that the last word in human history will not be said by the atomic bomb, or by a satellite orbiting about a burned-out earth, but by an older, more elemental and stronger force—the unconquerable power of loving-kindness.

REFORMATION SUNDAY

Luther and Ourselves

Reverend Roland H. Bainton, Ph.D.

A MINISTER OF THE METHODIST CHURCH AND PROFESSOR OF CHURCH HISTORY, YALE UNIVERSITY DIVINITY SCHOOL, NEW HAVEN, CONN.

Dr. Bainton is the senior member of the Yale Divinity School Faculty, where he was appointed to teach in 1919. He was born in Ilkeston, Derbyshire, England, on March 30, 1894, and came to the United States in 1902. He attended Whitman College, Washington, then took his D.D. and his Ph.D. at Yale, with church history his major study at Yale. He is now Titus Street Professor of Ecclesiastical History at Yale, a position formerly held by George Park Fisher and Williston Walker. Most of Dr. Bainton's writing has been in the field of Reformation history.

His best-known book is HERE I STAND: A LIFE OF MARTIN LUTHER

(1950). His most recent book is a biography of his father, PILGRIM
PARSON, *describing his father's successive pastorates in England,
Canada, the Pacific Northwest, and Connecticut, and his concurrent spiritual migration. His interests have included work with the
Quaker Unit of the American Red Cross. He is a member of the
American Church Historical Society. In this sermon he draws upon
his knowledge of the Reformation to apply the theme of reformation
to our own time.*

SERMON THIRTY-TWO

PROTESTANTS in the United States must come to terms with the
fact that they have come to be a minority. This statement, recently
made, is not factually correct for the country as a whole, but it
is correct for certain sections of the country, and particularly for
the greater portion of the Atlantic seaboard. The fate of certain
Congregational churches in New Haven, Connecticut, well illustrates
the point. The Davenport Church, named for John Davenport, the
pastor of the Pilgrim congregation which founded the city, has now
in its front yard a sign which reads, "Bingo Every Night." The
Plymouth Congregational Church, named for the first Pilgrim settlement in the land, is now the Keser Israel. The Howard Avenue
Congregational Church has lost its spire. The rose window has been
replaced by the image of an oriental potentate and the church bears
the label, "Hejaz Grotto." In other words, the Catholics, the Jews
and the fraternal organizations have taken over. This of itself does
not mean that the Protestants have diminished. It may mean only
that they have moved out of town; and there are in fact new Congregational churches in the suburbs. But there is no denying that the
Protestants are outnumbered. They are not, as once they were,
the dominant group, but only one of the smaller constituents in a
religiously pluralistic society which includes the Catholics of various
complexions—Irish, Italian, Polish and German; the orthodox
churches, Greek and Russian; the Jews, Orthodox, Conservative
and Reformed, plus all the holiness sects.

The reduction in the number of Protestants is not due primarily
to defections. Conversions to and from Catholicism and Protestantism cancel out. The reduction is due rather to a change in the complexion of our society, to the importation about a century ago of
large numbers of workers from Catholic lands. A similar shift has

223

taken place in our own day in Germany, where in the west the Catholics predominate because this area includes the Rhineland and Bavaria, the Catholic stronghold, whereas Saxony and Prussia, the Protestant centers, are in the Soviet zone. What all of this adds up to is that nowhere can any religion be assured of permanence.

But if we have lost a position of dominance, we have no cause to be downcast. To be a religious minority is neither a disgrace nor a misfortune. All of the great movements in the history of the Church, including the Church itself, began as minorities. Were not all Christians at one time the offscouring of the earth? Did not Jesus refer to His followers as a little flock? When, ever, was there a queueing up at the narrow gate? Some of the great orders of the Catholic Church had to struggle for recognition and even existence, such as the Franciscans, and a later branch of that order, the Capuchins. The Protestant movement, at the outset, was distinctly a minority, and at certain moments almost a minority of one. Martin Luther, when placed under the ban of the Church and the empire, and an exile at the Wartburg, felt that he was utterly alone, and was plagued by the question put to him at the Diet of Worms whether he, a single individual, could be right against the tradition of fifteen hundred years. He took comfort in the thought that Noah, when he obeyed God and built an ark on dry land with not even rain in sight, must have seemed to his neighbors to have been out of his mind. They were eating and drinking, and would not credit his predictions of a flood. Only eight went with him into the ark. How often he must have said to himself, "Are you alone wise?"

The Lutherans were a minority at the Diet of Spires, when they received the name Protestant by reason of their protest. The evangelicals were a minority in England when Tyndale, Latimer, Ridley and Cranmer went to the stake. So was it also in Scotland when George Wishart, the teacher of John Knox, was burned. Curious as it may seem, the very Puritans were a minority in Puritan New England. The saints, who inaugurated the enterprise and contributed its ideals, were often only a tenth of the population. The Nonconformists in England were a minority, subject until comparatively recently to disabilities, denial of Christian burial, exclusion from the universities and from some professions. And the Catholic Church in the United States began as a very small minority.

There is something to be said for being a minority. For one thing, a minority, particularly if subject to social pressures, is less likely to attract the indifferent and the social climbers. Unpopularity makes for sincerity. Moreover, minorities are good for majorities.

When the Congregationalists were dominant in New England, they were saved from too great complacency by the opposition of the Baptists, Quakers and Episcopalians. In old England the Anglican Church was made more alive by the critique of the Nonconformists. And the observation is not unjust that Catholicism is nowhere more estimable than in those areas where it is confronted by a stout Protestantism. All of this incidentally raises a question whether it would be well to have just one church for the whole world. There appears to be a place in the economy of God for competition, rivalry and mutual criticism.

Minorities have their place. Minorities have their rights. And this is a point at which Protestants are disturbed. We are fearful that if Catholics grow more numerous they may impose upon us several legal restrictions, that we may be reduced to private worship as in Spain or that Protestant marriages may be deprived of full legal status as in some of the Latin lands. When Catholic leaders tell us that in all consistency the Catholic Church in a completely Catholic society would have to demand that the state forbid the public exercise of other cults, we are not reassured to be told that this is not likely to happen because there is no completely Catholic society. If this is what would happen, it behooves us to see to it that there shall be no completely Catholic society. As a matter of fact, this practice is in vogue in Spain, and the question is whether the Catholic Church in the United States would, if it could, impose the Spanish pattern. Some Catholic spokesmen say emphatically that it would not, others say that in consistency the door must be left open.

We do well to be watchful and firm. Minorities have rights, be they Catholic or Protestant. But while we are watchful we do not need to be hysterical. There is good reason to doubt whether the pattern of Spain could be transferred to the United States. Spain has had a history unique even in Europe. Caught between Islam and Christendom, she decided for the cross against the crescent, and then sought by constraint to unify her culture. The Jews were caught between the two, and the techniques first employed against Moors and Jews were later turned against Lutherans. This whole background has made of Spain the most illiberal Catholic land in Europe. That American Catholics, reared in our democratic and tolerant tradition, would wish to imitate Franco is extremely dubious.

We can find a better use for Reformation Sunday than to voice our fears and assert our rights. Reformation Sunday will not be a wholesome exercise if it becomes merely an annual blast against

Rome. We do well to recall that those Lutheran princes who gave rise to the name "Protestant" at the Diet of Spires declared, "We protest and testify," and they were more concerned to testify than to protest.

As a matter of fact, Reformation Sunday may well be applied to ourselves. We all need reformation. Only about one tenth of the Protestants where I live attend church. In West Germany the percentage is said to be only six.

We need first of all a revival of faith. Luther's primary word was not that the Pope is wrong but that God is right. To believe in God is not easy. For Luther belief was not easy. That it was hard for him and that yet he believed may make it easier for us. Luther himself was both amazed and helped by the faith of those biblical characters who both doubted and believed. The Virgin Mary was for him an example. How astonishing that she should have credited the annunciation of the Angel Gabriel! She did indeed express a momentary doubt and said, "How can these things be?" And the angel answered, "Mary, you have asked too high a question for me, but the Most High will overshadow you and you will not know yourself how it happens." And Mary believed. How amazing, again said Luther, that the shepherds, when the heavens were opened and the angels sang, should have believed that a Saviour was born in Bethlehem and would be found in a manger! Well might they have said, "This cannot be. God would not have opened the heavens that angels should sing to shepherds. Surely He would have made the announcement to Herod or the high priest." Again, how astonishing that the shepherds should have believed that they would find God's Son in a stable! Luther marveled that the Wise Men believed when they came to Jerusalem and found no festivities for the birth of a prince. All was still. There would have been more commotion if a calf or a lamb had been born. The Wise Men might well have gone home. Instead they inquired and searched the Scriptures, and did not disdain to go to little Bethlehem. How even more remarkable that the Canaanite woman should have believed, when Christ appeared to be comparing her to a dog! Instead of being repulsed, she took the Master at His word and argued that she be not denied the portion of a dog. Again at Cana when the wine gave out, and Mary went to her Son and He rebuffed her, well might she have been too crushed to speak. Yet she went to the servants and said, "Do whatever he tells you."

Luther was astonished that all these believed where he would most assuredly have doubted. Because they held to the yea beneath the nay, he was strengthened to trust in the promises of God when all life appears contrary.

Luther was not credulous. His was no amulet religion. He would have had no sympathy with those who thought that the first American earth satellite failed because it did not carry an image of St. Christopher. He thought that the bones of the Wise Men allegedly at Cologne were probably those of some Westphalian peasant. Odd, said he, that in matters of business a German farmer will in the smallest transaction ask for a receipt, but in religion will credit anything.

Yet, many in our day may feel that Luther was credulous, or at any rate that he believed a great deal more than we can believe, as to miracles, for example. Yes, Luther believed and we may be unable to believe, but we do well to recall that his faith did not center at this point. The Gospel, he said, is not so much a miracle as a marvel. For him the great marvel was what God has done for us. Luther's faith was directed to the stupendous, inconceivable, incredible act of God in saving the world through our Lord Jesus Christ. Think of what this means. The Most High God, the Lord of heaven and earth, Who created and controls all things, this God made man, conferred upon him all things richly to enjoy. And this puny creature, who owed all to God, was not only ungrateful but rebellious. What then should God have done? Luther knew what he would have done. He would have wiped out the human race with brimstone. But God chose rather to send His Son Who took the form of a slave and humbled Himself even to death on the cross. He endured not only pain but reviling. The thieves suffered pain, but not mockery. And so did Christ suffer for our sins as to identify Himself with us and take to Himself the iniquities of us all so that with us He felt Himself estranged, alienated and forsaken by God. What man would ever have endured so much for his brother man? This reason cannot grasp, nor intelligence fathom. This is the amazing, redeeming love of God which we have only to accept, that we may be accepted despite our unworthiness by Him as just.

This is a transforming faith which redeems not only us but also our social relations. At this point take again Luther's sermon on the wedding at Cana. The wine gave out at the wedding. It always does, said Luther, at every wedding. You see some couples enamored of each other who in six months are quarreling, and you see some who have been together for many years who still fall out. The devil is very busy breaking up marriages. The wine turns to water. Now Christ does not take away the water. It has to be there. The hard things in marriage and in life have to be. But Christ turns them into wine, and how blessed is a marriage where the water has become wine, only those know who have tasted of it.

So also it is in the world. The angels proclaim peace on earth, and where this baby Jesus rules there can be peace on earth, but without Him there is only anger, reviling, wrath and contention.

Faith in God's immeasurable goodness transforms all relations. It makes us new creatures and so fills us with gratitude for God's unspeakable gift that what Christ has done for us we seek to do for the neighbor. The Christian must become a Christ, ready to take the form of a servant, and to minister to his fellow in need. Surely such a reformation in faith is relevant as much for Luther's spiritual sons as for any others, and as much on every day of the year as on the anniversary of the posting of his theses.

A Certain Dumb Man

Reverend David Oliver Woodyard

DIRECTOR, UNIVERSITY CHRISTIAN ASSOCIATION, UNIVERSITY OF CONNECTICUT, STORRS, CONNECTICUT, AND A MINISTER OF THE AMERICAN BAPTIST CHURCH

This sermon is by a younger man, his first to be published. He seems destined to make his mark on the preaching world. His use of the I-narrative form in this sermon is unusual and effective.

Born April 27, 1932, he studied at Denison University from 1950 to 1954 and at Union Theological Seminary, New York, from 1954 to 1958, where his major study was homiletics under Dr. Paul Scherer. His thesis was on the subject "Myth and Preaching."

During 1956 and 1957 he was Danforth Intern and Assistant Chaplain at Pomona College, Claremont, California. He was appointed director of the University Christian Association at the University of Connecticut in September, 1958. His work now includes preaching, teaching, and counseling.

MY NAME IS UNKNOWN TO YOU. That is of no matter. I have no significance in and of myself. Men and women in the Bible never do. There are no heroes in the Scriptures—only God, and He is not a hero, but a Redeemer. All you know of me is found in one verse. It was read for you this morning. "Now Jesus was casting out a demon that was dumb; when the demon had gone out, the dumb man spoke, and the people marveled." I was that dumb man. My concern now is to share with you the story of my life. I want you to understand, for one thing, the dumbness which was mine. Through me you may see something of yourself. Then there is also the healing which took place when I stood before the Christ. He stands in your midst too. I ought to finish with a few words about the rest of my life. It was lived under a commission to preach the Gospel and relate the whole of life to God.

I

I could begin with my early life, but that is of little consequence. What is important is that I was possessed by a demon which made me dumb. I could not speak. The mention of demons may offend some of you. It's pre-scientific talk, you say. But turn your heads from the words you reject to the reality you understand. Walk through a psychiatric ward like the one at St. Luke's Hospital. Notice the patients who stare aimlessly into space, who talk incessantly and incoherently, who close their eyes on the world and look into the abyss within. Or read a newspaper account of a governor who in the name of decency and Christianity opposes all which is Christian and decent. Glance at an apartment in Harlem where Rosie and her five children live in one room awaiting the return of a drunken and irresponsible husband and father. Don't be upset because I use the word demon to explain it. You understand the reality. Let that be enough.

But there! We got a bit off the subject. Return to the fact that I was dumb. Do you have any idea what it is like when you cannot speak? It's to hear a community sing "Praise to the Lord, the Almighty, the King of creation" and not be able to join in the refrain. It's to know that a person cares for you and not be able to say those magic words, "I love you." It's to know that God

229

speaks to us through the words of another. Our words become His Word. But my lips are sealed. It's to know that speaking is what distinguishes us from the animals and allows us to communicate with one another. Not so for me. God, I hated those days of dumbness! I could look in, but never speak out. I could reach in but never reach out. I was bound on all sides by myself. My world was none other than a dark, murky, moldy snake pit.

Maybe you find yourself like that. Oh, it's apparent that you can talk. In fact, many talk too much. That may be significant. Often there is an endless flow of words because there is no life and no meaning behind them. There is much talking but little speaking out of the depths. There is much listening but little hearing of the heart and soul of another. It is as if an iron curtain had been dropped about us. There's no communication with anything outside ourselves.

You don't have to be on a subway to understand this miserable isolation. It sits closer to home than that. It's that neighbor across the hall who doesn't speak to you any longer. It's that man who works next to you at the office. There's something between you that a hundred thousand words cannot break through. It's that child or parent you don't understand. They are a complete mystery to you. Sitting in the same room you are miles apart. After a day of broken relationships like that you turn to your mate and say, "I've been beside myself today." That's not it at all. If you could only be beside yourself once in a while, there would be some hope. But the hell of it is that most of us are bound inside ourselves. We are tied up tighter than a mummy in a coffin. We couldn't speak or relate to anyone if our lives depended upon it.

To make matters worse, we can't talk to God either. How many times in the Bible and in your own life does a voice curse heaven with the words of Jeremiah, "Wilt thou be to me like a deceitful brook, like waters that fail?" or those of Job, "Oh that I knew where I might find Him." Sometimes God seems so remote. We doubt if He still cares, if He ever did. Think not that it is His fault we feel this way. He's not unapproachable. He's not trying to hide. He's not playing games. By our own determination to go our own way and forsake His, we have built a wall about ourselves. And when the mortar has hardened, as it has for many of us, we can't get out. Brick by brick we have built God outside our lives. Then we have the audacity to curse heaven!

They called me a dumb man, and so I was. I could not speak. But this may not be the story of my life alone. This sophisticated world of yours is crawling with men and women who cannot communicate with anything outside of themselves. They are tied up inside themselves unable to speak to God, to their neighbors, and in the last resort, to themselves.

II

Back to my story. You see that I talk now. I was healed. I don't want to make it seem too simple, but in a sense it was. One day I met Jesus of Nazareth. I had heard *about* Him, I suppose you have too. As long as it was only *about* Him, He had no power over me. Perhaps that's how it is with you on Sunday morning. You hear sermon after sermon *about* Jesus but are never brought face to face with Him. That's the tragedy of all life, whether in your time or mine.

But it pleased God to set this man before me. You may be wondering what He was like. To tell the truth, I can't remember! Was He tall, or was He short? Was He dark, or was He light? Was His hair short, or was it long? These things didn't seem to matter then, and they don't now. One thing did. In Him I saw God. The Father drew near to me in His Son. God had moved in upon my life. This is impossible! Why would God in heaven come and stand before one who was of no consequence? That question did not persist long, though I have thought about it since. The fact is, He was there, He did care, and I was of consequence. It's hard to express the effect this had upon me. I had been dumb, but suddenly I could speak. For the first time I had a world outside my own. And I could enter into it. I was no longer tied up within myself. The shackles which bound me were broken asunder. I can no longer remember the first words from my lips. But the memory of the release I experienced will never leave me.

You would be interested in one thing. This event happened before a crowd. How mixed their reactions were! Some marveled. They knew something had happened which was of God, and they praised Him. But believe it or not, others tried to discredit Him. They did not deny the miracle, but they claimed He had performed it through the power of Beelzebub. That was a sure method of smearing a man. It was like calling him a Communist today. In a flash He derailed his detractors with a simple bit of logic. "If I am in league with Satan," he said, "why would I be casting out demons? That would be like a house divided against itself. Satan is smarter than that."

And Jesus didn't stop here. He pushed on to interpret what had happened to me. He proclaimed that the power of God had been manifest before our very eyes. It was by "the finger of God" that He had cast out the demon and freed me. In this very moment the kingdom of God was breaking in upon men. We had long awaited the reign of God, but expected it at the end of time. Now its power was known in our midst. In the person of Jesus, a new age had come upon men. Satan had had his day. But this was the day of the Lord. I remember a curious little parable with which He drew out this point. He spoke of a strong man and how his palace is safe so long as he has his weapons and power. But when one who is stronger comes along, the armor in which he trusted and his spoils are taken away from him. In that moment I knew what had happened to me. I had been helplessly bound by forces of evil. I was possessed by a strong man. And I could not free myself. But One Who was stronger had come along and made me His prisoner. It was a different sort of bondage in which I was now held. It was one which set me free—free for God, free for the neighbor whom He had set beside me, and free to be myself.

In this very moment, that same Christ stands in our midst. He's disfigured now. A sorry sight indeed. The spittle of His enemies is oozing down His chest. His side is bruised where they threw stones at Him. Blood trickles down His brow from the crown of thorns upon His head. His hands and feet are torn and swollen from the nails which pierce them. What are you going to do at the sight of that Christ? What are you going to say? For God's sake, get down on your knees—over there with His disciple, Thomas. And make the words on his lips your confession—"My Lord and my God."

Those of us who will so receive Him, who will offer up their lives to Him as a living sacrifice, will no longer be dumb, but will be lifted up into the Holy of Holies, will stand before the Presence of God and for the first time be one with their Father, their brother, and themselves.

III

Now I have spoken to you of my dumbness and the healing which was wrought by God in Christ. As far as the biblical narrative goes, my story ends here. Nothing more is heard of me. I didn't become a central figure in the Church like Peter, I was not a theologian of sorts like Paul, I wasn't even a bishop. My life was quite ordinary. Returning to my homeland, I found a wife and settled down. We had three children. Each morning found me trudging off to work with the other laborers. Each evening I came home to the enthusiastic embraces of the children and my wife. We had our hard times—such as when all of us were sick at the same time. And we had our good times —as when the first girl was married. If you had passed me on the street or visited our home, you wouldn't have noticed anything which marked me off from other men—or for that matter from yourselves.

But one thing was different about my life. I put it to you. How would you feel if this Christ had come and stood before you? How would you feel if you had been freed from a dreadful affliction? I dare say you wouldn't have sat around meditating about what a grand thing it was—and neither did I. From that day forward my life was lived under a commission to preach the Gospel of Jesus Christ. A hundred thousand horses couldn't have restrained me. I had been given the power once again to communicate, and I had to use it to the glory of God. That's why I am here this morning.

Now don't get me wrong. I didn't wear a pulpit robe and become a preacher in the sense you may be thinking. No one called me "Reverend." They just thought of me as another Christian like you who are here this morning. We all understand what being a Christian means; it means that we have been brought to God through Christ. Those who have known this experience have found themselves under a commission to move out into their daily life with this God. They had to relate Him to the humblest of tasks in their lives and the lives of others.

After I had had this encounter with Christ, I didn't look on life in the same way. It was no longer something from which I had to wring out every ounce of pleasure, comfort and contentment. I understood that every blessing I received was from Him, everything I did was before Him and in His sight, every sin I committed was against Him, every tragedy which befell me was His sorrow too. The whole of this life was God's. Every moment of it. Life became for me the concrete area of my responsibility to this God I had met in Christ. Each event was an opportunity to serve Him. Each word was an occasion to speak for Him. Each moment was a time to praise Him. I came to know what Jesus meant when He spoke of scattering with Satan or gathering with Him. Life can go off in either direction. A man can either associate or dissociate the whole of his life with God.

I knew that I was scattering when I saw a man hungry and did not feed him, when I saw one lonely and did not yield him my presence, when I saw one lost and did not drop everything to help find him for God, and when I saw one torn with grief and did not comfort him. But I was called to gather. The whole of life was God's and it was my commission in proclaiming the Gospel to relate it all to Him. When I entered a church on Sunday morning, I was no longer looking for a lift for living. In humility I prayed to be prepared to receive the Word of God. When a day ended, I no longer counted the change in my pockets to determine its worth. I offered its thoughts and labors to God for His judgment and His use. When I got down on my knees at night, my concern was no longer to boast of my own righteousness and barter for the best deal He would give me in return. I could only say "God be merciful unto me a sinner" and "not my will but thine be done."

To gather or to scatter. Those were the only two alternatives before me—or any man for that matter. But to the end of my life I was haunted with a thought Jesus left with me and the crowd. Evil spirits like to come back and haunt their old homes. And when they do, they bring their friends and make matters worse. My dumbness might return. I might again be all tied up within myself. The prospect of that—of losing my relationship with God and my neighbor—has driven me to forsaken my scattering ways and to gather with Him.

SCRIPTURES

For a Thousand Tongues

Reverend Laton E. Holmgren, D.D.

AN EXECUTIVE SECRETARY OF THE AMERICAN BIBLE SOCIETY, RE-SPONSIBLE FOR ITS OVERSEAS PROGRAM IN ASIA AND AFRICA AND A MINISTER OF THE METHODIST CHURCH

This sermon was preached on the WOR Radio Chapel on Universal Bible Sunday, December 14, 1958. In it Dr. Holmgren presents some stimulating figures and a challenge to Christian people to make the message of the Bible more vital in the world and in their personal lives. He shows the need for spreading the Bible to the rest of the world and reveals the startling fact that most of the world does not read and does not want it.

234

A minister of the New York Conference of the Methodist Church, Laton Holmgren is a younger religious leader of vision and courage. He studied at Asbury College, took his theological degree at Drew University, and has done graduate work at the University of Minnesota and at Edinburgh University. Illinois Wesleyan University recently awarded him the honorary D.D.

For five years he was Associate Minister of Christ Church, Methodist, New York, then spent three years as minister of the Tokyo Union Church in Japan. He played an important part in the rebuilding of the bombed church in Tokyo, the oldest English-language Protestant Church in the Far East. He worked with the National Christian Council of Japan and edited the Japan Christian Year Book. In several Japanese universities he lectured on "The Christian Backgrounds of American Democracy" and was a consultant to the Japanese Foreign Office.

During the Korean war, he conducted a series of spiritual retreats for the United Nations Chaplains at Corps Headquarters near the front and visited POW camps. He has made three trips around the world for the Bible Society.

SERMON THIRTY-FOUR

TODAY HAS BEEN DESIGNATED as Universal Bible Sunday, a day set aside around the world to emphasize the importance of our Christian Scriptures. In most countries, from pole to pole, Christians today will be studying the Bible, singing hymns about it and listening to sermons on its importance for the living of these days.

Honestly, though, the claim that this is Universal Bible Sunday is somewhat exaggerated. That word "universal" is too sweeping and gives the impression that all men everywhere in the world today are going to take from their shelves copies of the Bible, read their favorite passages and carry the Good Book with them to their churches to study its pages and sing its praises. Unfortunately this "universal" attention to the Bible isn't going to happen at all, not even in Christian America.

For one thing, there are in the world millions of *people who don't know the Bible*, probably have never even heard about it. To be sure, there are Christians in almost every country on earth but they are a very small minority in most places outside of Europe and the Western Hemisphere. Let me give you a few figures on the Christian population of some of the countries in Asia which I recently visited. Japan, for example, has a population of about 90 million people, of whom only 500 thousand are Christians. Korea has about 30 million people, of whom only about 2 million are Christians. India has nearly 400 million people, of whom only 8 million are Christians, and in Southeast Asia, Thailand has nearly 20 million people with only 15 thousand who are evangelical believers. There are, you see, millions of people in the world who don't *know* the Bible.

For another thing, there are even greater numbers of *people who can't read the Bible.* No one quite knows how many illiterate people there are in the world today but a recent survey by *The New York Times* reports that in the 198 countries and territories of the world there are more than 700 million adult men and women who are totally illiterate. In 97 of these countries, more than half of the people can neither read nor write. So you see even if they had a copy of the Bible, these millions couldn't read it.

Or again, there are still greater numbers of *people who don't want the Bible.* These include vast numbers of the youth of the world, being educated in secular schools of scientific materialism, who regard all kinds of religion as outmoded and old-fogy. The Bible for them is a book of crass superstitions and naive absurdities. There are also those who look upon the Bible as a threat to their own ancient faiths. They have their own religious convictions and their own Scriptures and they do not welcome what they call "foreign faiths." They do not want the Bible to be published and distributed in their countries and use various means to discourage it. Then there are those who oppose the Bible because they are militantly antireligious, such as most Communists. They seek grimly to destroy men's faith in God and have been known cruelly to crush those who teach and distribute the Word of God. Don't forget on this Universal Bible Sunday that there are millions of people in the world who do not want the Bible.

All of this describes the dimensions of our task, for if in fact the Bible is not being universally revered and used today, it is our mission to see that it becomes known, and read, and loved throughout the world. The plain truth is that we are engaged in a global struggle for the minds and souls of men. If we are to win in this struggle, we must take to them a message that will be at once commanding and convincing. Such a message it seems to me must have at least four characteristics:

In the first place, it must be *clear enough for all to understand it.*

236

This obviously means that the message of the Gospel must be in a man's own language. It does the peoples of the world no good to send them newspapers, magazines and books—even the Bible—in English, when they speak Spanish, Portuguese, Swahili, Kituba, Bengali, Ifugao and three thousand other languages and dialects. If this is to become in fact a Universal Bible Sunday, we must see that "men from every nation under Heaven," to quote The Book of Acts, shall once again have the Gospel in their own languages.

It may surprise you to know that by the year 1800 the Bible had been translated into only 70 of the world's languages. It was in the beginning of the nineteenth century that the Bible Societies were organized, in London and New York. From that day to this, a period of only 150 years, the number of languages into which the Bible has been translated has been increased from that mere 70 to 1,127! Today, through the efforts of the Bible Societies, it is possible for 95 per cent of the world's population to read the Bible in their own language.

It is quite impossible to describe the magnitude of this achievement. Probably no one can ever measure the privation involved, the depth of dedication, the hours of devoted study, the suffering and hardship endured to make these translations possible. Let me try to illustrate it in this way. I am thinking of a language in Central Africa which has never been reduced to writing. There are an estimated 100 thousand people who speak the language but no one has ever gone to their remote tribal villages to master their tongue, reduce it to writing, and translate the Bible for them. Suppose you agree to undertake this important task. You will probably fly to Leopoldville on a great modern airliner, then to Luluabourg in a smaller plane. From there you will proceed by bus as far as it goes, and then by canoe far up a tributary of the Congo River. After that you are on your own. It may mean miles of trudging through lonely jungle to reach the first Kiyanzi village. Remember now, you can't speak a word of their language nor is there anyone there who can speak a word of yours. You will doubtless be looked upon with considerable suspicion. Why have you come? Why do you dress so strangely? What do you have in that leather bag? It may take weeks or even months of silent friendliness to convince the people that your intentions are not sinister. Then begins the long tedious task of learning, word-by-word, the meaning of the strange language they speak, with its grunts and snorts and squeals. Years later, you will probably be ready to begin a translation of the Gospel of Luke and the Christmas story:

And so it was, that while they were there, the days were accomplished that she should be delivered. And she brought forth her first-born son, and wrapped him in swaddling clothes, and laid him in a manger; because there was no room for them in the inn.

Multiply this example a thousand times—in the jungles of Africa, in the mountains of Asia, in the hills of Mexico, and you have the story of how the Bible, on this Universal Bible Sunday, is going to men who speak in more than a thousand tongues. I say, if we are to win in the struggle for the minds and souls of men, we must speak to them in their own languages.

Or, again, if we are to win in this global conflict, we must provide men with a message that is *attractive enough for them all to want it*. The first task of the American Bible Society is the *translation* of the Bible; its second task is its *publication*. The Bible Society endeavors to publish the Scriptures in a form that will appeal to people, especially those who are unfamiliar with its contents. For most of us in America, the Bible is a sacred book, bound in somber black covers, with royal gold edges. But to many people in the world, these plain black covers are not attractive or appealing and may even be misleading. I was in the Belgian Congo recently visiting the Kituba people in the Kasai Valley. The first New Testament in their language was on the press in the United States. The Christian Kituba were really excited about the prospect of having the whole New Testament in their own language for the first time. As I sat at lunch one day with some of the African pastors, I showed them my English New Testament with its black covers and gold edges and asked if such a book would appeal to their tribal people. They looked at my book with uncertainty. Black, they said, was regarded by their people as the color of the devil, and I remembered that in English we have a phrase, "black magic"! They said that were we to offer this book to a Kituba unbeliever, he would likely run for the bush in fright. The black covers would surely make this book seem to be some message from the devil. Instead, they asked that we publish their Bible with bright yellow covers and today if you were to wander through the jungle of the Southern Congo you would see the Christians carrying their bright yellow New Testaments to church.

Throughout the world, The American Bible Society is producing Scriptures with these attractive illustrated covers, with helpful photographs interspersed through the text, in sturdy bindings that resist the attacks of weather and insects and with good large type for new readers. I repeat, if we are to win in this global struggle, the message we take to men must be attractive enough so they all will want it.

Furthermore, the message must be *easy enough for all to reach it*. This involves the American Bible Society in its vast program of the distribution of the Bible in the United States and in more than fifty countries overseas. The task of reaching the growing numbers of people in the world with the Scriptures is staggering. The United Nations estimates that world population is growing at the rate of 5,400 persons every hour or an increase of 47 million people every year. Careful studies project a world population of 6.3 billion people by the year 2000. The largest total increase will be in Asia, which in 42 years will have more than 60 per cent of the world's population; whereas the U.S. and Canada will have only 5 per cent of the world's total. But the supply of Scriptures for the whole of Asia, as well as Africa and South America, depends *solely* on the Bible Societies; for in none of these places are there commercial publishers of the Bible as there are in the U.S.A., Great Britain and Northern Europe. At the present time, however, there are twice as many persons being born every year as there are Bibles being distributed by all of the Bible Societies in the world. If we are to keep pace with the world's increase in population, not to mention reaching the hundreds of millions who already are alive and without the Gospel, we will have to double the present circulation of Scriptures every year. As you listen to my voice this morning, hundreds of devoted men and women are trying to do just that. They are carrying the Bible into the remote places of earth, so that men who speak more than a thousand languages may hear—often for the first time—the gospel story, from Bethlehem to Calvary. Sr. Antonio Parisi is trudging up the steep Andean slopes in Argentina. Juan de la Cruz is taking his books on a bus to the suburbs of Rio de Janeiro. Sabia Shenuda is riding his gray burro along dusty roads to the villages of the Upper Nile and Khun Sawai is chugging along the jungle canals of Central Thailand in his Bible launch.

We are, you see, making the Book easy enough for all to reach it.

Finally, if we are to win in this tremendous struggle, the message we take to men must be *great enough so they all can be saved by it*. Men everywhere are seeking answers to the distressing problems of our time. They are looking for a light that will lead to life. They are looking for a way that will lead to peace. That light and that way will be found only by accepting Him Who is revealed on the pages of the Bible.

This search for a way of salvation is characteristic of all the great faiths of the world. Too often we Christians fail to appreciate the important insights of the other great historic religions. Our own Scriptures tell us that "God has nowhere left Himself without witness." These other religions have produced great teachers who have told their people of the difference between the broad easy way that leads to death and the narrow difficult one that leads to life, and their people have tried to avoid the one and find the other. But despite their best efforts, they stand in the presence of good and evil and cry with the Apostle Paul, "The good that I would, I do not; and the evil that I would not, that I do. Oh, who shall deliver me?" It is only when a man meets Christ on the pages of this Book that he finds the Saviour he has been seeking. For Christ not only tells men the difference between good and evil, but, in their struggle to avoid the one and pursue the other, He takes them by the hand and says, "Let us walk this way together." Only when Christ enters their lives do men find the answer to life's most perplexing problems, its most distressing frustrations and its most terrifying fears. If we are to win in the struggle for the minds and souls of men, we must take them this message in more than a thousand tongues, so they may know the Saviour of the world, their Saviour and ours.

SERMON IN VERSE

The Death of Judas Iscariot

Reverend Herman J. Smith

RECTOR OF ST. LUKE'S EPISCOPAL CHURCH, CHARLESTON, WEST VIRGINIA

Herman J. Smith has a reputation for original and unusual sermons. In "The Death of Judas Iscariot," he employs blank verse to portray the moral struggle of Judas after his betrayal. The theology underlying the poetic drama is stimulating and will cause many people to ask themselves, "What is real repentance?"

The Reverend Mr. Smith was ordained a deacon in the Episcopal Church in 1927 and a priest in 1928. He was at All Saints in Hoosick,

New York, from 1927 to 1934; at St. Mark's in Green Island, New York, from 1934 to 1937; at St. Margaret's in Margaretville, New York, from 1937 to 1942; at St. Mary Magdalene in Newark, New Jersey, from 1942 to 1948; and has been Rector of St. Luke's, Charleston, since 1948. In his ten years at St. Luke's he has built a new church, a new parish house and a new rectory, upon the foundation of new interest in the church among the people of Charleston.

SERMON THIRTY-FIVE

Judas, Judas,
Whither goest thou,
With rope in hand,
This dark and dreadful night?

> Go? Where can I go?
> What place is left for me?
> What spot is foul enough,
> Short of hell itself,
> For me to go?
> What place is left among the living
> For one who's lost his soul?
> For such a one as I
> Who's lost his soul?
> For one who has betrayed his Lord
> And lost his soul?
>
> How does the mem'ry hurt!
> How aches my stricken heart!
> He called; the Master called,
> "Come Andrew, follow me."
> "Come Peter, follow me"; and then
> "Come Judas, follow me,"
> That morning in the spring
>
> But three short years ago.
> I heard, and I was glad
> To follow and be numbered
> With the Twelve.
>
> I went with Him to Cana.
> Before Him on the Mount

I sat and listened
As He spoke of God,
The mighty God of Israel.
I shared with Him the hope,
The age-old fervent hope
Of every Jewish heart,
That God would send to men
Messiah, strong and bold.
I thrilled as did they all
To hear Him preach, "The time,
God's time, is now fulfilled;
The Day of God,
Great Day of God's at hand."

My heart almost stood still
At Caesarea Philippi
When Peter made reply
And said for all of us,
"Thou art the Christ."

The Christ,
The Christ of God!
And why have I this soon betrayed Him?
What devil laid his hold on me;
What evil spirit gave I sway,
That I, Judas Iscariot,
Have come to such an end as this?

Say not the devil, envy.
I did not envy Him.
I saw but glory for myself,
A Prince, with Him as King.
I never sought for more.
I wanted only that.

Say not a hateful spirit,
Nor deadly malice, black.
I did not hate Him then.
I do not hate Him now.
Not with the scribe and Pharisee
Sought I His death, and said
"Much better one should die

242

Than all the people perish.
A man, one man for the people."

And never filthy greed.
Not for thirty tainted pieces
Of imperial silver
Have I betrayed Him.
Not for that I kissed Him,
Kissed Him with the tragic
Kiss of Death.
Those thirty silver pieces
I threw into the faces
Of all those vile and vicious men
Who thought that for a bribe
A man does anything.

No thief am I.
Absurd the charge; obtuse the men
Who make the charge—a charge
Not worthy of the Master
Who knew the hearts of men.
But say He did, and say He chose a thief,
A pitied petty thief he'd be
To find enough to satisfy his bent
From out that straitened, stringent treasury.

A broken, worthless man I am,
Broken on God's unyielding strength.
I thought that I knew better
Than did God.
I thought my plan was better
Than was God's.
I sought my selfish way
Instead of God's.
And I have sold my stature as a man
To cold ambition.

I thought that through
The force of circumstance
That I could bring about
To force the issue,
And to crown Him King,
King of Imperial Israel;

And bring the great reward
To me and all the Twelve,
Forsaking all to follow Him.
I thought that I could make
The Christ a man of might.
I thought that we would know
The wrathful, conquering glory
Of that great Day of God.

A frail and senseless man
I am, as any other man
Who pits his plan 'gainst God's.
For God cannot be crossed;
He ever crosses out
The wretched, stupid sinner
Who veers from God's lone way.
He is the God of might; the Judge
Whose justice does untempered stand.
His wrath that brings a nation to its knees,
His unabated fury toward His enemies
Cannot but fall,
And falling, fall on me.
His word, His Law forever stands,
"The soul that sinneth, it shall die."

Christ laid His hands on me,
His strong and gentle hands
In blessing.
And I have laid my hands on Him,
These wicked, guilty hands,
In treason.
These hands are stained with sin,
Stained black with mortal sin.
These hands have made of me a traitor,
A devilish, heinous traitor,
A traitor of the Christ of God.
What place is left for me 'fore God?
Where go I now with rope in hand?

He goes to die,
And so do I;
I go to die.

He goes to die,
Nailed to a tree's strong limb
He did not choose;
And I to die,
Hanged on a strong tree's limb
Of my own choosing.
He goes to die,
Condemned unjustly criminal;
And I, the criminal,
To die, and do what's left for me—
Become a scarecrow,
The tattered, battered semblance of a man,
A scarecrow in the fields of God.

Judas, Judas,
Hanged and dead,
What think you now
Of what you said?

O God, had I but known
Before I made my dreadful final choice!
Had I but seen what now I see
From out this timeless vantage place!

Look there at Peter
Who denied his Lord. He said,
"I never knew the man."
And when the cock did crow,
Went out and wept, and weeping bitterly
By God was full forgiven.
Our God is not the God
I pictured Him.
He's not a God of wrath
Who crosses out the sinner
Save with the cross of Christ,
Save with the cross of love,
Of love, forgiving love.

Would God I could impress
On mortal men the truth
That one as I,
Whose sin was worse than blasphemy,
Need never die,

As I have died eternally.
They only must so die
If they as I
Seek only their own way
And never turn aside
From self to God.
So know, if you should choose
Your self and nothing else,
His love must let you die,
And die eternally.

Repent, O men, repent
While you have time.
Become like Peter; not like me,
Ever left to be
A scarecrow,
The tattered, battered semblance of a man,
A scarecrow in the fields of God.

Judas, Judas,
From hell's deep place,
What see you now?
What look you at?

From this far place I see the Christ
As now He goes from preaching
To the dead on Sabbath past.
It's morning in the world.
There dawns a great new day,
Great Day of God,
Great Day of Peace,
Upon a weary world.

God's trumpet sounds.
I hear His trumpet sound.
Christ rises glorious from the dead.

The stone is rolled away;
The empty tomb's in view,
Death's hold is broken now,
The hold of death and sin.
Now He who died does live,
And lives forever more,

The Master, Lord and Saviour,
The Christ, strong Son of God.

> God's trumpet sounds.
> I hear His trumpet sound.
> Christ rises glorious from the dead.

This day is Easter Day.
God's proclamation made:
God loves, and loving gave
His Son, His only Son,
That having faith in Him,
You may find life that's new,
And live not for the day,
But ever live in Him.

> God's trumpet sounds.
> I hear His trumpet sound.
> Christ rises glorious from the dead.

On Easter it's still true
To be a man as God made man,
The freedom you must have
To make your choice.
You must stand fully free
To know or not to know,
To do or not to do,
To pray or not to pray,
To follow or be led astray.
And even God's great love for you
Will never violate
The choice you make.

Make wise your choice,
You men who live
And know the joy of Easter Day.
You must not die,
As I have died,
A selfish, self-choiced man,
When you can find and know

Your worth, God's worth, in Him.
Be not those sinful men

247

Who choosing, choose themselves
To find as I have found
Who made that choice of self,
And given what I chose,
Now nothing have,
Now nothing am,
Only a scarecrow,
The tattered, battered semblance of a man.
A scarecrow in the fields of God.

Baccalaureate 1958

Nathan Marsh Pusey, Ph.D., LL.D., L.H.D., Litt.D.
PRESIDENT, HARVARD UNIVERSITY, CAMBRIDGE, MASSACHUSETTS; A
LAYMAN OF THE PROTESTANT EPISCOPAL CHURCH

This distinguished sermon was delivered by Dr. Pusey at the Harvard Memorial Church on Sunday, June 8, 1958, opening Commencement week. In a brilliant discussion he touches upon man's intellectual life and aspirations, his need of religion, and subtly shows that faith is the most important thing in human life. It is a privilege to include such a message from the President of one of the great universities of the world.

The man who has laid out the tremendous advance program for Harvard College—a program that involves raising $82,500,000 for additional endowment for new professorships, for new building, and a general enhancement of the educational program, was born in Council Bluffs, Iowa, April 4, 1907. His forefather William Pusey came to America with William Penn; when his father died, his mother taught school and sent him to Abraham Lincoln High School in Council Bluffs. He received the Charles Elliott Perkins Scholarship to Harvard, where he first met "the excitement of reading under the guidance of great teachers." His love of teaching came from these formative contacts; Conrad Aiken, the poet, was his tutor at Harvard. He graduated in 1928, studied in France and Italy for a year, then returned to teach at Riverdale Country Day School, New York.

In 1931 he studied Greek, entered the Harvard Graduate School, and took his Ph.D. in ancient history in 1937. In 1934 he won Harvard's chief literary honor, the Bowdoin Prize, and went to Greece to study as an Archibald Cary Coolidge Fellow from Harvard. In 1935 President Henry M. Wriston engaged him to teach at Lawrence College to help start Lawrence's "great books" course. Scripps College asked him to develop a similar plan for them, then he returned East to Wesleyan University in 1940 to teach in the new liberal arts courses. In 1944 Mr. Pusey taught physics to Naval V-5 students at Wesleyan. The same year he was asked to become President of Lawrence College, where he planned advanced experimental courses to stimulate student's minds with the reading and discussion of great books.

Of his educational philosophy and practice Dr. Pusey has said, "Today the colleges and universities of America are inextricably embedded in and have become indispensable to our national life. . . . The variety of the services they perform and the dependence of more and more areas of our life on their activity and on their graduates, now far transcend what was imagined even as recently as fifty years ago." He sees education, not as a series of jumps, but as a continuous growth from nursery school through graduate school and beyond. He believes in better teachers and in better paid teachers.

Harvard was founded October 28, 1636, the first "colledge" in America; it now has more than 3,500 scholar-professors, instructors, and fellows teaching at Harvard College, Radcliffe College, and in graduate studies. Several of the Harvard men today carry on some of the most advanced research in the major areas of human inquiry. Education and religion are a normal part of Nathan Pusey's own life and be believes in their value for others.

SERMON THIRTY-SIX

IT HAS BEEN AN HONORED CUSTOM for a long time for the graduating class of Harvard College to come together to give thanks before leave-taking. It was thought from the beginning—with unimpeachable propriety, it seems to me—that the only fully worthy object for such thanks was not one's good fortune, nor one's fellow students, nor one's teachers, nor one's parents—not even Harvard —but only God. Hence the Baccalaureate Service. I assume that many of you—I should hope a strong majority, virtually all of you

249

—continue to approve of this one of Harvard's customs whatever the form of worship you are accustomed to. For my part there still seems to me no better way for a graduating class to begin the events of its last few days than to come together in a service of thanksgiving. Graduation from college is surely a major moment, a "numinous" event in anyone's life. Indeed it is such a turning point that other kinds of prayer than thanksgiving may very well be in order.

I tried at this service last year to indicate one of the reasons why it seems to me hard to say anything appropriate to the occasion. This is because of the great cultural variety to be found in each recent Harvard Class—the disparity of faiths and backgrounds, which has made it exceedingly difficult to find an acceptable way to worship together. This promises to grow worse rather than better in the years to come. But there is a no less formidable reason for the difficulty to be found in the advance of secularization in the Western world. I should like this year to say a few words about this, for secularization is today, as we all know, a very serious stumbling block in our society.

We can assume that these services, originating in 1642, had their beginning in what was for all practical purposes still a pre-Copernican world. Certainly in early colonial Massachusetts the nearness and relevance of God had not begun to be questioned, and the process of secularization, which was even then beginning in other parts of the world, was in all probability here completely unknown. The Charles for whom our river is named, though he had departed from London, had not yet lost his head. Milton was only just coming to the great events of his life and to his greatest poems. Newton's birth was still three months in the future. It was not—certainly not at Harvard—a secular age.

I do not know that all the baccalaureate sermons which have been given in Cambridge since 1642 have been preserved. Even if they have, I doubt that there is anyone now who would have the patience to read through them. But if these two conditions could be met, one might very well discover reflected in them something of the intellectual history of the Western world during the past three centuries, but I should be very much surprised if there is much evidence in them of advancing secularization. . . .

Let me now before going further say what I mean by "secularization." The word denotes a growing attachment to a way of life in which there is neither need nor place for religion. It cannot be

250

defined positively simply as attachment to or concern for the world of human habitation, for this was and is the prior, characteristic point of view of various religions, notably Christianity, whose God, it will be recalled, so loved this world that He gave His life for it. It has, therefore, rather to be described negatively as a way of life, which, though its hope, like that of Christianity, is in the world, proceeds deliberately without concern for religion, that is without any dependence on or need for the concept of God. Indeed, in occasional instances, it exhibits rather fierce hostility to this concept.

It may well have been Herbert Spencer who first gave currency to this meaning of the word. I do not know about that, but whenever the beginning may have been, there can be no question that secularism is today a powerful force in the world—in the West as well as in the East. There are many forms and varieties of it. And wherever it is—even in academic communities!—it makes traditional forms of worship difficult because secularism has no need of the traditional object of worship which is God.

The understanding or knowing what to do in the face of this situation is made doubly difficult because up to a point secularism is indisputably a good thing. The dynamism it has unleashed has had a great deal to do with building the world as we know it. Indeed, so great have been its successes that it has itself become a faith and raised a hope that man can through his own efforts—without God—solve all the remaining problems which stand between him and a secular paradise on earth. Its temples may be laboratories and factories, perhaps also libraries! Its very laudable goals are the complete understanding of the physical universe and the mind of man, and then the shaping of these after the heart's desire. Individuals have been swept along in the advance of secularism, and have become fascinated if also perplexed by it. In the confusing, promising, but problem-ridden world it has created, a tragic result has been, as Sir Walter Moberly has said, that "some think God exists, some think not, some think it is impossible to tell, and the impression grows that it does not matter." [1]

The chief point I should like to emphasize to you today . . . is simply this, that in my opinion it *does* matter, hard as it is in our present situation to say it or to have it understood.

There can be no quarrel in a university with secularism in itself, but only with it as it comes hubristically in its turn to pretend to speak for the whole of life. J. H. Oldham, a British author knowl-

[1] *The Crisis in the University,* page 55.

edgeable about both the secular world and the religious, on whom I am dependent for much of what I am here trying to say, has defined in this way what is clearly one of the major problems of our time: "It is one of the many debts which we owe to Baron von Hügel," he says, "that he cleared up much confused thinking by showing convincingly in his great work, *The Mystical Element in Religion,* that there are areas or levels in human life that have their own proper autonomy over against the religious view and are governed by their own distinctive laws with which religion has no right to interfere. Religion, he affirmed, is both everything and *not* everything. Christianity not only acknowledges the rights of the secular, but is especially concerned to affirm those rights. The scientist must be free to disregard religious considerations in pursuing his studies in his special field. The modern world has been right to repudiate ecclesiastical direction in secular affairs. Where Christianity takes issue with the trend of modern society is the assumption that man's relation to the objective world is the whole of life." [2]

Mr. Oldham's own chief interest is in religion; his point is that man's relation to the objective world is not the whole of life, and that secularism, in so far as it proceeds on the assumption that it is, falls short, and must always fall short, of adequate ministry to human need. Here is the crux of the difficulty, for at this point, it seems, individuals will simply insist on seeing the same human situation quite differently. For my part I do not know how to make clear what is at stake other than by simply asserting that the questions which are finally of most importance to all of us in our private lives and for the health of our "selves" are not the questions which secular inquiry normally asks of nature, important as these are. They are rather the questions which religion *answers* for her believers by supplying meaning to life, by kindling hope, and by giving through faith in God a basis for ethical behavior. It is because religion does these things for her believers that it is so important; just as it is that as religion does them her truth is validated.

It is fair to ask why a part of life or an attitude toward life which promises so much has among such wide segments of society fallen into disfavor. The attractiveness of secularism supplies part of the answer, but not the whole of it.

The impression of the irrelevance of religion has been mightily strengthened among thoughtful people by the shortcomings they

[2] J. H. Oldham, *Life Is Commitment,* page 25.

252

have sometimes observed among those who would advance its cause. Too often, for example, they have found in the churches juvenile conceptions of God, primitive notions of a large-size man who exists to be pleased, like an old-style father, or a stern, perhaps even petulant judge, or at best of some kind of anthropomorphic figure Whose conduct could be compared to that of our own more virtuous human beings only to His disadvantage, as Homer's gods with Homer's heroes. It has been my impression that atheists often have in mind some such gods as these, and so it is not surprising, though it is ironical, that in so far as the unbelievers kill them off, they undoubtedly also serve the cause of religion.

The churches have failed again and again at this most central point to help their people to understand that though God cannot be seen as an object is seen, nor met face to face, He can be felt, if we let Him enter our lives, as all-pervasive, concerned in all the experiences of life, and is to be experienced as very close to us indeed in every redeemed human relationship. We can be taught not to be afraid or scornful of mystery and to live in trust with the simple fact that a God who can be fully encompassed by our minds cannot really be God.

There have been other shortcomings from the side of religion which have aided the advance of secularism—aesthetic failings, poor music, impossible hymns, unhelpful, moralistic sermons, the mistaken notion that churches are for "good" people rather than for sinners, or that one goes to church as a favor to God—above all, the failure of the churches to rouse themselves, to cease contending among themselves—indeed one might say to "desecularize" themselves in order to be concerned not for their own selfish interests but, lovingly, for the whole of the world and the whole of life within it. When one considers how inadequately churches have served the needs of people in this new technological and secularly attractive age it is not so surprising that many have withdrawn from or remain outside churches, to the advantage of the growing secularization. It is even more to be wondered that not more people have been put off, or that having once been put off, they ever come back.

But there have, of course, also been shortcomings on the part of those who have insisted on having nothing to do with the churches, such things, for example, as the cultural ignorance which has come from neglect of Scriptures, unexamined persistence in immature conceptions of God, excessive confidence in self, failure to support the churches and to strengthen the ministry (which you will remember was an original purpose for the founding of Harvard College), indifference, above all perhaps the loss of the practice of prayer. But my purpose is not to redress a balance.

It is no part of a college's obligation to endeavor to give or rather to impose answers, but a college should help her sons to ask the right questions—and all the questions. This is a very large and very difficult responsibility. It is of it that I have wanted today especially to speak. For in my judgment this college or any college cannot properly discharge this responsibility if, because of a doctrinaire approach or a prejudiced view of the value of religion, it tends to concentrate attention on a part of human experience and abandons the effort to try to see it whole.

There was a time not so long ago when religious fundamentalism worked to prevent a free play of mind and spirit—was restrictive, unenlightened, fearful, limiting. Unfortunately there are those who honestly believe, in spite it seems to me of a vast amount of contrary evidence in music, art, and personal behavior, that religion's influence must always be of this nature. But with the advance of secularization there has come into being a new kind of fundamentalism, a secular variety. And whereas the old kind, at least in academic circles, has long since been unmasked and put to flight, the new kind, which would forcibly eschew all attention to religion, unfortunately has scarcely as yet been identified, with the result that its noxious influence—noxious I believe to spirit, imagination, and so also, in the long run, to mind—works among us almost unopposed, and at times indeed with approval.

We are members of a secular university in a society which, despite the many churches to be seen in all the towns and cities in America, is fundamentally more secular than we like to admit. It does not follow from this fact, however, that we should be afraid or scornful of religion, or be upset by the fact that following ancient practice at the end of four years of largely secular learning we have come together here for a few moments to offer thanks to God. . . .

It is as hard to explain human virtue in terms of a secular world as it is to explain pain in terms of an omnipotent God. And yet Harvard is still interested in human virtue . . . and as eager to see it grow in each of her sons. Mr. Oldham, coming close to the very heart of the case for religion, even in a secular society, speaks of "the infinite obligation men owe one another."

The infinite obligation men owe one another? Why? It seems to me that this must be for no other possible reason than that God wills it so, for if it is not so from Him, from the very center of the creativity in our world, then it is not really so. In my judgment Mr. Oldham illuminates the basic problem which is posed for us by the advance of secularization in our time when he asks, "Why should we rule out the possibility that the deepest secret and meaning of life should be found, not in the exploration and manipulation of a world of things, but in communication and dialogue, encounter and response?" [3] To this question it seems to me if we are truly thoughtful we can only echo, "Why indeed?"

And so I conclude. Your college hopes that among all the untrammelled study you have done here, from your activity outside the classroom, in association with your friends, perhaps in part from experience in this or some other church—that in one way or another Harvard has helped you to find a meaning and a center for your life. If you have found this outside religion, so long as you have found it for yourself, there can be no fault in that. Agnosticism can be an honest and, at least in the face of false gods, an entirely healthy state of mind. But the experience of many seems to indicate that it is not one in which one can long dwell, for trust we must in someone or something, surely, for our spiritual and mental health, not merely in ourselves. The final answer must, we hope, be God.

At the end of your four years in College we come together in a service of thanksgiving as graduating classes have been doing at Harvard for more than three centuries. Secularization, like cultural variety, has had the effect of making worship increasingly difficult for us. But it has not in my judgment made it irrelevant. Indeed it would seem to me to be a very superficial intellectual credo which would imply that the questions of religion can be ignored in or out of college. For this reason it is my very sincere wish, and my prayer, that with all the other goods which it is to be hoped Harvard has given you she will not have failed you at this most crucial point. You have undoubtedly learned much here. For this and other reasons there is a great deal to be thankful for. Now as you depart from Harvard College I should like to leave with each of you a very personal wish. This is that the total experience each of you has had here will help you again and again in years to come to realize the enlightenment and joy of belief.

[3] *Ibid.*, page 58.

On Being Lukewarm

Reverend William Graham Cole, Ph.D.

CHAIRMAN OF THE DEPARTMENT OF RELIGION AND DEAN OF FRESH-
MEN AT WILLIAMS COLLEGE, WILLIAMSTOWN, MASSACHUSETTS

*This wholesome, practical sermon was preached to the students
of Williams College, and is the type of sermon students will remember long after they graduate from college. Enthusiasm for life
and faith are important, and that importance is shown here.*

*Dr. Cole attended Mt. Hermon School and Columbia College; he
took his B.D. at Union Theological Seminary and his Ph.D. at
Columbia University. He was ordained minister of the Presbyterian
Church in June, 1942. He served as assistant minister at the Church
of the Covenant, Cleveland, Ohio, as chaplain and lecturer in
Church History, Western Reserve University, as visiting chaplain
at Stanford University; and then became counselor to Protestant
students, Columbia University. He was next chaplain and Assistant
Professor of Biblical Literature and Religion at Smith College, and
is now Dean of Freshmen, Cluett Professor of Religion and chairman of the Department of Religion, Williams College.*

He is the author of SEX IN CHRISTIANITY AND PSYCHOANALYSIS,
articles in PASTORAL PSYCHOLOGY, CHRISTIAN CENTURY, *and* THE NATION.
*He is a Fellow of the National Council on Religion in Higher Edu-
cation, chairman of the Williams College chapter of the A.A.U.P.,
and often preaches at eastern colleges and preparatory schools.*

SERMON THIRTY-SEVEN

> "Because thou art lukewarm, and neither cold nor hot, I
> will spew thee out of my mouth," Revelation 3:16

THERE ARE FEW THINGS in life more distasteful than a lukewarm
cup of coffee or a half-melted dish of ice cream. Food should be
hot or cold, but not that miserable middleness which is neither.
So it is with people. We admire those who have a definiteness about
them, a distinctiveness which makes them what they are. They may
be violent in their enthusiasms and lethal in their hatreds, but we

always know where they stand. The mediocre soul, the bath water of whose life is always at a tepid temperature, never hot enough to warm anyone nor cold enough to make one shiver, is a pitiful sight to see. Lukewarm. The word is a symbol of indifference, which means literally *not different*, lacking in individuality, in distinction, in character. All things are the same. Indifferent people, says our text, are neither cold nor hot and therefore God spews them out of His mouth. He prefers the chill blast of an atheist's unbelief to the lukewarm blandness of a man who simply does not care, to whom it makes no difference.

I

There are many sources of indifference. The Book of Revelation suggests that these Laodiceans are lukewarm because they feel self-sufficient. Their citizens are pictured as saying, "I am rich and increased with goods and have need of nothing." One is almost always indifferent to that for which he feels no need. The healthy man leafs casually past a magazine article describing the cure for some obscure disease. He has no sense of need for such a cure. He is indifferent. But the man who suffers with that ailment is far from indifferent. The page will seize his attention like a steel trap. He needs such a cure desperately.

The current lukewarmness toward religious faith springs from the absence of any feeling of need. Many today are saying, "Religion is all right for those who need it, but I don't need it." They are not cold. They are not militant atheists, attacking Christianity as an opiate of the people, as a dangerous delusion. They are simply lukewarm. They are not interested. Religion is for them a matter of indifference. One can scarcely blame them. Most of them look upon religion as a series of statements which they find it impossible to believe. They are not sure whether or not there is a God, and they do not think that it matters very much one way or the other. They are perfectly willing to concede that Jesus was a very good man— perhaps the best who ever lived—but they do not see why the Church talks about His divinity, His being part of a God Who is one in three and three in one. The creed of Christians seems to them ancient, unintelligible and, worst of all, irrelevant. If there are men and women who choose to believe such things, that is their own affair. Our lukewarm moderns are not at all hostile toward the faithful. They are simply indifferent. They cannot see that their acceptance of Christian faith would change anything in their daily lives. They have no sense of need. And as a matter of fact one must admire their honesty. They are right to reject the answers of religion, because they have never asked its questions.

For the heart of the religious enterprise is not primarily a matter of answers. These change from age to age and from individual to individual. Religion is rather a series of questions. Albert Schweitzer pointed this out to the reporters who interviewed him on his first trip to the United States several years ago. They asked him for his solutions to the troubles of our times—the atomic bomb, the tension between East and West. He replied that he had no such solutions, and went on to say that the great minds of the past have not been those which have given the right answers but those which have asked the right questions. This is the business of religion—to lead men to ask the right questions, and indifference to this enterprise is literally impossible. For who can be indifferent to the meaning of his own life? Who can remain lukewarm when he looks forward to his own death? It is with these ultimate questions that religion deals. Why were you born? What are you doing here? What are your goals in life, what standards of value direct your day-to-day existence? What do you hope to accomplish before you die? Is there anything for which you would be willing to sacrifice your life? These are only a few of the questions with which religion deals, and these are scarcely matters of indifference to any of us. They make all the difference in the world—the difference between life and death. No one else can answer these questions for you. That is why the atheist is quite right to refuse to accept the easy affirmations of the pious. The whole point of the Book of Job is that the three friends are far too quick to offer their solutions to a problem that is not really theirs. Job asks the ultimate questions, born out of the agony of his sufferings. He is almost blasphemous as he rejects the orthodox answers of his friends. And in the end, God vindicates him, praising him for his honesty and integrity, while the three friends are rebuked for their easy solutions to a profound mystery. It is not the business of religion to offer its answers to a world that does not ask its questions. The world is quite right to be indifferent to such answers. The first task of religion is to confront men with the mystery of life, the depth of existence. Then they will begin to ask the right questions. And out of the fiery furnace of their own experience they will forge their own answers, which are after all the only ones which have any real relevance to them. They may find themselves at the end within the bosom of Mother Church. Many an earnest soul in these perplexing times is returning through the flame of self-searching to the faith of his fathers. But we must not seek to avoid the flames. Unless the questions have been asked, the answers are sterile and hollow. Unless they come out of the deep places of the soul, they are answers without questions. They are lukewarm, and they produce indifference. God spews such out of His mouth, be they ever so orthodox, be they ever so pious. Their answers are not their own. They have borrowed from the anguish of another. Better the freezing cold of the man who faces the mystery of life and can find no answer than the tepid mediocrity of him who timidly takes the answers of others.

II

Part of our indifference to religion, then, springs from our rightful rejection of answers without questions, and if we deal seriously with the ultimate mysteries of life, our indifference is overcome. Still another source of our lukewarmness springs from our fear of questions without answers. We are afraid to look into the depths of existence, afraid to probe too far into the dark places of reality lest we discover the life has no meaning, that our questions have no answers. Those who could not solve the riddle of the Sphinx, you remember, were hurled to destruction. It seems safer to avoid the path whereon the Sphinx lies crouched, to walk the easier road of indifference. The lukewarm waters may be neither so cleansing as the hot nor so invigorating as the cold, but at least they are safe. No one was ever scalded or frozen in them. So we simply do not ask the ultimate questions of life. We bury them deep beneath the surface of our awareness and refuse to deal with them. We lead a life of carefree indifference, devoted to the pursuit of pleasure and the avoidance of pain. We are gay and unconcerned. But we dare not stop for very long in our rapid run through life. We cannot stand to be alone with nothing to do except to think. For it is in such moments that specters rise to haunt us. The ghosts of buried questions cannot rest. They walk through the corridors of our consciousness whenever those corridors are for an instant uninhabited by the trivia of our daily lives. So we turn on the television set, or go to a movie, or seek out a friend for conversation. Solitude we cannot abide. For it is then we must stand and deliver. Questions flood the mind—why am I here? What is the meaning of my life? What is the answer to the mystery of life? From these we flee, pretending that they do not matter, pretending indifference. But we flee to our own destruction, for we must move faster and faster, close off larger and larger areas of our lives, dwelling more and more in a world of illusion. As Paul Tillich has observed, "Beside indifference, cynicism is a way of salvation."

For at least cynicism faces life's questions with honesty and with courage. Its icy blast may freeze the blood and chill the heart. It proclaims that there are no answers, but it does not pretend that there are no questions. It knows the inevitable necessity of these ultimate problems. It knows that man has some structure deep within which impels him to search, to ask, to knock. The cynic does not try to stop such a quest; he merely warns that it is futile, that the truth must be faced with courage. His answer to the questions of life is, in short, that there is no answer, that life is meaningless apart from the individual patterns of meaning which each man can impose on the face of reality. Man struggles against darkness in the midst of a universe that is blind, uncaring and without purpose of direction. The things he values most are utterly at the mercy of the things he values least. The cynic looks deep within the abyss which is life and murmurs, "Nevermore!" and the echo of his own voice responds hollowly, "Nevermore!"

It is cold—ice-cold. But it is courageous; it is honest; it leaves the way open. The cynic cares. He is not indifferent. He does not pretend that these questions do not count. And one day he may discover that there is some answer. One day he may become convinced that it is more than some cruel joke that man should be so made that he must forever ask and ask. He may discover that the reason man was made to ask is in order that he may be answered. Gertrude Stein is reported to have sat up in bed just before she died and asked her companion, "Alice, what is the answer?" To which Alice responded gently, "There is no answer, Gertrude," whereupon Miss Stein cried out, "Then what is the question?" and fell back dead. Questions demand answers. And there are those who believe that the structure of reality is such that man's questions are not empty and in vain. They are forged out of life itself, and to them life replies.

III

We are lukewarm because we see religion as answers without questions. We are indifferent because we fear that religion may be questions without answers. And there is still one further source of our turning away. We may have learned to ask the right questions instead of turning a deaf ear to other men's answers. We may even be convinced that there is meaning to be found at the heart of reality. But how can we ever know what that meaning is? How can we be sure that we are simply indulging in wishful thinking, while others with whom we disagree have actually discovered truth? We do not wish to take the risk! Fearful of being hurt, we shrink back from the struggle. Our indifference protects us from possible harm. We do not have to invest ourselves, to throw ourselves into the midst of life's battles, there to be winded and wounded. We stand aloof from all parties, all causes, all movements—spectators of life rather than participants in it. Such was the goal of the ancient Stoic. He sought to protect himself from hurt by avoiding too deep an attachment to anyone or anything. His ideal was *apathia* for in himself he could not be hurt; he could not be proven wrong.

But if we think to save ourselves in such a way, then ours is the height of folly. For all those who have peered deeply into the depths of existence, of whatever age or creed, all those who have drunk at the well of wisdom give back Amen to the words of Jesus: "Whosoever seeks to save his life, the same shall lose it, but whosoever loses his life finds it." Dante, you remember, put the lukewarm, the timid souls who feared the risks of life in a dark plain just outside of hell. Even the Inferno would not receive them. The damned at least rebelled, but these pale creatures were only for themselves. Even the frigidly cynical sages of modern European existentialism agree that to live is to act, to venture, to risk. To hover anxiously on the sidelines is not life at all but death. Your heart may be beating regularly and your respiration excellent, but you are dead if you do not care, if you do not dare. And conversely, the man who throws himself into the midst of life may be killed, his pulse and nostrils quiet forever, but still he lives. Is Abraham Lincoln dead? Do Socrates and St. Paul speak no more? Is Jesus vanquished and defeated? Besides these shining immortals, where are the "safe" ones of the past? To live is to care, to care is to risk, to venture, to try, to be hot or to be cold, to walk forth into the dark and unknown places of life.

That is where the questions and the answers of religion meet— in the dramatic daring of the man who has the courage not alone to wrestle with the mystery of life, to ask the questions of existence, but also to test his answers with his very life. For the meaning of reality is not to be found just with the mind. It is discovered only by the whole man making the word flesh in every hour of his existence. And that involves risk. You may be wrong. You may be seeking to advance your own petty will against the eternal structure of truth. But that is a venture which every man must make. Did Jesus know beyond all doubt, past all questioning that He was right, that God would vindicate Him in His struggle with the Pharisees? The frequency of His going apart in prayer, the agony and sweat of Gethsemane suggest otherwise. Why did He cry out, "My God, my God, why hast thou forsaken me?" if He knew, if there were no uncertainty, no risk? Did Martin Luther know as he stood before the assembled might of Europe and declared, "Here stand I," know that he was speaking in the name of God? The record shows that he was tortured by doubt until the day of his death. No man knows. No man can be sure. He can only act. He can only venture. He can only risk and then leave the issue in the hands of God. When you feel the heat of Calvary, are burned by the heroic courage of the noble army of martyrs, seared by the faith of all those great souls who have dared to ask and then to trust their answer, can you still hang back, lukewarm, indifferent and afraid?

IV

You are not called to accept the dogmas of other days. Rather you are called to face the questions of your own day, your own life. You are confronted by the mysteries of existence. Do you dare to look into them, to enter into them, to wrestle with them? You may be chilled by the cold of no answer. Or you may be scalded by the blast of an answer which will take hold of you and shake you and drive you into dangerous paths of living. That is what religion means. You may embrace it with heat or reject it coldly, but you cannot be lukewarm. For such as these God spews out of His mouth.

SERMONS FOR STUDENTS

At the Edge of Mystery

Reverend Russell J. Humbert, D.D., LL.D., D.Let.

METHODIST MINISTER AND PRESIDENT OF DEPAUW UNIVERSITY, GREENCASTLE, INDIANA

Russell Humbert is one of the brilliant young minister-college presidents who combines a knowledge of the church, religion, and education with an understanding of the educational needs and aspirations of young people today.

"At the Edge of Mystery" discusses man's mental and spiritual hunger and his need to discover the mysteries behind the material and spiritual forces of life. His sermon brings the testimony of the New Testament, of outstanding leaders of our time, and his own convictions in support of the Christian point of view.

Dr. Humbert was born in Barberton, Ohio, and attended Wooster College and Boston University School of Theology. He was ordained to the ministry of the Methodist Church in 1930, was pastor of the Methodist Church at Beech City, Ohio, from 1933 to 1935, of Firestone Park Methodist Church, Akron, from 1935 to 1940, was called to Epworth Church in Toledo, 1940 to 1944, and from 1944 to 1951 was pastor of Trinity Methodist Church, Youngstown, Ohio, one of the largest Methodist Churches in the United States. In 1951 he became President of DePauw University. In 1952 he published A MAN AND HIS GOD. His educational philosophy and his deep religious faith are exemplified in this sermon.

SERMON THIRTY-EIGHT

"We are God's children now; it does not yet appear what we shall be, but we know that when he appears we shall be like him, for we shall see him as he is," I John 3:2.

WHAT I AM ABOUT TO SAY to you is the outgrowth of two facts—the one is a mood, the other a condition. The mood is yours, or may I say ours, a normal mental and spiritual hunger which causes us ever to ask questions and seek answers. The condition of which I speak is the state of our world, which, noisy as it is, causes some persons to be lost in a sea of modern babel while others find it a challenge to move beyond the sonic barrier of confusion and doubt to the place where they have faith and certainty.

As a basis for our thinking I go first to a rather strange source, a sophisticated magazine, *The New Yorker*. The lead editorial dealt with a television interview which Edward R. Murrow had with the noted physicist, J. Robert Oppenheimer, who said he was not unworried about the results of the atomic bomb experiments being currently conducted in various parts of our world. The editorial concluded with these words of spiritual value: "In his Columbia University speech, Mr. Oppenheimer used a phrase that is memorable: he said, 'We live at the edge of mystery!'"

Curiously enough, there was a small news item about the same time that beautifully illustrated his words—the announcement that a certain substance in human tears was believed to have an arresting effect on cancer cells. Here is the edge of mystery for you: love, sorrow, beauty causing tears, tears arresting cancer: ergo, love arresting cancer. The fine edge of mystery.

Today in a different way we are standing at the edge of mystery. This is not new, for in a very real sense our birth and continued existence is a mystery. The manner in which we develop as human beings is an unknown quantity. Here we may well adopt the words of the writer of First John when he says, "We are God's children now; it does not yet appear what we shall be, but we know that when he appears we shall be like him, for we shall see him as he is."

Our interest is in education. We are supposed to be professionals and as such, continual learners. Every day we stand at the edge of mystery and these poetic lines best express my own feeling:

I love preliminary things, the tuning up of flutes and strings . . .
The little scrolls that musicians play
The varying notes to feel their way . . .
The hush, the hum with which it dies . . .
But most, I love to see the curtain rise . . .

As the curtain rises and we stand at the edge of mystery may we explore our own mood and prepare to move into the unknown together.

WE STAND TODAY AT THE EDGE OF MYSTERY
IN THE AREA OF THE MATERIAL

Some people complain about our materialism; they deplore our gadgets and they go so far as to damn our discoveries. No doubt we have become more and more aware of things, but along with this awareness we are conscious of the limitation of things. The many things with which we live have also made us aware of the creative mind back of the material. This results in a sense of real humility. Some of you will remember the editorial and the telecast to which I referred a few moments ago, and the almost startling humility on the part of the great physicist, Oppenheimer, which was climaxed with this statement: "We guess in the night and then correct our guesses by day."

The nature of the real is becoming more complicated and even more of a mystery. As Americans, we do not worry about all the frontiers having been conquered; they are greater in number and extent than in any period of man's history. An expert in the field of electronics declared recently that the place where we stand today in electronic development is comparable to that in exploration at which Columbus stood when he pulled up the gangplank of the Santa Maria. This challenge gives us reason to pause and find a trustworthy chart and compass. A complicated and uncharted future can best be met by the trained, yet humble mind. From the sensitive mind of the eighteenth-century poet William Cowper came this statement in "The Task":

> Knowledge is proud that he has learn'd so much;
> Wisdom is humble that he knows no more.

We are in a position to take advantage of the challenge presented by the ever-growing complexity of the material world. Man at his best is constantly curious about the nature of reality. In a much less academic area, a celebrity in the field of entertainment was complaining about his passing the fifty-year mark; he made this complaint in the presence of Charles Kettering, the man of practical engineering fame who was himself past seventy years of age. Mr. Kettering reminded the celebrity that this did not bother him greatly because he found it best to "co-operate with the inevitable." This is not blind submission but the challenge of the unknown in the area of the material. One of the world's leading men of science, President Lee DuBridge of Cal Tech, recently implied that science is one more path to greater human understanding of our material world when he said: "Men climb Mt. Everest, explore the bottom of the sea, sail to the far corners of the earth, explore the atom, the crystal and the stars—all because they are born explorers. . . . Are science and engineering just the tools for man's amusement and for his ultimate destruction? Let us say, rather—and more truthfully—that they are his . . . tools in his eternal struggle to achieve his highest . . . spiritual ends."

Yes, we stand at the edge of mystery in the area of the material; and it does not yet appear what we shall be.

WE STAND TODAY AT THE EDGE OF MYSTERY IN THE AREA OF THE MENTAL

A preceding generation was known as the "Age of Reason," another, the "Age of Doubt," and those who follow us may refer to this as the "Era of the Mind." Great advances have been made in our lifetime in the understanding of the human mind, yet we stand at the edge of mystery in this area of the mental.

With all good conscience we can say the mind has come of age in our generation. The wise providence of God has timed this well, for when men are surrounded by their own creations they are forced to sharpen their God-given minds to guide their creative abilities. Our culture is the result of our co-operative thought, and this process is still in its infancy. Gilbert Highet, in his well-known book, *Man's Unconquerable Mind*, says it well: "All important cultures are manifestations of the power to think. Western civilization is the product of systematic thought. It would be easier to destroy mankind physically than to destroy it mentally." No wonder the writer of the Wisdom literature of the Old Testament said: "A wise man is strong; yea, a man of knowledge increaseth strength" (Proverbs 24:5).

It is important that we feel the tug of the Eternal as we stand at the edge of mystery in the area of the mind. Man by himself can become arrogant, deceitful and destructive. We need the nudge of the Divine to become moral constructive agents. Out of his rich experience as an experimenter and inventor Thomas A. Edison made this observation: "I know this world is ruled by Infinite Intelligence. It required Infinite Intelligence to create it and it requires Infinite Intelligence to keep it on its course. Everything that surrounds us —everything that exists—proves that there are Infinite Laws behind it. There can be no denying this fact. It is mathematical in its precision." The realization of God's power and presence will have a transforming effect on each of us as individuals. A vision of truth and beauty moves us to accept truth and emulate the beautiful. This must have been what Jesus meant when He said: "Blessed are the pure in heart; for they shall see God," and what Paul meant when he said to the Romans: "Be ye transformed by the renewing of your minds" (Romans 12:2).

Since this is the era of the mind, this era needs not only the spiritually aware, but the mentally curious and the divinely discontented. I think it is an accepted fact among the psychologists that the happiest people are those who are discontented, those who are not satisfied with things as they are and find happiness in trying to improve them. The Pulitzer Prize novelist of a few years back, Oliver LaFarge, penned these lines: "Were it not for the twin forces of curiosity and discontent, man would still be living in caves and brush shelters, inadequately clad in crude skins, and nourished by half-burned, half-cooked gobbets of whatever animals he managed to kill with the crudest stone-tipped weapons. Curiosity is not

266

unique in man, but man alone fortified it with speculation . . . so that he could wonder 'why' and 'what would happen if.'"

There is little doubt concerning human ability; this is proved by our record and our accomplishments. We have a body of self-secured knowledge, reasonably trained minds; now we must supply the power and drive for the future. We could well embrace the idea of Emerson when he said: "What I need most is something to make me do what I can." We have confidence in the truly educated moral person. This person has discovered how to teach himself and will forever be a learner. In the area of the mind, we stand at the edge of mystery and it does not yet appear what we shall be.

WE STAND TODAY AT THE EDGE OF MYSTERY IN THE AREA OF THE SPIRITUAL

Because man's religion is spiritual and personal, religion and mystery have usually been associated. Our training and aptitude will help us explore this normal area of life. As we think of this continuous quest we do so in the spirit of the seventeenth-century writer, Henry Vaughan, when he said, in "The Search":

> Search well another world: who studies this,
> Travels in clouds, seeks manna, where none is.

Standing at the edge of spiritual mystery, we live in a predictable, friendly world order. If we were in need of witnesses to support this claim, they could be found in every discipline and area of education. Let me rely upon four men, leaders in the field of science. It was Sir James Jeans who said in 1930: "Thirty years ago we thought, or assumed, that we were heading toward an ultimate reality of a mechanical kind. It seemed to consist of a fortuitous jumble of atoms which was destined to perform meaningless dances for a time under the action of blind, purposeless forces and then fall back to form a dead world. . . . Today there is a wide measure of agreement which, on the physical side of science, approaches almost to unanimity, that the stream of knowledge is heading toward a nonmechanical reality. The universe begins to look more like a great thought than like a great machine." Robert A. Millikan said, at about the same time: "The idea that God is not a being of caprice and whim, as had been the case in all the main body of thinking of the ancient world, but is instead a God who rules through law. . . . That idea has made modern science, and it is unquestionably the foundation of modern civilization." Another of world renown in this field, Arthur H. Compton, said in 1946: "In their essence there can be no conflict between science and religion. Science is a reliable method of finding truth. Religion is the search for a satisfying basis for life. . . . Beyond the nature taught by science is the spirit that gives meaning to life." Then sometime before his death Albert Einstein added his testimony when he said: "God is not playing dice with the universe." Yes, we have learned that God and man must work together within those predictable laws which govern the universe. What we discover in one small area of learning helps us make even greater discoveries in another. With Dante Gabriel Rossetti ("The Sea-Limits"), we say:

> Gather a shell from the strown beach
> And listen at its lips: they sign
> The same desire and mystery,
> The echo of the whole sea's speech.

Another assumption upon which we build life at the edge of spiritual mystery is that man at his best is a trustworthy creature. Not only can we trust the predictability of the universe, but we can trust the persons who live in this world order. Today we think of the many persons to whom we are indebted: members of the family, teachers, benefactors and a host of others. The influence of a great person is like a trail of trust; he leaves a trail in the sky of mankind like the vapor trail of a high-altitude plane. Integrity of character is a normal quality for the truly educated person; this person we can trust.

In addition to our faith in a world order and God's persons, we come to a climax of trust and faith as we experience God—a knowable, understanding, loving Father. Here, too, we know few of the answers; we stand at the edge of mystery.

Here we move more surely into the area of faith. Life is more like the artist and his painting than it is like the accountant and his his books. Some people are content to look upon life as a mechanical accounting procedure, counting the length of days, number of years, amount of money and other tangibles. From this point of view everything is predicated upon dimension and substance. But from the Judeo-Christian point of view we have a God Who is more than an accountant; He is a creative artist, concerned with beauty, truth, growth and those personal qualities which make for eternal satisfaction.

With the full realization that I am negative, let me mention some modern mental robbers that plague us at the edge of spiritual mystery:

(1) Those who worship objectivity and bland neutralism rob the mind of a needed intellectual curiosity.

(2) Those who set materiality at the center of life rob the soul of spiritual satisfaction.

(3) Those who move away from strong moral foundations are robbed of a future house of life.

(4) Those who are cynical and professional doubters rob some of a healthy faith and cause them to flounder in a purposeless doom.

(5) Those who see only the failure of mankind to build a lasting peace rob some of their hope for a better mankind tomorrow.

Each important level of human experience produces new mysteries waiting to be explored. This is the motive power and the abiding purpose of the truly educated person—to continue to explore the unknown. We stand at the edge of mystery in the area of the material, the mental, and the spiritual. The late Russell W. Davenport, out of a rich and colorful experience as a man of letters, helps us find an historical perspective at the edge of our mystery today in the words of this poem, "The Dignity of Man":

> The vision that the world is waiting is
> The same that raced its way in wagon-tracks
> Across empurpled plain and precipice,
> And whispered in the starlit tamaracks
> Where travelers told of freedom in the West
> Around the fires of hopeful bivouacs:
> The vision of a mighty purpose, pressed
> By all the peoples of the earth, to make
> The hidden truth within them manifest:
> And as this continent was free to take,
> And thus awake the hope of all mankind,
> So now, in hope, we hear the future break
> On the unsovereigned beaches of the mind.[1]

*

We are God's children now; it does not yet appear what we shall be, but we know that when he appears we shall be like him, for we shall see him as he is.

I John 3:2

[1] From *The Dignity of Man* by Russell D. Davenport (Harper & Brothers, 1955). Used by permission of the publisher.

Sedatives or Solutions

Chaplain Charles I. Carpenter, S.T.D.

UNITED STATES AIR FORCE ACADEMY, COLORADO SPRINGS, COLORADO

Chaplain Carpenter exemplifies the minister facing war and applying the message of Christ to military men in action and behind the lines. He went through World War II in the Pacific, and in Europe, flying with the army, then later with the Air Force, taking courage and faith wherever he went.

"Sedatives or Solutions" shows his way of bringing men face to face with the reality and glory of faith in Christ, a faith that lifts men and nations.

Born in Wilmington, Delaware, January 13, 1906, he attended Bucknell University, studied theology at Drew Theological Seminary under Lynn Harold Hough, and took his S.T.D. at Boston University in 1950. He was ordained a Methodist minister in 1928, was pastor at Fort Lee, New Jersey, and Federalsburg, Maryland. He then entered the chaplaincy of the United States Army in 1936 and was stationed at Fort Wright and Langley Field, then was sent to Ft. Randolph, Canal Zone, 1937–39. He was Air Chaplain, U. S. Army Air Corps, 1942–45, became Staff Chaplain, U. S. Strategic Air Force, Europe, 1945–46, was at Air Force Headquarters in Washington after the war, and was Chief of Air Force Chaplains, 1949–57, with the rank of Major General.

During the war he almost literally covered the globe with flights, visiting men in action, preaching wherever men could listen (and listen they did, for "Carp," as he was affectionately known, has something to say that made life worthwhile), burying fallen men with dignity, counseling generals and enlisted men.

After the war, he continued to visit Air Force bases all over the world. To see him in action is an event: it was once my privilege to accompany him to several air bases where morale was low and to watch him take hold of and elevate the spirits of hundreds of men.

In recognition of his work, Dr. Carpenter was awarded the Legion of Merit, Oak Leaf Cluster. At present he is directing the training of chaplains at the U. S. Air Force Academy at Colorado Springs and holds the permanent rank of Colonel.

"And he drank of the wine and was drunk," Genesis 9:21.

THIS INCIDENT, described in the ninth chapter of Genesis and the twenty-first verse, happened many years ago, yet it obviously has present-day applications that might be interesting for us to examine.

God was about to vent His wrath upon the world. He directed Noah to prepare an ark and to take into it two of every living creature as well as the members of Noah's own family. Noah built the ark. God then sent great rains upon the earth. For forty days the rains descended, and Noah and those with him floated safely within the ark. Then the rain ceased, and the floods went down, and Noah, his family, and all the animals in the ark came out upon dry land. God then made a covenant with Noah never again to allow His anger to be felt upon the earth, and as a sign of that covenant God placed a rainbow in the sky. Through this experience, Noah was given the opportunity of building a new world. Everything had been destroyed. All was to be made new. Here was man faced with a great opportunity and as always a comparable responsibility. Everything was to be made new through the use of imagination, ingenuity and industry. Noah was to create a new world. What did Noah do? It is stated in the Scripture—"And Noah began to be an husbandman, and he planted a vineyard: *and he drank of the wine and was drunk.*" Here we have an example of an individual who failed in his responsibility and missed his great opportunity.

This is a disgusting picture; yet it is not an unusual one. Of this group here today some of you, possessed of the key to change the world, will end your lives amid confusion, frustration and failure. Some here, who have the opportunity of solving the problems of a modern day, will instead become part of these problems. You will seek sedatives for yourselves rather than solutions for the world. The group in which you will be found will be decided largely by your point of view concerning the meaning of life. What is your interpretation of life? Does life mean to you, "Get what you want, satisfy your own needs, gain position, power, wealth, learn to win friends and influence people?" To be successful must you hold completely to an egocentric position or will you have a vision of the vastness of the world, and dare to use your knowledge to find a solution for the problems of the world?" Will your life be centered in the accomplishment of your own selfish interests or will you recognize the challenge of the needs of others?

A friend of mine tells a story of his little boy. The child playing in the back yard of his house was a "big shot." He talked to his father of "*my* flower bed," "*my* sandpile," "*my* tricycle," "*my* yard." One day the father took the boy to see the circus, and, as the two walked amid the strange new wonders of the circus world, the youngster, looking at all that was about him, reached up and said, "Daddy, hold my hand." Basically, all of us are as the little child, our lives centered on ourselves. The tragedy is that so often we never leave our own back yard.

It is assumed that each of you is prepared to cope with the business of living. Are you now ready to make a living, or have you a vision of the needs of the world, and are you challenged to the belief that, through your own strength, blessed by God, you can change that world? We've now brought God into this discussion. When we talk of God, we begin to talk of religion, for religion is man's search for God and his ultimate understanding of God. We might then ask, "What is your religion?" "Have you thought of God as a part of your education?" "Is personal religious faith even necessary of consideration?"

Let me present this thought in another way. One of the great forces in the modern world is Communism. What is it about Communism that intrigues so many of the peoples of the world? Bishop Gerald Kennedy has attempted to give a clue to that which intrigues in Communism as he tells the story of a Red soldier and an American soldier in Berlin at the close of the war. The clue is found in the statement of the Red soldier; "We are happy not because we are rich but because we know where we are going." If this is true, the Communist concept of life may be opposite to yours, but at least it has given its adherents a sense of direction. It may be that your own concept of life presents a tired philosophy fighting a holding campaign. Why not have that concept, through faith under God, dare to create a better world? All of this discussion should lead you to analyze your personal concept of religion. Halford Luccock writes, "Much of the message of the Church of today is in the realm of peace, poise, and power in perpetual possession." If this is so, then religion becomes only a search for "peace of mind" or "control of fear." Religion becomes a sedative. Human beings lose themselves in a search for that which satisfies selfish want or desire. This was never the dynamic message of the Christ, and this was not Christ's interpretation of religion.

You remember an occasion when a rich, young ruler came to Jesus and said, "Master, what must I do to inherit eternal life?" In modern terminology, the young man was seeking a sedative. Listen to Jesus' reply, "Go, sell what thou hast, give to the poor, and come follow me." The emphasis was on action, "Go," "Sell," "Give," "Come," "Follow." The entire responsibility for success was placed on the young ruler. Within the assumption of this responsibility was found the solution to the problem. The solving of the world's problems lies not with God but with you. You have the key to the problems of the world. You are capable of finding the modern solutions. The ruler's thought was, "what can I get out of life?" Jesus advised, rather, to give something to life. Many people think that since the young man had kept all the ground rules of the religion of his day, and obeyed all the laws, he had a right to expect compensation comparable to his conduct. Actually compensation was not to be given on the basis of his conduct but on the basis of his contribution. In other words, "it's not enough to be good; you have to be good for something." Vital religion is not a sedative— something to live on; but a solution—something to live for. A sedative eases pain. It does *not* cure pain. The world today needs something to live for—a cure of its ills. There is no easy way of meeting life. Life is a struggle, and we are all caught in the whirlpool. Life is action; life is the repeated demand for decision; life is continual conflict. The solution for the present day is found in the "sense of a task" and when we have that "sense of a task," we rise to the heights of accomplishment which the task demands.

Jesus one day came across a man named Simon, a fisherman. Simon had lived his entire life around the Sea of Galilee, and as a fisherman was an expert. Jesus took him away from the Sea of Galilee (out of his own back yard), and gave him a vision of the world. Subsequently, Jesus said to him, "Thou art Simon. Thou shalt be Petras, a rock, and on this rock I shall build my Church." At this point in the life of Peter a strange thing happened; Peter began to act like a rock. The days of denying were over. For the sake of Jesus, Peter defied all danger. For Jesus' sake, Peter finally died a martyr's death. It is true there was a time when Peter backed away from the challenge. Around a fire one night, he sought to calm his fears by saying, "I never knew Him." There came a time when Peter could no longer shirk his duty but devoted his life to the creation of a new world. Twenty centuries of Christianity are not the result of tranquility and evasion on the part of men but rather the result of the courage and vision of men who accepted the challenge of the cross. There is a cross in all solutions. You can be assured that, if you are to find the solutions to the problems of the world, you will be required to pay the cost.

Life Magazine has called this age, "The Silent Age." If this statement is true, because human beings are afraid to express their convictions, then this generation is indeed in great danger; a danger greater than that from the hydrogen bomb or any future form of nuclear fission. Solutions today will be found by individuals of deep, serious convictions motivated to dynamic action. They must live their faith, whether it be political or religious. It would be very simple for those here to become great crusaders. If people could give themselves to the accomplishment of some world-shaking task, if the crusade into which they entered would be headlined in all the papers, and men would marvel at their daring, most people would enter such a crusade. What must be realized is that the significant thing about living is that, in whatever niche in life they find themselves, there they must give their best. It is not the headlines one makes that indicate success but rather the sincerity of the work done in the area in which he dwells. When Lindbergh flew the Atlantic, he was lauded for his skill and courage. Little was said of the mechanic whose ability had brought that lone-engine aircraft to its peak of performance, yet he too had achieved success. An individual cannot move mountains every day, but by expending his best effort, it is possible for him to write "success" into life.

As the team takes the field next football season, most of the people in the stands will be cheering the flashy backfield man running, swivel-hipped, through the opposition. The most important man on the team in the minds of the fans will be this hero. All along the forward line will be the individuals whose names may never make the headlines, but whose consistent blocking and careful fulfillment of their apparently routine assignments on each play will vitally aid in team success.

It has often been said that this is a young person's world. This is a trite statement, but it's extremely true today. I have an opportunity to observe young people of America at their many duties throughout the world. American young people in military uniforms are today everywhere in this world. They can be found living in some forty different countries. They are in Japan, Germany, France, England, North Africa, the Philippines and Korea. Dispersed American young people live in the midst of the differences in the customs

274

of the Oriental countries. These young Americans are faced daily with temptations and the necessity of making decisions between right and wrong. Every decision will affect their own lives, but, in addition, every decision they make will leave an impression on the minds of the natives of the country in which the American Armed Forces are living. Today, American young people in the military uniform have become the representatives of democratic America as well as representatives of Christian America. Yesterday, this country of ours was represented before the countries of the world by three groups: the diplomat, the Christian missionary, and the tourist. The diplomat, trained by the State Department, represented America at the seats of foreign governments. The Christian missionary, true to his divine calling, went into far distant countries to preach the Gospel. The American tourist, blessed with much money, wandered the travelways into many strange places.

Today, a fourth group has been added as our international representatives, and that fourth group is by far outnumbering all the others. We find American young people in the uniform of this nation representing America in forty of the countries of the world. At the conclusion of the last war America missed its greatest opportunity to convince the world of the reality of the democracy and Christianity of America. When our victorious armies entered Germany and Japan, instead of giving real Christian examples through our conduct, we preyed upon the civilians of the conquered countries. We took from them their most priceless possessions for a few odd cigarettes or pounds of coffee. Physical passion overcame and overpowered all personal principles as we "shacked up" and lived among the people. The close of this last war was our great opportunity to begin the creation of a new world. Like Noah, ours was to be a new day, and like Noah "we drank of the wine and were drunk."

Some of you here may have fallen under the influence of that false idea that *"years of military service are wasted years."* You resent the interruptions of your plans for life. You would much rather be about the business of developing a career. I shall not debate with you the question of the modern military emphasis. I submit that the only wasted years are the years you waste. Military service, or any position in life today, is important in its every aspect. Success will not be found at the time you develop a career in law or medicine or science. Success comes when you live your best at whatever task is yours, contributing to life all the idealism and creative ability that have been entrusted to your stewardship. Now is the time to make

275

your contribution to the development of a new world. As when in the Battle of Britain our allies fought against great odds to stand off the vast military resources of Hitler, so you must fight against the breakdown of the moral standards of America. This fight is an individual contest. Your contribution to victory, success if you would call it such, is made as you maintain a personal life representative of the religious tradition of the nation.

You will need, in making your contribution to the building of a new world, all the intellectual resources of which you are possessed. You will need in addition to your personal strength a contact with God, a personal God, Whose power is unlimited and available to those who call upon Him. I challenge you to the all-important task of contributing through life to building a better world. If you can meet this challenge, then I am sure there will be written as a final summation of your life a better epitaph than written of Noah: Noah, the man who failed to meet the responsibilities of his day; Noah, the man who found a sedative rather than a solution. For of him, it was finally written in the conclusion of the chapter from which our text is taken—"And all the days of Noah were nine hundred and fifty years, *and he died*."

THE SOCIAL GOSPEL

Hearts Waiting for What?

Reverend Gardner Taylor, D.D.

PASTOR, CONCORD BAPTIST CHURCH OF CHRIST, BROOKLYN, NEW YORK, AND PRESIDENT, THE PROTESTANT COUNCIL OF NEW YORK

Gardner C. Taylor was born in Baton Rouge, Louisiana, June 18, 1918, the son of a minister. He studied at Leland College in Louisiana and Oberlin Graduate School of Theology. Leland College has since awarded him the honorary D.D. in recognition of his work.

Before beginning his present work as Pastor of the Concord Baptist Church of Christ, Brooklyn, New York, in 1948, Dr. Taylor served successively and successfully as pastor of Bethany Baptist Church, Elyria, Ohio; Beulah Baptist Church, New Orleans, Louisiana; and Mt. Zion Baptist Church, Baton Rouge, Louisana.

In his present pastorate, Dr. Taylor ministers to a membership of more than ten thousand. He is a member of the General Council

of the American Baptist Convention, and president of the Protestant
Council of the City of New York.

In 1947 he preached in Copenhagen, Denmark, during the
World Baptist Alliance. In 1950 he preached at the World Baptist
Alliance in Cleveland, Ohio, and in 1951 gave the commencement
address at Colgate-Rochester Divinity School.

He has spoken at many universities, and delivered a series of
sermons to the Annual Convention of Canadian Baptists. In 1953,
Oberlin College conferred upon him one of its First Alumni Cita-
tions for his influence as a preacher. In 1955, he addressed the
Golden Jubilee of the World Baptist Alliance in Westminster Hall,
London.

In 1952, the Concord Church was destroyed by fire and Dr.
Taylor has taken the lead in the rebuilding of the church at a cost
of $1,200,000. On April 1, 1956, he led the Concord Congregation
into its new church. In 1958 he was elected president of the Protestant Council of the City of New York, the first Negro to hold this
office. On March 28, 1958, he was sworn in as a member of the
Board of Education of the City of New York.

SERMON FORTY

> "And it shall be said in that day, Lo, this is our God; we
> have waited for him, and he will save us: this is the Lord;
> we have waited for him, we will be glad and rejoice in
> his salvation," Isaiah 25:9

IN "TINTERN ABBEY," William Wordsworth, in words among
the sweetest in the English language, speaks of the haunting sense
of high destiny which belongs to us. He speaks for all of us when
he describes an inward yearning toward something worthy which
he has not yet reached, a persisting, poignant compulsion toward a
fulfillment not yet achieved. In heart-breakingly touching language,
Wordsworth says:

> And I have felt
> A presence that disturbs me with the joy
> Of elevated thoughts; a sense sublime
> Of something far more deeply interfused,
> Whose dwelling is the light of setting suns,
> And the round ocean and the living air,
> And the blue sky, and in the mind of man. . . .

There hangs over each of us the awareness of moving toward something, of becoming something far finer than we have ever been. Ah, we may wince, but we are never for long free of that yearning to become better, that instinctive squirming to be let loose from some imprisoning and crippling web in which we are caught. This sense of inward struggle toward something, of awareness of some huge, approaching wonder forms the basis for the earth's finest literature, informs and indwells the world's worthiest crusades and fashions the splendor, the most glorious splendor of our humanity. We speak of this characteristic in us in many ways, as "getting ahead," or "bettering our condition," or "our ship coming in," or "the pot of gold at the end of the rainbow." Whatever the term, we are aware of something about to happen—big, wonderful.

In all the sweep of the Bible there is this constantly recurring note. Hearts waiting—for what? The Bible pulls the tinsel from around this awareness and says quite honestly that we are waiting for God. This is our contract with life. For the coming of the Lord God into our arena of action, into our theater of operations, the righting of wrong by the aid of the Divine arm—for these things our world waits.

So it was with the ancient prophet, this strangely haunting poet whom we call Isaiah. In a day of darkness for his people, as black as midnight, the man speaks of the coming of God in power. Hungry masses will have set before them God's feast, pride and arrogance shall fall and the fortresses of evil shall be leveled with the dust. Beneath the events that fill the Bible there is this continuing theme of God in the act of bringing something unspeakably wonderful to pass. This is the evangel.

"And it shall be said in that day, Lo, this is our God, we have waited for him, and he will save us: this is the Lord; we have waited for him, we will be glad and rejoice in his salvation." We need a God Who can get in it with us and we need a God Whose power and might are set against evil. In that day shall we say, "Lo! this is our God."

It has been repeatedly pointed out that a fatal flaw in Greek religious faith as it is represented in Greek mythology is the distance of the gods on Olympus from the heat and fray of life in Athens and the other Greek city-states. Almost all of the Greek tragedies end in the death and disgrace of all of the principals. No one survives, the good die with the bad and there is no vindication for either right or wrong. The gods of Greece were too far from the needs of men, and so the cause of righteousness never knows a certain and worthy end.

Any man who would bless the lives of people must somehow "sit where they sit." Wilfred Grenfell became the angel of Labrador because he went and lived with the people of that needy place. If Christians are going to bless their community, it must be because they have entered the same sorrows, felt the same temptations, known the same heartbreaks as those to whom they would speak. As you know more about life you speak less easily about it, but what you have to say carries more weight. Arthur Gossip, so long the prince of the Scottish pulpit, said that shortly after his wife's bewildering and sudden death, when he had finished preaching in a church of a certain Sunday, he heard a woman say to another as he passed, "If I could only believe that man knows what he is talking about, I would start all over again." Another replied to her, "He does. His wife died but the other day." The world does wait for men and women who speak with spiritual authority because they have walked slippery ways and have found and can report that "underneath are the everlasting arms, and the eternal God is our refuge."

God Himself to be our God must enter the arena of our troubles, the theater of our operations. This is at the heart of the Good News we call the Gospel: We have a God Who comes where we are. I hear in the distance the cry of a man who has stood over a fallen and wounded race, and has watched the God of all the earth feel their loneliness, participate in their heartbreak. He cries, "In all their affliction he was afflicted." We have no less a Gospel than that God is kin to us. One hears the words of the brave old Book and takes hope, for our hearts wait for a God Who can feel our sorrow and share our heart's desires.

Dare we hope that God throws His strength in on the side of truth and justice? Or is raw power forever on the throne and the heartbroken disinherited forever on the scaffold? Are we to fight these battles for peace, for a land of equal opportunity by ourselves? Granted the brilliant dedication of those who labor in the cause of true freedom in this land, is this all the strength we have? Is our last court of appeal our own Supreme Court, or is God going it with us? Is He near enough to know the hard fight of downtrodden people? Can He hear the groan of the slave?

A man in the South, a Negro handy man, was asked by his white employer, a bank president, "John, why are the colored people spending all of their money going to court to get equal rights? All of the money and power and government in the South are on our side. How do you hope to get the things you want if we fight you?" The Negro thought a moment and answered, "S'pose God say so?" Does He?

There is great sorrow these days in the hearts of many Americans who love this land and who believe that God has for it some worthier destiny than our bitter divisions of race and region. Of course, we must in sorrow and shame confess that we are reaping the bitter harvest after a long season of sowing expediency and sub-American ideas and attitudes. For the forseeable future we shall doubtless find ourselves in a painful period of being purged and cleansed of our great national sins.

We can all take comfort and courage in the awareness that there is Another who throws in His strength on the side of justice and a fairer, juster world. Our problems are huge, the road we must travel in this nation and in our world toward peace and harmony may be a long and arduous one, but God travels it with us, or better still, leads us along the road we must journey. Our land, America, has a better day on ahead. We shall yet stand together in this land with all races and regions united in liberty's holy cause to the Glory of God and in the vindication of our democratic assumptions. For God is in it with us.

There are signs almost beyond number of His presence in the struggle of our nation toward its democratic fulfillment. Our history seems to say that God has presented all of us in this nation with the holy possibility of bringing to pass on these shores a society of unity and mutuality in the midst of all our diversities of color and creed and national origin. Step by step, sometimes in a way that we could not comprehend, we have been led to the fulfillment of that destiny. To the glory of this nation, no matter how dim the vision of the better society has become betimes, it has never died in the hearts of millions of Americans. And at times, once in the great national sorrow of civil conflict, the vision has been the paramount concern of our American people.

Take our lives one by one and there is a long chronicle of failure and mediocre living. Is He close enough to sense our broken dreams and our blasted hopes, our failures and our yearnings? How does He look upon our cemeteries of wasted years? The old Book puts it bravely: "Like as a Father pitieth his children, so the Lord pitieth his children." In this we can take hope.

280

James Stewart reminds us of a poem of Coventry Patmore. "The Boy," it is called, and tells of how one day Patmore's little son, having been disobedient, was sent to bed without supper and unkissed. The poem goes on to tell how the father, his anger cooling, crept up later that night into the room where the child lay asleep, his face still damp with tears, and around him to comfort his sad little heart, the sleeping child had gathered some of his favorite toys. The father leaned over and kissed those childish tears away, and left some of his own. As he did it occurred to him that God might feel the same toward His children. He wrote:

> When Thou rememberest of what toys
> We made our joys
> How weakly understood
> Thy great commanded good
> Then, Fatherly not less
> Than I whom thou hast moulded from the clay,
> Thou'lt leave thy wrath, and say
> I will be sorry for their childishness.

"Like as a father pitieth, so pitieth the Lord his children."

Always the Gospel proclaims God's nearness to our need. Always in our poor stained humanity there is an anguished cry from broken generations, "Is there no balm in Gilead, is there no physician there? Why then is not the health of the daughter of my people recovered? O that my head were waters, and mine eyes a fountain of tears, that I might weep day and night for the slain of the daughter of my people!" And there is the answer of God, the tramp of His foot far off—thundering down the road of the centuries toward our relief and redemption, the cry on His lips, "O Israel, Fear not: for I have redeemed thee, I have called thee by thy name; thou art mine. When thou passest through the waters, I will be with thee; and through the rivers, they shall not overflow thee: when thou walkest through the fire, thou shalt not be burned, neither shall the flame kindle upon thee. For I am the Lord thy God . . ."

God close to my crying heart, God close to our broken society! —that is the Gospel of the New Testament.

Hiroshima: Our Guilt and Our Atonement

Reverend Arthur W. Mielke, D.D.

MINISTER, PARK CENTRAL PRESBYTERIAN CHURCH, SYRACUSE, NEW YORK

This sermon was preached in Park Central Church on Sunday, April 20, 1958. It discusses a point which most Americans prefer to sweep under the rug: Are we guilty as a nation and as a people, especially as Christians, for dropping the hydrogen bomb on Hiroshima? Dr. Mielke has carefully documented it with facts about the event itself and its aftereffects. He presents a sermon which will cause Christian men and women serious thought.

As minister of Park Central Church, Arthur Mielke has taken a place of leadership in Syracuse and is known among the people of the city and the members of his congregation as a preacher who believes with deadly seriousness in the Gospel as the way of life.

Arthur Mielke was born in Danville, Illinois, in 1912. He attended the University of Illinois, from which he received his A.B. degree in 1933, and received his B.D. degree from Yale Divinity School in 1936. He then spent a year at Mansfield College, Oxford, England, on a Yale Divinity School fellowship. Hamilton College conferred the D.D. upon him in June, 1958.

He was ordained a Presbyterian minister in 1938, and served the First Presbyterian Church, Cooperstown, New York, from 1938 to 1942. From 1942 to 1945 he was minister of the First Presbyterian Church, Middletown, New York, and during most of that period (1943 to 1945) he also served the Middletown Congregational Church. He has been pastor of the Park Central Presbyterian Church since 1945.

Dr. Mielke is active in denominational work and is now serving as a member of the Permanent Judicial Commission of the New York Synod. He is also a member of the Board of Christian Education of the United Presbyterian Church, U.S.A. He has taken part in the Church Officer Training Program of the Presbyterian Church and is coauthor of one of the textbooks used, YOUR CHURCH AND YOUR

JOB. *In addition to serving his downtown church, he has led his members to take significant steps to minister to the interracial neighborhood in which the church is located.*

SERMON FORTY-ONE

"But Jacob said, 'I will not let you go, unless you bless me,' " Genesis 32:26, R.S.V.

AT ABOUT SEVEN O'CLOCK in the morning of Sunday, August 6, 1945, the Japanese radar system reported the approach of a small force of enemy planes. Hiroshima and the surrounding towns were alerted. By eight o'clock it was determined that only three planes were in the group. The alert was removed on the assumption that the planes were on a photographic-reconnaissance mission. Shortly after eight-fifteen the National Broadcasting Company of Japan noticed that the Hiroshima radio was off the air. Attempts were made to reach the station by telephone, but no answer was received. At eight-thirty the radio officials were so worried that they asked the railroad telegraph station in Tokyo to try to reach Hiroshima. They were told that the telegraph lines had been cut. It was also reported to them that a large explosion at Hiroshima had been seen by people about thirty miles from the city.

The radio officials, still not knowing what had happened, decided to notify the central government. The government, through military channels, tried to reach Hiroshima by radio, but received no answer. By this time the government officials were also growing concerned. They knew that the various communication centers in Hiroshima were miles apart from each other, and that there was no ammunition dump in the city. They could not imagine what kind of explosion could have occurred to destroy all lines of communication. Further, the three enemy planes which had been reported in the vicinity could not possibly have destroyed all the communication centers or caused the magnitude of explosion which was reported.

So, the Japanese army sent a colonel to Hiroshima by plane to investigate the situation. When he was still a hundred miles from the city, he saw a sight which he could not comprehend—a huge pillar of smoke that stretched unbelievably high into the air. As he approached the city, he circled and looked down in utter amaze-

283

ment at the devastation beneath him. Unable to land at Hiroshima, he finally set his plane down at an airfield thirty miles away. By that time some people who had escaped from Hiroshima reported to him that a large bomb had been dropped on their city, that terrible fires were raging through most of its streets, and that thousands must surely have perished.

As was later revealed, one of the three American planes had dropped the first atom bomb ever to be dropped on a city. It exploded with the power of twenty thousand tons of T.N.T. and with a blast equal to that of all the high explosives which could be carried in a fleet of two thousand heavy bombers. The bomb fell near the geographic center of the city of 343,000 persons, a city of about the size of metropolitan Syracuse, and completely destroyed 60 per cent of the city. The heart of the city was completely pulverized. One army officer remarked that the city seemed to have been ground into dust by the foot of a giant. It was later found that twenty-six of the thirty-three fire companies had been completely destroyed, that two thirds of the approximately eight hundred firemen had been killed, that 260 of 300 physicians and surgeons had been killed, and that 1,800 of 2,400 nurses had been killed. Deaths numbered more than one hundred thousand and another hundred thousand were injured. They died as a result of the shock wave, burns, falling debris and the damaging effects of radiation. Many more have died from effects of radiation since the bombing.

We are told that the bomb which fell on Nagasaki a few days later was of a different type, but the results were much the same—the tremendous flash and the billowing mushroom of smoke, followed by death, destruction, suffering, pain and bewilderment.

Harrison Brown, an atomic scientist, wrote in his book, *Must Destruction Be Our Destiny?*:

At Hiroshima man committed what must without doubt be the greatest single slaughter of human beings that has occurred in any one day in history. We remember the horror of Lidice and our shock at the mass butchery in the German concentration camps; we have read of the mercilessness of Attila, the rape of Nanking, the Black Hole of Calcutta, and the Death March of Bataan. In terms of mass slaughter, all these are but flimsy shadows in comparison to Hiroshima. It is fortunate for the Japanese that they surrendered shortly after the second bomb, as it is, indeed, for our own consciences, that more were not used.

It certainly is. For the burden on our consciences is heavy enough for having dropped the first atom bomb on a defenseless civilian population—and also the second—without having to live with the memory of dropping more. The finger of history has already written. The indelible record cannot be changed. Our nation was the first to use this unbelievably terrible weapon of destruction, and to use it without warning. It is unpleasant to dwell on this fact, but it remains a matter of record that the first nation to do this was not a backward, uncivilized, unchristian nation, but our own beloved country.

At the time we rejoiced because the two bombs brought the war with Japan to a speedy close. It was argued then, as it is still argued, that such drastic action was justified because it saved the lives of thousands of young Americans and Japanese by ending the war. For this we are all grateful; but our consciences are still deeply troubled at the thought that the moral price we paid for victory was so high as to amount to a moral and spiritual defeat.

Some will say that the decision to drop the bomb was made for purely military considerations, that all is fair in love and war, that if we created the bomb first we had a right to use it first, and that, since the war is over, we should forget about the moral implications of what was, at the time, a military necessity. But the trouble with this argument is that we have not let the Nazis and Communists off so easily. Our nation took the lead in bringing the leaders of Nazi Germany to an international court in order to condemn them in the name of the conscience of mankind. And we have just as strongly condemned the leaders of Communist Russia for their inhuman treatment of political enemies and satellite people. Since we all stand under the judgment of the same God, we cannot expect Him to bring our enemies to judgment while letting us off. Either we should treat the Nazis and Communists as lightly as we want to be treated, or we must acknowledge that we, too, have sinned. Any sensitive Christian knows that in the long run there is no alternative but the latter. Somehow we must face up to our guilt in dropping the first atom bomb.

Others will say that our deed was only tit for tat, since Japan had first committed the treachery of Pearl Harbor. But two wrongs have never made a right and never will. We firmly believe that Japan stands condemned before God for Pearl Harbor, but this is her spiritual problem, just as Hiroshima is ours. Paul gave us some clear advice at this point when he wrote to the Romans: "Beloved, never avenge yourselves, but leave it to the wrath of God; for it is written, 'Vengeance is mine, I will repay,' says the Lord."

Still others maintain that the difference between dropping an atom bomb and the saturation bombing of a city like Tokyo is but a matter of degree, and that we should be no more disturbed at one than at the other. However, the atom bomb marks a distinct breakthrough in scientific achievement and now makes possible the extinction of whole cites and nations. The atom bomb and its successor, the hydrogen bomb, are so unbelievably destructive as to usher in an entirely new era of warfare. Those who would use such a bomb must reckon with the intense moral problem of releasing a force which now makes it possible for one nation to destroy the cities of another nation before the victim could do anything about it. The many terrible moral problems presented by war come to a tragic focus in the atom bomb, so that we are now at the point in history where we must either learn to live together in peace and mutual trust or face the real possibility of self-destruction.

If some people are still able to justify our dropping the first atom bomb ever to be let loose on a city, it is very clear that two groups of people—the scientists and the churchmen—are deeply troubled. The atomic scientists in particular are frightened, disturbed men. To read their writings leaves no doubt that they wonder whether they have created a Frankenstein which will devour its creators. They leave no doubt that it is now theoretically possible for one nation to destroy another nation. They speak and write like Old Testament prophets, foretelling destruction if we do not speedily develop a world government and the will to live with one another in peace. The old days of antagonism between science and religion are gone, for scientists have taken to their pulpits like preachers to warn against the potential evil of what they have created. There is a moral urgency in their writings, and we can understand why. They know the terrible consequences of the misuse of this new power.

A friend of mine, a minister of a church in Princeton, New Jersey, tells of a visit paid him by the Rev. Kyoshi Tanimoto, the Methodist minister who miraculously survived the blast at Hiroshima. Mr. Tanimoto asked to meet Dr. Einstein, because he, a man on whom the first atom bomb fell, would like to meet the man who made the atom bomb possible. The great mathematician was pleased to welcome the visitor from Japan. One can only imagine the drama and emotional excitement of that meeting at the professor's home. As the conversation was reported, Dr. Einstein ventured to suggest that the bomb should never have been dropped on a city, but that it should have been dropped on water or waste land. The Japanese minister, in the gracious manner of his people, tried

286

to set Dr. Einstein at ease by suggesting that surely the Japanese would have dropped the bomb on America if they had been the first to develop it. With firmness in his voice and with moral conviction, Dr. Einstein replied, "Even if you might have done it to us, this would still have been no excuse for us to drop the bomb." He was saying that wrong is still wrong and that there are no extenuating circumstances in God's moral kingdom.

Churchmen seem unable to match the moral fervor of the atomic scientists, but they have not been silent. The Federal Council of Churches meeting in March, 1946, adopted this clear statement:

The surprise bombings of Hiroshima and Nagasaki are morally indefensible. They repeated in a ghastly form the indiscriminate slaughter of noncombatants that has become familiar during World War II. They were loosed without specific warning, under conditions that virtually assured the deaths of 100,000 civilians. No word of the existence of the atom bombs was published before the actual blasting of Hiroshima. A prior demonstration on enemy soil (either in vacant territory or on a fortification) would have been quite possible and was actually suggested by a group of scientists concerned. Japan's strategic position was hopeless. Even though the use of the new weapon last August may well have shortened the war, the moral cost was too high.

True, we may find that we have won a Pyrrhic victory. We won the war, but at the terrible cost of a crushing moral defeat. We have not yet found any satisfactory explanation for not trying first to drop the bomb on water or waste land as a warning of what would come if Japan failed to capitulate. To those who argue that this would have availed nothing, we reply that we did not give ourselves or them a chance to find out. So, we live with our gnawing guilt at having dropped the first atom bomb on a civilian city, and having done so without making an attempt at a warning. A sense of impending doom and helplessness hangs over us. We fear that another nation might initiate an atomic attack on us, and we know, in our heart of hearts, that we would not be in a position to pass judgment on their deed.

But, having recognized our guilt, can we find some way of atoning for it? We, like Jacob, are troubled by the dark memory of what we have done. Jacob secured the birthright, but he did so at the cost of a clear conscience. He cheated his aged, blind father and his twin brother. But his conscience would not let him rest. One night he had it out with God in a spiritual struggle so violent that it left him with a physical handicap. He limped for the rest of his days. As he described the experience, he said that he dreamed of an angel of God who wrestled with him till the break of day. So intent was he on resolving his problem of guilt that he said to the angel, "I will not let you go, unless you bless me." Shortly thereafter, Jacob sought out Esau, and they were reconciled. May we hope that out of the struggle within our consciences we may be moved to seek reconciliation with those we have so painfully hurt?

This desire for atonement is already finding expression in many ways.

For one thing, consider the terms of the peace treaty we made with Japan at the close of the war, and the clear purpose of our occupation forces to lay the foundations of democracy in that country. John Foster Dulles, the chief architect of the treaty and of that policy, spoke in 1952 as follows:

The treaty placed no limitations upon Japan's trade and no dismantling of her shipbuilding or textile plants. Future reparation was to be limited to the use of Japan's two surplus assets; namely, surplus industrial capacity and surplus labor.

No limitations were placed upon Japan's right to defend herself since none of the Allied Powers had accepted any limitations of armaments for themselves.

Never before in history have victors in a cruel, costly and prolonged war offered the vanquished a peace of such unqualified reconciliation.

This treaty, and our occupation policies, went part way toward atonement of our sins at Hiroshima and Nagasaki.

A second expression of this desire for atonement is found in the many quiet acts of reconciliation which are going on between Americans and Japanese. An incident which dramatically symbolizes this activity took place some months ago on the television program called, "This Is Your Life." Those who saw it tell how the Rev. Mr. Tanimoto, the Methodist minister in Hiroshima, and the pilot of the plane from which the bomb was dropped, were introduced to each other before a nation-wide television audience. Both parties were reasonably nervous at the prospect of the encounter, but they were soon engaged in conversation by the master of ceremonies. When asked what thoughts first went through their minds, Mr. Tanimoto said that he fell to the ground and said to himself, "Oh, God, what has happened?" The pilot said that when he circled the city and looked back at the tremendous mushroom of smoke and fire, he cried out, "Oh, God, what have we done?" Then the two men shook hands, giving expression to their obvious feeling of common regret and to their relief at this chance for reconciliation. How many other incidents like this have taken place in less dramatic situations? We cannot know, but we are sure that there have been many.

A third episode in the drama of atonement took place several years ago when the so-called Hiroshima Maidens were brought to this country for the treatment of burns suffered in the bombing. Like many others in Hiroshima, they had been unable to secure adequate medical treatment. In 1953, a group of young women gathered together in the church of this same Mr. Tanimoto. At the time of the bombing, they were young children. But when they met in the church, they were young ladies trying to find a place for themselves in society. Marriage seemed remote. Gainful employment was difficult because of their appearance and their disabilities resulting from arm and hand burns.

Meanwhile a number of Americans began to promote ways of bringing these maidens to our country for medical treatment. It is difficult to know to whom credit most belongs, though Norman Cousins, Editor of *The Saturday Review,* took a prominent part in the project. Mt. Sinai Hospital in New York deserves special mention for its offer of facilities. Many persons, including Christian ministers, participated in the arrangements which finally brought twenty-five of these Japanese girls to this country. They have now returned to Japan, grateful for the loving care and treatment which helped to heal not only the burns on their bodies but also the scars in their souls.

In trying to assess the motivation of those taking part in the project, the small committee of leaders sat up late one night and asked themselves why they were doing this. The first reason they gave was a deep-seated and underlying sense of guilt and strong personal responsibility for the first atomic weapon used against human beings.

When the final arrangements were made, a group of Hiroshima girls went together to the railroad station. The group included those who had been chosen to come to America and over forty who had to be left behind because of necessary limitations on the number who could be cared for and health reasons which would have kept them from America under any circumstances. Those who would remain behind wanted to say "good-bye" to their friends. They seemed more jovial than usual, almost as if they were sharing in the spiritual benefits of the atonement which was being wrought for them through the twenty-five who were chosen.

When the project was announced, there was another vivid incident. *The Saturday Review* received a phone call from a man who identified himself as Robert Lewis. "I just wanted to say how personally grateful I am for this project," he said. "I was captain of the plane that dropped the bomb."

A fourth way of atonement is seen in the establishment of the Japan International Christian University. Though Christian leaders have dreamed of a great Christian university in Japan since the turn of the century, it was the Second World War which gave it the necessary impetus. The president of the student body recently expressed what many have known to be true, that "I.C.U. was born from the ashes of the A-bomb." He went on to say, "We must not forget the agony and earnest prayers of mankind which gave it birth." By training Christian leaders for Japan's next generation, we can help atone for our guilt, and, like Jacob, make a blessing out of a terrible wrong. Just as Jacob was given a new name, Israel, after his spiritual struggle, we may gain the new name of "benefactor."

Opened unofficially in 1953, this university has already established itself as one of the great educational institutions of the Far East. The first graduating class consisted of 165 students. At present 666 undergraduates are enrolled. The freshman class of 167, which was enrolled just a few weeks ago, was selected from 2,474 applicants, of whom 38 per cent were women. Not only does the large number of applicants testify to the quality of education offered there, but there is further evidence of this high quality in the positions commanded by graduates. In a country where competition is keen and even fierce, one I.C.U. graduate was one of fifteen selected from eighteen hundred applicants for a position in the diplomatic service, and was the first in years to be selected from a private university. Four of the twelve positions in Family Court, for which there were 990 contestants, went to I.C.U. girls. The influence of I.C.U. is being felt increasingly throughout the whole nation, so that we may confidently expect the next generation of leaders in Japan to show the influence of Christian democracy. If, in some future international crisis, Japan finds herself at the crossroads of momentous decision, it is now certain that Christian voices will be raised in high places. Who can tell whether these voices may make the difference between peace and catastrophe? As we continue to support this most significant Christian enterprise, we may truly feel that our atonement for our guilt at Hiroshima is being used by God for mighty purposes of peace and reconciliation.

Though we can never change the record of human history, and though the scars of our souls are deep, we may still atone for our guilt, just as Jacob made his peace with Esau. Driven by this worthy motive to put good into the world in place of evil, and to try to overcome a wrong, we shall become partners in shaping the new world for Christ.

If we, like Jacob, wrestle with the angel of God until He leaves His blessing, we shall know how truly God can make the guilt of men to serve Him.

WORSHIP

Look Who's Here!

Reverend Clifford Ansgar Nelson, Th.D.

PASTOR, GLORIA DEI LUTHERAN CHURCH, ST. PAUL, MINNESOTA, AND CHAPLAIN OF THE MINNESOTA STATE SENATE

This distinguished sermon on the meaning of worship is based on the old story of Isaiah and King Uzziah, and shows the importance of the mystic communion between God and Man.

Dr. Clifford Ansgar Nelson studied at the University of Minnesota and Augustana Seminary, Rock Island, Illinois, and was ordained in 1929. He studied theology and church music at Leipzig, Germany, in 1929 and 1930, and received the honorary Th.D. from the University of Bratislava, Theological Faculty, Bratislava, Czechoslovakia. He has held pastorates in Minneapolis, Minnesota, and Rock Island, Illinois; he has been pastor of Gloria Dei Lutheran Church in St. Paul since 1935.

He is a frequent contributor to theological and church journals, and writes a weekly sermon in a column called "Lift Up Your Hearts" in the LUTHERAN COMPANION. *He is the author of* THE CROSS IS THE KEY *and* WITH HEARTS UPLIFTED; *co-author of* MY BOOK OF PRAYERS; *translator of* FAST FALLS THE EVENTIDE *by Olle Nystedt (1956) and* MESSAGE OF THE CHURCH FOR A WORLD OF CRISIS *and* THE HAMMER OF THE LORD *by Bishop Bo Giertz (1955 and 1959 respectively). Since 1953 he has been Protestant Chaplain of the State Senate of Minnesota.*

Dr. Nelson traveled in war-torn Europe for the Lutheran World Federation in 1946 and has since traveled in Europe, South America,

*Palestine and the Near East, Australia, Japan, and Hong Kong. He
was a member of the Joint Hymnal Commission to create the New
Service Book and Hymnal; he is a member of the Permanent Commission for the Lutheran Hymnal, and the Commission on Church
Music of the National Council of Churches.*

SERMON FORTY-TWO

"In the year that king Uzziah died I saw also the Lord
sitting upon a throne, high and lifted up; and his train
filled the temple," Isaiah 6:1

IN HIS AUTOBIOGRAPHICAL BOOK called *Report to the Creator*, Mr.
Jerome Ellison tells a fragment of his life story in the form of a
conversation with God. It is the record of a turbulent life of success
and failure, of joy and sorrow in the pilgrimage of a sophisticated
modern who, try as he will, cannot get away from his responsibility
to God. He is literally haunted and pursued by the thought of God
"down the arches of the years," to use the phrase of Francis Thompson.

A most interesting chapter bears the title which I have used for
this sermon: "Look Who's Here!" He tells the story of how as a
lad he was in church at worship on a Sunday morning. To him it
was a gripping experience, and it seemed to him in his boyish
enthusiasm that he had felt the very real Presence of the Spirit of
God most vividly. He had found an other-worldly lift and inspiration in the hour of worship. And that day as he went out of church,
he felt under compulsion to talk with some of the grown-ups about
what he had felt so deeply. But when he made a fumbling attempt,
he was keenly disappointed. They were clustered together in little
friendly groups talking about their business, their pleasures and all
sorts of trivia. He was deeply hurt when they politely ignored him
and someone even made a witty quip about how church had been
hard on him. It was the beginning of a sense of disillusionment
with religion in his life.

Later, many years later, he went back to church. And this time
too he sensed the Holy Presence of God. As before, in his childhood,
there were the people who ignored his talk and tried to turn the
conversation away from what seemed to them a most embarrassing
subject. But this time he was an adult. He knew the value of a

profound experience of worship. He knew what he had been missing all these years. And so he insisted on talking about it to his fellow churchgoers. And he writes of how he felt like shouting to those about him: "Look Who's Here!"

I think that all of us know something of that experience and are shamed by it. All too often we have spent our moments after worship indulging in all kinds of cheap and irrelevant talk. It may have been about the Saturday-night fun we had, or even about the decorations for the next church supper. But to some impressionable youth it may have been a sign of how little we have caught the splendors of what worship means. It may be that we have too lightly understood the meaning of worship, or we may have been sharing a worship that was less than the adoration before what Rudolf Otto liked to call the *mysterium tremendum.* Most likely it was the former, and we need to learn constantly afresh the mystery and miracle of the meaning of Christian worship.

Isaiah is telling his ancient story of that high moment in the temple when suddenly, and unexpectedly, familiar things became wondrous and he was arrested by an experience of the Presence of the Almighty. God came alive to him, the common ritual and order that he had gone through so many a time before when he worshiped was strangely real. The altar which he knew so well was luminous with God, the music was like the singing of cherubim and seraphim, the smell and smoke of the incense conveyed to his senses the atmosphere of another world. It was as though instead of being in the temple made with hands he had arrived at the very court of heaven and there was a dialogue between God and himself. It was a moment that he could never forget. It changed his life. It sent him on a new mission in life. It was the revealing moment when he made a commitment that made his whole career a passionate crusade for the kingdom of God and His righteousness.

Neither has the world of believing souls been able to forget the experience of Isaiah. The record of his experience as it is told in the sixth chapter of this magnificent prophetic volume has inspired the life of religion ever since it was written. The great liturgies of the historic churches have been patterned on the rhythm of Isaiah's worship experience. The singing of the great Trisagion "Holy, Holy, Holy is the Lord of hosts; the whole earth is full of his glory" has become the call to worship of believers everywhere.

Now I would not suggest that the transcending experience of Isaiah could possibly become the everyday or even every-Sunday

293

experience of a Christian in our world today. That would be asking too much of frail human nature. Rather the glowing account of the prophet is that of one of the high and holy moments that may come only once in a lifetime. But I would like to suggest that there is something in this story that speaks to each of us about the mood and the attitude of expectancy that we must cultivate and covet if we are to know even occasionally something of this reality that ought to be present when we worship God.

For look who's here! If we have really worshiped when we have gone to the house of God, we know Who it is. It is none other than God Who has been lifted up before us. It is the Lord Christ Who has been with us. Should not our hearts be exalted and our spirits glow with the exciting wonder and beauty of it all? Is not this the thrill of our being together in the sanctuary, that we find the fulfillment of His word that where two or three are gathered together in His name, there He is among us? Our Lord promised that to His friends. And ever since, Christians have known that sacred joy in their sharing of praise and prayer and sacrament together. Sometimes more than others, perhaps when our hearts are ready either because of poignant need or because of eager faith and ready mind and heart, it has seemed as though heaven were opened and the Spirit of God descended like a winged dove of peace upon us. The number of fellow worshipers has been immaterial, the place has not been too vitally important, but the sharing of Word and sacrament has opened inner springs of refreshing inspiration.

Call it mysticism if you will; it is not something that is beyond the reach of any plain believer. It is the kind of rich inner sense of the reality of God that can come to any man if he is at all spiritually sensitive. It is not reserved simply for those who have a religious quality about them that makes them respond to some vague esoteric mysteries. It belongs to any plain man who is in earnest about his religion. It is one of the surprises that might happen to any one of us in a cathedral or the plainest chapel, in liturgical or non-liturgical worship.

Never underestimate the value of worship. Never go to it without a sense of hunger and anticipation. Never neglect it because your mood is dull, or your spirits are down. It may be at that very moment that God will be found in the familiar words and the pedestrian gestures and acts of our worship. Years ago I was impressed by the intimate story of Archbishop Yngve Brilioth, of the See of Upsala, Sweden. He tells it in the pastoral letter which he issued when he was first made a bishop. His awakening to the life of religion came in the days when he was a college lad. That Sunday morning he had gone to the little rural church in his home parish. The old minister droned the liturgy in his usual dull manner. The boy was his own careless and indifferent self about such matters. But in the midst of the communion service, as the pastor read the ancient call to prayer: "Lift up your hearts," something broke within the boy's soul. It seemed as though those words were a personal call to him. It was the summons from eternity, deep calling to deep, that he should lift up his own little heart to the heart of the unfathomable God. So religion came alive for him. It started him on a career of leadership. It brought heaven to earth. Time and eternity came together in his soul.

It is something akin to that which might happen to any of us when we worship. For, you see, God is here. And He is the seeking God. We take the risk of meeting Him when we go up to pray, God is a living God and the place of worship may be vibrant with His Presence for you when you are in the place where He has planned to meet us. It may be an unexpected surprise, or it may be the touch of His hand that you have been hoping for and looking for. The religion-in-general which bedevils us so much may become religion-in-particular; the God of our vague deistic faith may come alive as the God Who has dealings with our own souls. The risk is very real when we do not "neglect the assembling of ourselves together, as the custom of so many is."

Look who's here! God's Word is here when we worship. From the time of St. John's prologue to his Gospel we have become accustomed to making the Word of God a personal thing, actually a Personality. And there is good theological reason to do that. When we speak of the Word of God we are not at all limiting ourselves to the words of a book, not even the words of the New Testament Scripture. Our concept of the Word of God is that of a Voice, an eternal Voice from beyond, that speaks with a haunting human accent ever since the Incarnation made the world aware that the living God speaks in human language and makes Himself intelligible to us through the living Word. It is that living Word that is here when we worship. "God keeps up a continual conversation with every creature," is the way the French writer Paul Claudel put it once. That conversation is not confined to people sitting in church, to be sure, but worship is one place where we dramatize the divine conversation and where we can hear the still, small voice if we will be quiet enough to listen for it. I like Martin Luther's simple definition of worship when he wrote: "that we may come together to act and to hear God's Word—that our dear Lord may speak to us through His holy word and that we may speak to Him, in turn, through prayer and songs of praise."

The Word of God is our designation for the living and active voice of the Eternal which is seeking to break through our calloused world with its many sounds and noises, its distractions and irritations, its fevers and anxieties, to speak to us the message of a saving and healing God Who is seeking to speak with us. One of the great parables of worship is the page from the Danish philosopher Kierkegaard where he is writing of worship as being like drama. He was actually writing a satire on the superficial way in which the people of Copenhagen in his day went to church. They went to church as they went to the theater. They went to be inspired by the eloquence of the gifted preacher and to be entertained by the artistry of the choir and the organist. Let it be so, he insists. Going to church *is* like going to the theater. But with this difference: the actors are not the preacher, the liturgists, the choristers, the musical performers. The stage is not up there where the altar lights are gleaming and the service is being performed. Ah no, instead, the word that is being spoken and sung is the Word of God Who is the Great Author and Playwright. The preacher is but the prompter. The stage and arena for the drama are down in the souls of those who listen and hear. It is there that God's Word is being acted out. It is there that the destiny of men is being spoken and action is being formed. Worship and preaching become the place of a divine-human encounter that makes being in church a significant thing. The message of the philosopher may have irritated the fashionable people of the capital of Denmark, but they speak poignantly to us today. Worship is the stage of a divine drama being played out, not at the altar alone, but in the hearts and minds of each of us.

William Temple spoke of worship as the one thing that could save our world from chaos. And of course he was speaking in much larger terms than of simply saying our prayers or going to church. But he goes on to give a succinct outline for the meaning of all worship when he says: "To worship is to quicken the conscience by the holiness of God, to feed the mind with the truth of God, to purge the imagination with the beauty of God, to open the heart to the will of God, and to devote the will to the purpose of God." If we could get hold of the meaning of that sentence when we worship, it would begin doing things for us in our anticipation and expectancy that might quicken every conscious contact we seek in the fine art of worshiping our Lord.

But look around you when you worship. Look who's here! We have not understood the meaning of worship when we have looked only at ourselves and God. Granted that they are the most significant elements in the act of worship. But worship is a social thing. Man is a social creature. Our great Judeo-Christian tradition of worship reminds us, as over against the solitariness of much of Eastern mysticism, that when we meditate and pray we must find the rhythm of alternation between ourselves and God and our fellow man. Worship means an awareness of our brother. It heightens our feeling of our common humanity. Any worship that simply drives our souls into a splendid introspective isolation is false when measured by the standards of our biblical religion. Look at the story of Isaiah as he sees God high and lifted up, and you will hear him calling out in concern for his own uncleanness and that of his people: "Here am I, Lord, send me." Worship in its true meaning always moves from the individual to the crowd, from God to man in its personal relationships:

Out of the world of the Many
Into the world of the One;
Out of the world of the One,
Into the world of the Many.

Our little church where we go to pray may be at an obscure crossroad of the world, but if it is God's church, the church of the Master, it will be the place where we are quickened to think in terms of all men everywhere. The walls of our own church become transparent and we are made to be one of a great company whom no man can number gathered before Him in all the earth, and of the great company of all souls gathered before the throne in heaven. The church where we pray may be filled with upper-middle-class segregated Protestant Americans, but the company with whom we have fellowship is made up of all of God's little children; the shabby and the hungry, the last, the least and the lost, the black-skinned brother and the oppressed refugee are all there. The preacher may relate the kingdom of God to the streets of our own city or village, but he represents One Who spoke of a kingdom that must come on all the earth. The mind must be broad to encompass Christ's meaning, the heart must have a spacious sympathy that reaches out to the needs of a whole world. For when we worship, if we are aware at all of the implications of our faith, we are a part of the beloved community, the great fellowship, the family of all who are encompassed in God's concern. We find ourselves called to march with Christ into all the world. We hear the anguished cry of all humanity when we look up to His cross and rub shoulders with His friends. We are joined together to follow Him Who wants to enlist us in His cause.

Look who's here! Think of that when next you go to the house of God. If you find somehow that you have been directly confronted with the goodness and the severity of God because you have been there, you have worshiped aright. If your heart has been warmed by the comfort of the Gospel and your spirit has been stirred by the urge to be a better person than before, thank God and take courage. If somehow you go back to your home and to your job feeling a bigger person, and challenged to be of help to God in His enormous task of bringing redemption to yourself and others, then worship is fulfilling its true function.

Look who's here! It is He, the only One Who can make life decent and useful and strong for you and the world where you are commissioned to serve Him. Pray for grace to be aware of Him and to meet Him when you go up to the temple to pray. Ask that the Lord will show Himself when the Word is spoken and the sacraments are shared in your church. Then worship becomes what someone suggested once:

> The beggar knocking,
> The sinner prostrate,
> The sinner looking into the Master's eye,
> The child speaking to the Father,
> The pardoned man resting,
> The saved man thanking, and
> The saint rejoicing.

Long ago, as far back as the fifth century, there was a lovely prayer included in the ancient Liturgy of Malabar which shows the transforming meaning of worship:

Grant, O Lord, that the ears which have heard the voice of Thy songs may be closed to the voice of clamor and dispute; that the eyes which have seen Thy great love may also behold Thy blessed hope; that the tongues which have sung Thy praise may speak Thy truth; that the feet which have walked in Thy courts may walk in the region of light; and that the souls of all who have received Thy blessed sacrament may be restored to newness of life.

Look Who's Here!

Index

This index has been prepared for clergy and laity alike, but particularly with the needs of the busy pastor-preacher in mind. It has been designed to be suggestive, helpful, and convenient for the man in search of sermon ideas and illustrations. To make the book his own, the reader should add other words and pages as he finds them useful.